'Oliver James has done it again – a brilliant, brave and peppery defence of the primary role of nurture over nature in matters of the mind. This gloriously readable book combines fascinating cases from his practice as a therapist with a trenchant analysis of the scientific evidence about how much we have neglected such factors as early abuse in the origins of mental illness later in life.'

– *Professor Ian Robertson, Director of Trinity College Institute of Neuroscience, Dublin University*

'*Not in your genes* not only buries some powerful genetic myths, it re-focuses our attention on the crucial importance – for the future of humanity – of how we treat our children, especially in their early years. Oliver James accomplishes these dual task with a wonderful jumble of research evidence, logic, passion, personal stories and humour.'

– *John Read, Professor of Clinical Psychology University of Melbourne*

'This book is that rare thing, intelligent and easy to read ... All parents must read this brilliant book.'

– *Philippa Perry, Psychotherapist, broadcaster, writer; author of* How to Stay Sane *and* Couch Fiction

not in your genes

not in your genes

genes

The real reasons children are like their parents

oliver james

Vermilion
LONDON

1 3 5 7 9 10 8 6 4 2

Vermilion, an imprint of Ebury Publishing,
20 Vauxhall Bridge Road,
London SW1V 2SA

Vermilion is part of the Penguin Random House group of companies whose addresses
can be found at global.penguinrandomhouse.com

Penguin
Random House
UK

First published by Vermilion in 2016

www.eburypublishing.co.uk

A CIP catalogue record for this book is available from the British Library

Hardback ISBN 9780091947668
Trade Paperback ISBN 9780091947675

Printed and bound in Great Britain by Clays Ltd, St Ives PLC

Penguin Random House is committed to a sustainable future for our
business, our readers and our planet. This book is made from Forest
Stewardship Council® certified paper.

MIX
Paper from
responsible sources
FSC
www.fsc.org   FSC® C018179

This Be Yet Another Verse

They fuck you up, your little ones
They know just what to say and do
To drain your world of joy and fun
Then blame the misery on you.

But they'll be fucked up in their turn
By children they can't understand,
Who'll teach them what we had to learn
That nothing ever goes as planned.

Child hands back misery to man
It spreads out like a lifeless plain.
Eject them early as you can
And never speak to them again.

Paul Bamborough (2014), *pace* Philip Larkin

To my sisters, Jessica, Mary and Lucy

Contents

Preface   1

Introduction   3

Chapter 1:   The Real Reasons Children are Like their Parents   13

Chapter 2:   Why was Peaches Geldof so Like her Mother?   39

Chapter 3:   Not in Your Genes   61

Chapter 4:   Maltreatment and Love (Why Siblings
             are so Different, Pt 1)   75

Chapter 5:   Your Role in the Family Drama (Why Siblings
             are so Different, Pt 2)   111

Chapter 6:   Why Traits Run in Families   141

Chapter 7:   The Real Causes of Ability   165

Conclusion: It's the Environment, Stupid!   211

Appendix 1: Not in Your Genes: Time to Accept the Null
             Hypothesis of the Human Genome Project?   217

Appendix 2: Twin Studies: A Discredited Method   243

Appendix 3: The Fatal Flaws of the Minnesota Twins
             Reared Apart Study   251

Appendix 4: The Perils of Geneticism: The Advantages
             of Believing in a Flexible Psychology   257

Endnotes   267

References   293

Acknowledgements   331

Index   333

Preface

The latest evidence from the Human Genome Project is proving that it is not genes which make psychological traits run in families. There are physical traits that pass down genetically, like height, looks and eye colour, but it now seems very much as if variations in things like mental illness, smartness or shyness, have little or nothing to do with the sequences of DNA which pass from parent to child.

Rather, it is proven that patterns of nurture make us like our parents and grandparents: what travels down the generations is precise kinds of bickering, humour, snide asides, delicious food preparation, beatings, hugging, short-temperedness.

You are like you are because you were related to by both your parents in very particular ways, good and bad. When you have children, you are liable to do exactly the same, or something similar, in many respects, or else react against it.

How you were cared for, especially in early life, was critical. This, in turn, was caused by the way your parents were cared for, all the way back to your grandparents and beyond. The best evidence suggests that nine out of ten maltreated children develop a mental illness as adults. Seventy per cent of maltreated children become maltreating parents themselves.

Much nurture is positive, the love and sensitivity, the teaching of skills, the intimacy. But in almost all families, there are toxic patterns. The implication is that we do not have to go on repeating the past.

Politicians play on our desire to improve our material circumstances in order to provide a more affluent life for our children. If only we could see that, once a basic level of material security has been achieved, it is far more important to pass love down the generations than property, or stocks and shares.

Introduction

I only ever excelled at one skill: dribbling footballs. Alas, I was never an excellent footballer for the simple reason that it's a team sport. It is true that I once scored a goal after dribbling around ten players but, when practising with my friends, they used to chant 'Selfish James never scores'.

When my son was aged two he could dribble a football remarkably well and from around aged five, he was doing it in a way that was startlingly similar to how I used to. Aged seven, I sometimes witnessed him dribble past the whole of opposing teams and score.

The interesting thing is that it is impossible that my son could have learnt this from me.

At nine, he was at pains to point this out. Something of a barrack room lawyer, he recorded the following interview with me on my iPhone:

Son: Oliver James, is it true that when you were young you used to dribble exactly like me?

Me: Pretty much true, yup.

Son: Okay. And is it true that you are disabled and I have never seen you play?

Me: It is true.

Son: And is it true I have never seen a photo or a video of you playing football?

Me: That is correct.

Son:	So you have to admit that I dribble exactly like you, yet I've never, ever, ever, ever seen you do it? So is it true that that came from genes?
Me:	No.
Son:	Why so?
Me:	Errrrrrr…
Son:	That's all we need.

(The reader can listen to this interview at www.selfishcapitalist.com/ and see a clip of him dribbling. The interview was recorded whilst driving in my car and includes poignant interruptions from the GPS instructing me how to get our destination. My son labelled the file 'Oliver James Wrong'.)

For 27 years I have suffered from multiple sclerosis and for the last 15 that has somewhat impaired my walking. I was not able to dribble from well before my son's birth ten years ago, and there are no recordings or pictures of me performing when young. Neither my wife nor I hothoused his dribbling when small, he was a born dribbler.

Like him, you might have thought that it must be some genetic dribbling code that he has inherited. But the odd thing is that it seems extremely unlikely that his skill was passed through genes, even though we share half of them in common. The latest research cannot find genetic codes that significantly influence the transmission of psychological characteristics from parent to child (dribbling is in large part a matter of psychology). Whether it be specific genes, groups of genes, or large numbers of variants, they have not been shown to play any important role in explaining our intelligence, personality or mental health.

I appreciate that this last sentence will be met with incredulity by some readers but they are a fact, not my interpretation. The consensus in the scientific community is that studies of genetic variants can only explain, at best, a tiny amount (1–5 per cent) of our psychological individuality.[1] The scientists have invented something called the 'Missing Heritability'[2] as a way of describing this finding. Because they were so sure that genes would explain us, based on the results of studies of identical twins, they devised the idea that the genes are still there, it's just a matter of finding them.

Now, this is where my interpretation does come in. Normally, when hundreds of studies have contradicted a theory, the theory gets dropped. I maintain that the impact of genes is not missing, the Human Genome Project – HGP – has proven beyond little doubt that it is largely non-existent. Enough studies have occurred for us to have reached that point. I believe it is safe to say that genes hardly influence why we are like parents or different from our siblings.

In the case of mental illness, for example, by 2011 there had been 115 HGP studies of it[3] and several dozen have been published since. They have looked everywhere that the genes could plausibly be found and the believers in genes are beginning to admit defeat.[4] Hardly any scientists now believe that DNA codes which directly determine us will be found, the only question is whether they have indirect effects.

I assume the general reader does not care for more detail about this than what I have presented in Chapter 3. Those with a scientific bent should immediately turn to Appendix 1, which reproduces my peer-reviewed, published scientific paper setting out the evidence. If you think that studies of identical twins have proven the importance of genes, think again: Appendix 2 explains why such studies are now all but disproven. Those who have been tricked by the much-publicised American study of identical twins who were supposedly reared apart[5] should read Appendix 3: it's a study which is bogus, hyped by ill-informed journalists and TV producers. Those who want even more detail should read my forthcoming scientific monograph, called *It's The Environment, Stupid!*, where still further substantiation is provided.

Of course, if genes do not seem to explain us, parents can still physically pass traits down to their children. For example, it seems extremely likely that at birth many autistic children's brains have not developed properly, that some children are born with autism[6] (loosely defined as an incapacity to know that others have minds). But that does not need to have anything to do with genes. It could be largely or wholly because of what happens in the womb and there is some evidence it may be so, in some cases.[7] This is in accord with the fact that one third of babies are born 'difficult'.[8] It has long been accepted that this is mostly not caused by genes, the difficultness of neonates results from the pregnancy and birth.

Going back to my son's dribbling, I have little doubt that he has acquired this trait from me through a physical, biological mechanism. One theory is that in becoming an exceptional dribbler myself, my body released chemicals that switched certain genes on or off.[9] This pattern of chemicals, rather than any particular genes, could have been passed on to my son through a process known as epigenetics, although this is very much a speculation.

Just as it now seems highly probable that genes do not cause our individuality, and whilst there are almost certainly other, as yet undiscovered, physical causes of it, there is a mass of solid evidence that how we are nurtured makes an enormous difference to how we turn out, for good and ill.

My son is a far better footballer than I ever was. When he was seven he was spotted by Southampton FC and trained with them for two years, aged eight and nine. He was twice invited for trials to become a member of their academy, not far from joining one of the best under-nine-year-old teams in the country.

This is because he is better adjusted than I was. Although he was selfish and did not pass the ball when small, unlike me, as he grew up he was able to see the need to cooperate with his teammates. I have good reason to suppose his superior personality and mental health resulted from the highly responsive care he received from my wife, and because he felt loved by both of us. He was able to tolerate others getting the glory of scoring a goal he had created, able to realize if he passed to teammates, sometimes they might pass to him, giving him his moments in the sun.

By contrast, I was sometimes a snarling, angry child because the early care I received was often rejecting and unresponsive. In later childhood, despite repeated attempts to persuade me to be more of a team player and despite my best efforts to be so, my personality got in the way. Looking back, I would speculate that my dribbling was a form of aggression and a way of feeling in control (literally of the ball), one that my mother very much encouraged and enjoyed, and which she had originally nurtured by making me such an angry and powerless boy through her irritable and sometimes violent nurture (don't get me wrong, at other times she was loving and very much on my side). If I did pass this skill to my son through epigenetics, the fundamental cause was not genes, it was the nurture my mother provided.

It is also worth mentioning that when very small my daughter was just as good at dribbling as my son. I have little doubt that if she had lived in a society where that skill was valued in girls and if we, as parents, had valued it in her as much as we (particularly me) valued it in our son, she would be an outstanding female footballer. Thus, it is possible that both our children were born with the physically (but not genetically) inherited potential to be exceptional dribblers, but whether that was realised depended wholly on how we reacted to them as parents (especially me, with my desire for my son to be the footballer I was not) and what was valued in our society. As you will see in story after story in what follows, this is absolutely typical of how parents cause the way children turn out. Insofar as anything is inborn, albeit not inherited through genes, the critical factor is how parents respond.

Richard Dawkins portrays us as mere carcasses that enable DNA to be transmitted onwards, if we reproduce. As far as psychological traits go, the Human Genome Project is proving him emphatically wrong. The truth is that the good and the bad in you results to a large extent from the unique care you received. This is incredibly good news. As parents, if we get it right, the outcome will be positive.

There is now overwhelming evidence that childhood maltreatment is a major cause of mental illness. Even the World Health Organization acknowledges that 29 per cent of mental illness worldwide is attributable to it,[10] almost certainly a considerable underestimate.

7

For example, the single best study found that 90 per cent of children who had been maltreated had a mental illness at age 18.[11] Think about that: nine out of ten children who were maltreated developed a mental illness. It implies that nearly all maltreated children become distressed adults. There is plenty more evidence of this. The more childhood maltreatments you suffer, and the worse the kind of maltreatment, the greater your risk of subsequent mental illness.

Equally, there is strong evidence that children who suffer no maltreatment very rarely develop mental illness.[12] The presence of early love and responsiveness creates emotional health and inoculates against later adversity.[13] Whether loved or maltreated, the impact of parental care cascades down the generations.

The implications of genes being so insignificant and nurture being so vital are mind-blowing, hard to get your head around. If you are a parent, once you stop thinking of your child as having been 'born that way', there is so much you can do to alter the trajectory of its life and consequently; the lives of your grandchildren. At the simplest level, just by believing its abilities are not fixed, a child can improve its academic performance, the same goes for the beliefs a parent or teacher has about the child (see Appendix 4). Forget about having your genes tested to identify psychological traits, it is science fiction. There will never be gene therapy for mental illness or any other psychological traits. Mental illnesses run in families because of nurture, not genes. If unhappy patterns are broken, they will not be passed to the next generation.

If you are a troubled adult who thinks that this is your genetic destiny, or if you just have some irritating quirks that you had always assumed to be genetically inherited, it will be empowering to you to find out that they are not set in genetic stone. The brain is much more plastic than used to be believed, change is possible in adulthood, albeit often hard won. The studies show that if people diagnosed with a mental illness believe it is inherited, they fare worse. If their relatives, or the professionals caring for them believe the same, the prognosis is more pessimistic (see Appendix 4).

The late Paula Yates, the television presenter and ex-wife of Bob Geldof with whom I worked in the 1980s, is an example of the baleful effect of believing mental illness is genetically inherited. When I knew her, she told me that she did not drink because her father had been mentally ill and she was convinced she was at high risk of that too, because it was in her genes. Indeed, mental illness and substance abuse did befall her in the last few years of her life. But it was nothing to do with her paternal DNA, for it turned out that Jess Yates, the man who raised her, was not her biological father (that was the TV presenter Hughie Green). The true cause of her vulnerability was the care she received as a child. That she believed it was in her genes made it harder for her to overcome her problems.

All of us have been in the grip of hugely powerful intergenerational processes that dictate how we function. Only by awareness of them can we gain some control and change. This is illustrated in Chapter 6 with the tale of four generations of mothers who blamed their daughters for their difficult behaviour, with no awareness that they were causing the problem through their mothering. With the help of therapy, the last mother was able to break the cycle and her daughter is freed from it.

If you are the parent of an inexplicably impossible child or have a crazy or obnoxious partner, it is understandable that you want a clear medical label for the problem and even better, a pill that will change it. The psychiatric profession and drug companies know this, and ruthlessly exploit that longing for a simple solution. Fully 40 per cent of the websites on the Internet that offer explanations of mental illness have drug company backing of some kind;[14] there is a deliberate and costly campaign to sell the genetic explanation and the drug solution.

I am not suggesting that genes play no part in what we are like as a species. Genes explain why we are not born with the necks of giraffes or the flippers of penguins. As well as physical traits, they confer fundamental human psychological traits, like language, humour and putting ourselves in the minds of others. What the Human Genome Project seems to have proven is that the extent to which we have these and other psychological traits is not governed by variants in specific genes. This makes evolutionary sense.

As explained in Chapter 5, all of us are born at a unique point in our parents' relationship, affecting how they respond to us. We have a place in the family, our birth order. Our gender means particular things to both parents. They are very likely to have different expectations for each of us. In order to thrive, it makes sense that we would be born with great plasticity, able to adapt to what is required by our specific place in the family and expectations from parents. To be born stupid with parents who wanted a clever child, to be born extrovert if parents wanted a quiet child, that would decrease our likelihood of winning their affections. Being highly adaptable would work far better.

Genes enable almost all of us to acquire language. But which one we speak is wholly dependent on the one we are taught by our parents and society. The same way, nearly all of us have the potential for psychological characteristics like liveliness, intelligence or depression, but the extent to which we develop them and in precisely what way depends largely, or completely, on nurture.

Enough of these generalisations. There is no point in dilly-dallying. We can get straight into the real reasons that children take after their parents as soon as I have briefly explained a few details of the sources I have used and some other book househusbandry.

Footnotes and other househusbandry

A good deal of this book is concerned with the causes of mental illness, more than personality or ability – even the last chapter's analysis of the causes of exceptional ability shows that maltreatment often plays a considerable role. Yet my main message is optimistic. To this end, at the conclusion of each chapter there is a section entitled WHAT WORKS? 3 TAKEAWAYS. These are not chirpy exercises in positive psychology: 'Hey, you can sort yourself out by a bit of mindfulness training and eating a large portion of beetroot for breakfast every day'. Rather, I provide you with mostly scientifically supported, practical implications.

Where I mention evidence for an assertion I make, I provide a footnote with details of the study or studies, with an asterix in the text. The footnotes section at the end of the book is divided into chapters, with the page number and the words for which I provide evidence.

The book is littered with case histories. Some are based on clients I have worked with and in these cases I have received permission to tell the story. Some are based on emails and subsequent phone or Skype conversations I have had with members of the public who contacted me and who have also given permission for their use. Unless otherwise specified, in all the case histories I change important details to retain the anonymity of the persons in the story.

There are also famous people used to exemplify points I am making. Chapter 2 is devoted to Paula Yates and her daughter Peaches Geldof, the sources for which are explained near the beginning of the chapter. Chapters 5 and 7 use some famous examples, mostly based on biographies and autobiographies. As in my previous books, these psychobiographical examples are based on reliable sources, like the famous people's own accounts of their lives, and in some cases, my own personal experience from working with them, or interviews I did with them for newspapers or on television. In using psychobiography, I am following the tradition developed by Sigmund Freud and Lytton Strachey, hoping to engage the reader through famous people with whom they may feel they already have some kind of relationship, through the media, or their artistic or scientific creations.

Chapter 1

The Real Reasons Children are Like their Parents

Human beings have the longest period of dependence on their parents for survival of any species.[1] Whereas most mammals are independent after a few weeks or months, humans require five years. For that reason, we start off highly attuned to our main carers, hoping to attract their loving and material resources. We may die, emotionally as well as literally, if we do not.

Although it sounds rather negative and is only one aspect of the parent–child relationship, I characterise the normal tendency of a child to attract its parent's resources and be highly protective of what they were like as *Offspring Stockholm Syndrome*.

Stockholm Syndrome was first identified when it was discovered that hostages in a Stockholm bank raid developed empathy for their captors and adopted many of their opinions. This is a rational survival strategy in the circumstances. Captors are less likely to kill you if they become attached and sympathise with you as a human being, just like themselves. One of the most famous instances was Patti Hearst, the American media heiress who joined the terrorist group that kidnapped her.[2] By endorsing their campaign, she survived. Hers was not just a cunning wheeze, she truly identified with them, just as children do with their parents.

Since small children are completely in the power of parents, it makes sense for them to do their best to ingratiate themselves. Like hostages, they adopt their 'captors'' opinions because, although we may prefer not to think about it, children genuinely are at risk of death from parents.

Most parents are desperate to do the best they can for their children, and that makes them prepared to put themselves second, or at least, to feel torn between doing so and meeting their own needs.[3] But small children are a tremendous burden. Their total dependence when they are infants, unable to move, feed or soothe themselves, is so extreme that it creates a potent guilt and urgent demand. At times, for most mothers (it is nearly always the mother who is the primary carer for the infant in the early months) this can be intolerable and insufferable.[4] Given the pressure, small wonder that fully half of mothers of babies under the age of one year report having seriously pictured killing their baby at some point[5] (in actual fact, the true proportion is probably nearly all of us parents, however fleeting the thought). For most mothers, the 24-hour demands are so intense that, on occasions, it becomes a case of 'one of us has got to die, this can't go on'.

Anyone who has cared for a small child knows how physically and emotionally exhausting it can be, due to loss of sleep, loss of autonomy and the feeling that you are out of time and beyond civilised society. In our atomised world, with so many mothers isolated for most of the day rather than feeling part of a community, no wonder it is so common to become depressed and furiously angry,[6] a mixture of despair and low-grade irritability which periodically explodes into severe anguish or an incontinent loss of temper, or at the extreme, into psychotic incoherence. Indeed, is it any wonder that about two babies a week are killed by their carers in England and Wales, or that the age group most at risk of being murdered is under-one year olds?[7]

It may seem an extraordinary and lugubrious suggestion, but the primary explanation for why children become like parents are the combined realities of the total dependence of small children and the threat this poses to the emotional survival of the carer, occasionally making them murderous. Children must find a way to attract parental resources and ingratiate themselves, otherwise they can die.[8] The easiest way for the child to attract parental approval is to copy them.

Teaching, modelling and identification as mechanisms by which children become like parents

Teaching

Parents implicitly and explicitly coach their children in the 'right' ways.[9] At the outset, everything that happens for infants, happens at the behest of the carer. As soon as they are old enough to understand, children are told how and when to eat, shit, pee, play and react to adults. As they get older, parents strongly encourage some activities and discourage others. Taught what pleases and displeases their parents, children adjust what they do accordingly. For example, when I am not shouting at them to leave me alone to get on with writing this book, I encourage my children to be playful and creative. Consequently, seeking their parents' approbation, they place a high premium on these attributes (and hopefully, too, because they find these states enjoyable). Equally, both my wife and I can be competitive and while we do not deliberately do so, we implicitly teach competitiveness to our children. I encourage and supervise my son to do sprint training because he likes to be better than other boys at football (yes, and because I want him to be). The explicit lesson is 'beat the other boys!' A proportion of the positive and negative features that children develop is the simple consequence of such teaching, things like regular habits, organised thought and a glass-half-full attitude to life – or their opposites.

Modelling

Distinct from being actively taught, children carefully study how parents behave and scrupulously copy it from a young age. When our daughter was about six months old, she witnessed me doing yoga every morning, part of which consisted of rapidly breathing in and out through my nose, rather noisily. To our amazement and amusement, she imitated this sniffling noise. As children get older they pick up on other tiny details like this, behavioural or verbal tics. In the exchange between my son and me with which this book began, my son asks 'Why so?' – it's an interrogative I sometimes use. They also duplicate less trivial patterns of behaviour, which range from punctuality to aggression to passivity.

While I may teach my children to be playful and creative, I also model patterns that are less wholesome. For example, I have always been a driver who is somewhat negligent of the regulations, whether that is not putting on my seat belt, speeding, or even using my mobile phone. I modelled this from the example of my father: I can still visualise the scene when I was seven years old in which our car broke down in a private London road that he used illegally as a shortcut to get us to school. Such modelled habits pass down the generations. Alas, I fear that when my children become drivers, they may imitate my attitude to traffic regulations. Interestingly, though, having witnessed my transgressions, as part of their identity they may do the exact opposite and be at pains to avoid such illegality, perhaps in an internal alliance with my wife's diametrically opposed attitude – she is a fastidiously law-abiding driver. As we shall see, family dynamics – the patterns of relationships between all family members – hugely affect what we model.

As parents, there are nearly always some gaps between what we teach and what we model: 'do as I say, not as I do'. For example, most parents teach their children that lying is wrong and yet, when our child picks up the phone, if it's someone we do not want to speak to, we frantically wave at our child to tell the caller that we are not there. Our children learn from observing us that there can be exceptions to rules and we do not necessarily mean what we say, there are mixed messages.

Where there are two parents, differences inevitably occur in their views about some issues, such as what constitutes healthy eating, how much screen time should be permitted and, in our family's case, traffic regulations. Parents differently model these issues to the children and the children sift through and select, according to what will attract parental resources.

When children do precisely duplicate parental behaviour, it is often assumed it must be genetic but it is nothing of the sort. My son did not inherit a gene that makes him say 'Why so?' They closely monitor parents' personal styles, characters and behaviour patterns. As assiduous students, they are scarily astute. More than anyone, my children can sometimes leave me with nowhere to hide when specifying my faults.

Identification

Whereas modelling is imitation, identification is the child experiencing some aspect of the parent as being them.[10] The child takes what the parent is like into them, making it one and the same thing as their very self.

At root, identification occurs out of love or out of fear.[11] If it is love, the child is being like the parent in order to make the parent feel good or not wanting to distress them by being different. For example, when my son was aged eight, he asked me about a book I had written on office politics. Having explained it to him, he started playing around with the ideas in his school life. Intrigued by the tactic of ingratiation, for instance, he employed it on a teacher by complimenting him on his tie, with gratifying consequences (though when he reported this to me I warned him not to lay it on too thick, as ingratiation backfires loudly when spotted). He was identifying with his beloved father's interest, applying it in his own life, and making it his own. Because I have shown him love, he loves me and wants to be like he whom he loves.

At the risk of disappearing down a tunnel of love, I can say much the same of my relationship with my father. His feelings about women were always mixed, and he was more at ease with males. I was his only son, the third of four children, with three sisters. Purely because of what was between my legs when I was born, he poured a great deal of affection into me, as well as his unfulfilled hopes, which caused me some difficulties

as well as having many benefits. He treated me very differently from
my sisters.

I was a delinquent, angry boy because my mother was overstretched,
caring for four children under the age of five at the point when my younger
sister was born. My mother smacked me (sometimes round the head) when
she lost her temper and could be very irritable and depressed, although in
later life she was also sensitive and I always knew she loved me. As a toddler, my father did his best to bond with me and once the hell – as far as I
was concerned – of formal education began, he showed great sympathy for
my reluctance to cooperate with it, as did my mother. They were united
in their loathing of the destruction of creativity that formal education can
entail. Indeed, given how lamentably organised British education is, I am
inclined to agree with them that one of its main purposes is merely to ware-
house children so that parents can work.

However, my father had mixed feelings about schooling. He was a
scholarly man who loved knowledge. Most importantly in relation to
me, one of his unfulfilled ambitions was to have attended a major public
school, and he wanted that for me. He had been made into a snob, in some
respects, by the slights of class inflicted by his background and education
(as it happens, St Cyprian's, the school where he endured his early education was described by George Orwell in his memoir, *Such, Such Were The
Joys*, my father attending five years later; it depicts a humiliating, snobbish
and dispiriting institution).

One of six sons, his father had been an exceptionally successful doctor and dentist,[12] but a tyrannical man who had been the son of the proprietor of two grocery stores in Northampton, aware of his humble origins.
Two of my father's brothers also trained as doctors, along with him. All
three attended the posh Magdalene College, Cambridge University, having been sent to a respectable but by no means posh public school. My
father's experience at university was that the ones who went to the majors
had the most fun, enjoying a Bertie Woosterish life of drink-fuelled gaiety
and playfulness, at least in my father's imagination. That contrasted with

the hard slog of my father's pursuit of his medical degree. His conclusion was that if he had a son, he should go to a major and to his Cambridge College because that would make him (his son, but also my father, by proxy – parents identify with children too) a member of an elite that also had the most fun.

Unfortunately, the mixed messages I received from my parents led to a bumpy academic ride for me. Throughout the long line of disastrous academic failures, my father closely supported and encouraged me in the face of strong evidence that I was as thick as the proverbial two short planks.

I did not get off to a good start. I can still picture the corner of the playground during the break time on my first day at school, aged four, when I randomly attacked two older boys, who, not unreasonably, grabbed me by the hair and pulled. My parents allowed me to withdraw from school for a year.

Until the age of eight I attended schools that put little pressure on me but then I was sent to an extremely strict one. This being 1961, I was regularly beaten by the headmaster with a rounders bat for my misbehaviour and lack of application. I did no work and consistently bumped along the bottom of all my classes (the order of performance was read out each week and the bottom three was always some permutation of Arendt, Carpenter, James). At ten and a half, the headmaster called my parents in and startled them by saying I was 'mentally subnormal' and must leave because I required special education (many years later, however, ha ha, my mother had the great satisfaction of sitting next to the headmaster at dinner and being able to answer with some relish the question 'Whatever happened to Oliver?'). Sent to a boarding school in Kent, I continued my bad behaviour and lack of academic commitment, proceeding to fail the entrance exam to the major.

I failed so badly that I was fortunate to be given a second chance. My father drove me down to a crammer, a boot camp for thickos, having pleaded with the major to let me have another go. He was sympathetic but also warned me that this was my last hope. Since he cared so much about me getting into a major, so did I. For ten weeks, I started every day (Sundays included) at 7 a.m. with a French and Latin word test before breakfast. Each Saturday morning we took the complete entrance exam and our progress, or lack thereof, was mercilessly exposed. I was still badly behaved and the punishment for this was to be sent for a run. During those ten weeks I must have jogged hundreds of miles but I was only beaten once (for throwing stones at the ducks on a pond). By the end I had doubled my marks and passed the exam with a respectable score. But, alas, on arrival at the major I returned to my old ways and at the end of the first term failed the school internal exam, dropping down a year.

I have the letters my father wrote me while I was there, at least two or three a week, as he gently tried to coax and advise me to apply and behave myself. Shortly after taking my O levels (now GCSEs) and before the results had been published he took me for a glass of Pimms at a pub. He did not read me the riot act, he was warm and kind, but he calmly posed three choices, ones that in retrospect seem curious. I could leave the school, there and then, and go and work on the railways in Swindon (why he imagined that city employed so many railway workers I never did discover), I could go and work as a stockbroker in the City, or I could stay at the school and go to Cambridge.

Having absolute faith in my father, I accepted this as a multiple-choice test in which there were no alternatives. Although I quite fancied the idea of the railways, I was not mad keen on the idea of relentless manual labour. In our family culture, working in financial services was akin to joining the SS, and a stockbroker was like being a guard at the Belsen concentration camp, so I did not consider that option. Which only left going to Cambridge. Being so much identified with my father, it did not occur to me to ask about the possibility of attending less academic universities. My dad warned me that I would have to work extremely hard to achieve this goal, since, at best, I was going to scrape a handful of O levels (indeed, my total was seven, all poor grades). Nonetheless, I signed up for the plan and worked like a super-nerd for two years, with brief periods of marijuana-induced anaesthetisation as light relief, sere-naded by Pink Floyd.

The reader may have guessed by now that when my A level results came they were not good (a B, D and E – but as I always tell my children, A levels were real A levels in those days, just as Firsts were real Firsts, not the namby-pamby grade-inflated metrics of today). Luckily for me, I was allowed to sit the exam for Cambridge. Finally, I managed to work out how to answer essay questions well enough to pass that exam quite well and was accepted by my father's old college.

Interestingly, however, once at university, I did not live out my father's dream of becoming Bertie Wooster. For one thing, this was 1973 and such behaviour was out of fashion (although only ten years later it was back in vogue, Mrs Thatcher's era dovetailing with a beautifully executed televi-sion dramatisation of Evelyn Waugh's *Brideshead Revisited*). But more profoundly, and much to my father's distress, I reacted strongly against the idea of being a major public schoolboy and a different identification emerged, that with my mother.

Although from a wealthy family, she had been primarily raised by an illiterate Tasmanian nanny, and she had great faith in what she called 'the integrity of the working classes'. In accord with this, I spent my gap year between school and university setting up a holiday play scheme on a hous-ing estate on the edge of Manchester (called Hattersley, it was where the notorious Moors Murders had occurred five years before). My Cambridge college being very posh, I rejected the port-swilling and letting off of shot-guns into the night, of some of my hunting, shooting and fishing contem-poraries (the college actually had its own beagle-pack). Instead, I grew my hair long, and spent a lot of time reading and pontificating. My relation-ship with my father never quite recovered from this betrayal of his unful-filled ambitions, although we continued to share the love of scholarship that he had modelled for me.

The main point of this lengthy digression is that my father never gave up on me and that it was because we loved each other that I kept on responding to his pleas to buckle down. Love can be the foundation of identification. It might be said that the very fact that I am expounding the ideas in this book is evidence thereof: my father was a psychoanalyst, and along with my mother, who also was one (and also had a big influence on my thinking), he was a compelling advocate of the role of nurture in determining what we are like. I did not genetically inherit my longstanding fascination with the nature-nurture debate, I identified with my parents' interest. But identification does not only work through love.

Very often it is out of fear. If so, the child is identifying in order to avoid unpleasant experiences, like criticism, punishment or, at worst, physical attacks. This identification with the aggressor is a way of pacifying them. It is saying, 'don't hurt me any more, I am who you want me to be, I am you'. That way, the aggressor is less likely to attack them.

Maltreatment as a cause of similarities between children and parents

Beyond the three mechanisms of learning (teaching, modelling and identification), maltreatment is the most tenacious cause of why children become like parents because it sets in motion a desperate and compulsive tendency to repeat the past.[13]

Teaching and modelling can be consciously spotted once we grow up, and we can choose alternatives. Identification can certainly be hard to unpick, since it is part of who we are. But the effects of maltreatment are hardest of all to overcome.

At its simplest, maltreatment causes the child to feel the same distress as the parent. If I am a depressed parent, I may be depressing to my child. If your parent upsets you in particular ways that create similar distress in you, sometimes a duplicate of their distress. The content of the depressive ideas may be identical.[14] If the parent is depressed about being fat and intellectually inadequate, those ideas may be planted in the child by a form of coercive teaching – 'you're fat, you're stupid'. They may also be transferred into the child by behaviour, such as proving that it lacks intelligence by humiliating it in front of others. 'I'm okay,' the parent feels afterwards, 'you're not.'

Maltreatment includes emotional abuse (like being victimised, being treated cruelly or seeing other siblings favoured over them), emotional or physical neglect, and physical or sexual abuse. If we are maltreated, it causes severe distress which becomes the way we experience the world. It remains intractably part of us because the child copes with the distress through re-enacting it in other relationships, including with siblings and peers, and in later life, in love, work and friendships.

For example, a woman had been the object of considerable negative attributions from both parents. Her father routinely humiliated her by showing her how much cleverer he was at mealtimes. Her mother criticised her for being fat, having in fact made the girl overweight by encouraging her to overeat. As a result, the girl had very negative ideas about both herself and how other people viewed her, expecting them to think her fat and stupid. Both in childhood and in later life, she attracted friends who continued the maltreatment by also calling her fat and treating her as worthless. Even though it made her unhappy, being related to in these ways was familiar, comfortable in a way that benign alternatives were not. Behind this lay a faint hope that, somehow, this time, with this new friend, it would turn out differently.

In studies, such emotional abuse is emerging as the single most destructive maltreatment.[15] If I persistently tell my children that they are stupid, ugly or foul, it's invidious and damaging to their psyches. If I favour one child over another, bigging one up and putting the other down, the injury is deep, the wounds hard to heal. Painful though it may be for us to admit, to some degree all parents unintentionally maltreat their children, and mostly without being conscious of what they are doing. Indeed, maltreatment is found in all relationships, including in workplaces and between friends. But it is particularly damaging when done repeatedly and extremely by parents to children, because of *Offspring Stockholm Syndrome* and the power imbalance.[16]

I call the projection of unwanted negatives on to others the *I'm Okay, You're Not* mechanism. If I am feeling angry or depressed, I may get rid of those emotions by provoking them in someone else. We use each other as dustbins for unwanted emotions in this way on a daily basis.[17]

If it is an infrequent or a mild, transient incident, it does no lasting damage. Hence, if you are feeling in a bad mood at work, you may send an email to a stressed colleague chasing up a document that they should have already supplied. Consciously, you think you are just doing your job; unconsciously, by choosing that particular moment to pressurise them, you are creating an irritant, which you know, deep down, will add to their stress levels, reducing your own by excreting it on to them. At a subliminal level, you know that when they open the email they will let out a little curse as they read it, stressed by the added burden. You feel a little bit better the moment you press 'send', knowing that after they open the document their heart rate will rise, their blood pressure increase and a frown will crease their face. Your body may relax a little, you may have a small and temporary relief from your bad mood.

All family members sometimes do this to each other. I may feel fed up and, instead of getting on with writing this book, send my wife a text asking if she has remembered to arrange the MOT for her car, causing her annoyance. It's part of the warp and woof of family life, humorously explored in the television series *Modern Family*. Most of it is ultimately harmless, causing only short-term dips in moods, but it has bigger effects when done by parents to children because of the power ratio.

If I see that my child is tired, has had a bad day and has still not done their homework, there are distressing or benign ways and moments to communicate the need for them to get the homework done. I can do it in an *I'm Okay, You're Not* way, or in one that does not dump my rubbish on them. If I choose the moment to suggest they do it when they are just settling into a much-anticipated new episode of *The Simpsons*, it is liable to annoy them. If I am in a hurry or feeling fed up after a difficult day's work, I may unconsciously choose precisely this wrong moment,

24

and because I am the parent, I have the power to impose my bad mood on them by switching off the TV and insisting they do their homework then. They cannot do the same to me, although their howls of rage may irritate me. It is easier for me as a parent to use my children as a dustbin for my bad feelings.

Although in itself a small thing, done repeatedly I can prime my children to anticipate such dumping of my emotional toxic waste on them. The patterns become a form of emotional abuse. If I play the 'turn the TV off' gag on them across a range of activities, I can get my children to live in unwitting fear of my bad moods. I may use what I cook for them as a means to induce negative emotional states – 'Dad, you know I hate too much pesto on my pasta'. I can drive the car too fast making them feel sick or scared, be persistently late picking them up at school, insist on dragging them round the golf course when they would rather be at home, use dozens of domestic arrangements to subtly torment them. It becomes an intimate terrorism,[18] so that I only have to mention a buzzword or display a gesture for that to signal to the child that the abusive pattern is about to happen. The child finds themselves walking on eggshells, looking out for signs that it's about to happen, living in fear of it.

These patterns on the part of the parent usually result from having been subjected to them by their own parents.[19] A client of mine was so victimised from a young age. Our work together enabled him to avoid repeating the pattern with his children. However, occasionally his childhood mistreatment would show up in his adult relationships. For example, he took in a female lodger who reminded him of his mother. He found himself feeling furious with the lodger. A key issue with his mother had been being in the right. My client constantly felt his lodger was in the wrong – she didn't do the babysitting she had committed to do, she came into parts of the house she was not supposed to, that sort of thing. He started to make her feel his rage by picking the right words and moments to upset her, much as his mother did to him. Because we were able to analyse the childhood buttons the lodger was pressing, he was able to calmly

deal with each problem as it occurred. Instead of upsetting her, he nego-
tiated the practical arrangements in ways that caused no grief. Without
that insight, he would have continued to act like his mother towards her,
making her feel the distress he did as a child.

In essence, he was identifying with the lodger as if she was his childhood self, then reliving the scenario of being tormented by his mother
by being the tormentor. As his mother, he could avoid the unpleasant
sensation of being the tormented child. In these ways, we often re-enact
past torments in the hope of a better outcome. Either we become the tormentor, or we find tormenting situations or people who do it to us. It does
not work, though.

What makes extreme *I'm Okay, You're Not* insidiously invisible and
hard to believe is that it becomes part of our internal emotional furniture.
It is so familiar that it is hard to notice it is going on, as familiar as the sink
in your kitchen. By contrast, other kinds of more overt maltreatment can
sometimes be more easily remembered and identified, such as physical
and sexual abuse.

As therapists we frequently hear of very exact attempts to recreate past
maltreatment, endlessly repeated in relationships, including the one with
the therapist. In doing so, whether reliving the role of tormentor or tormented, the client is hoping that this time there will be a better outcome.
They are trapped on a treadmill of trauma, which they hope by repetition
will be different next time. The core task of a good therapist is to help the
client gain insight into the real origins of these patterns and then provide
a different experience in the therapeutic relationship.

Because the maltreatment was like the air or light in a room, something they were so used to that they took it for granted, it is hard for them
to see. Almost invariably, I find myself having to help my clients *Believe
The Unbelievable*: that their parents truly did maltreat them and that it was
as painful as it really was. Like fearful hostages, clients are tremendously
reluctant to confront the reality that their parent was unloving or cruel.
Through the warmth and support of the relationship with the therapist, we

can give them a different experience, enabling them to relate differently to their intimates, friends and colleagues beyond the therapeutic sessions.

In adulthood, maltreated children frequently become exactly like their tormentor. This is at its most obvious in the extreme example of physical or sexual abuse: a high proportion of abusers of both kinds were themselves abused in that way.[20] Because of *Offspring Stockholm Syndrome*, all of us are defensive of our parents in many respects, very reluctant to allow ourselves to be critical of them. The child in us is still there, fearing what may happen if we oppose them. Abused children will go to astonishing lengths to protect their parents. At the outset of our work, I have heard the phrase 'I had a happy childhood' uttered by more maltreated clients than I care to remember.

One of the most remarkable examples I have encountered was when I met a daughter of Fred West, the serial killer and rapist, on a television programme. She determinedly defended her father and his reputation. This was despite the fact that she was aware that he had committed innumerable horrific crimes, including ones against her.

Modern views of mental illness place maltreatment rather than genes as the main cause. The Traumagenic Model[21] is a good example, developed by clinical psychologist John Read. Rather than an illness, it is conceived as a form of distress akin to post traumatic stress disorder (PTSD), or actually is just that. Tightly defined, the symptoms of PTSD are: intrusive thoughts and memories that erupt into the mind beyond the person's control, sometimes including hallucinations; avoidance of intimacy or of difficult issues; negative feelings and ideas that seem to come from nowhere; and being suddenly or easily aroused, a hyper-reactivity, over-sensitivity. Often those with PTSD try to douse these unpleasant states with drugs or alcohol. Components of this collection of symptoms are found in a great many mental 'illnesses'.

The latest evidence proves that there is not necessarily a mapping from one kind of maltreatment to one kind of mental illness.[22] Rather, all maltreated children show a hotchpotch of anxiety, depression, mood swings and delusions. In later life, they are more easily distressed than people who were less maltreated in childhood. The precise form of the maltreatment, like whether the child was called ugly or was neglected in some way, can determine the content of the distress. But the idea that there are isolated, discrete categories of mental illness that do not overlap with other ones has been disproved.

The new model is called traumagenic because almost all adult emotional distress entails the eruption of traumatic past experience into the present. The victim has been primed by their parents to expect threat. A small thing, one that others might regard as innocuous, triggers what seem to independent observers to be inappropriate, disproportionate reactions.

In the extreme, this is a person who was raped suddenly having flashbacks to the details of the attack, finding themselves back in the bedroom or back alley with the perpetrator forcing themself upon them. Tiny details, like a name or a sound associated with the trauma could be the trigger. The flashbacks are as real to them as normal reality, they are really happening when the 'video clip' of the trauma switches on. Just as dreams are as real as reality, so it is with those who are reliving trauma.

These 'experiential videos' are distinct from hallucinating sounds or sights. It now seems clear that many of the hallucinations of psychosis are simply versions of memories[23] – hearing a voice from their childhood telling the victim they are a bad person, seeing the real original tormentor on the other side of the room. But as time goes by the experience may be reinterpreted and represented differently. Hence, the experience of extreme powerlessness may be dealt with by hallucinating oneself as a supremely powerful person, a much safer person to be, like Jesus Christ. This is the true origin of delusion: it is not the mechanical problem, not the faulty brain caused by faulty genes, which the psychiatric profession has mistakenly insisted upon for over a century.

If a child was seduced by a parent and it was incorporated as part of their normal experience, when they realise its abnormality when they're older, they have to suppress those memories. Aspects of it may have been enjoyable, perhaps they even experienced elements of erotic arousal. The abuse may also have been the only situation in which they were shown love. That makes it even harder to integrate into their adult self this forbidden secret about which they have mixed feelings. The memories and secrets may start erupting as hallucinations or delusions, the content of which are based in the original trauma. A conventional doctor or geneticist will dismiss the patient's ideas as delusional nonsense, the product of a dysfunctional brain. In truth, the content of the delusions are highly meaningful.

For the most part, the experiences were painful and distressing. Whether extreme, like rape, or less so, like being shouted at or hit, they become established as patterns which erupt into the present. The nuclear core of all mental illness is reliving the past in the present, whether in the form of an actual memory being mistaken for the present, or a distorted aspect of a memory.

Those are the extremes, but all of us were maltreated sometimes, in some ways, without exception. Crucially, we were maltreated and loved in often radically different ways from our siblings, resulting in our unique kinks.

To summarise my explanation, the key mechanisms which make us like our parents are:

⟩ *Offspring Stockholm Syndrome,* in which the hostage-child does its best to make the captor-parent relate to and like them, by copying their traits. This is achieved through learning: teaching, modelling and identification.

⟩ The direct effects of maltreatment, or of loving care, in which the depressed parent may be depressing, or equally, the loving parent makes the child feel loved.

⟩ The *I'm Okay, You're Not* unconscious wish of a parent to make themselves feel better by inflicting the same or similar maltreatment upon offspring. This results in the child having the parent's feelings.

⟩ The maltreated child becomes someone who repeats the past, in the hope that this time it will turn out different. They may do this by putting themselves in similar or near-identical relationships and situations to the original one, or by provoking others to treat them in the way their parents did.

The reader may feel that this brief account of how children become like parents is bleak. It is important to stress that the positives about us are also transmitted by the mechanisms described above. *Offspring Stockholm Syndrome* leads us to be receptive to the teaching of positive traits, likewise to modelling and identifying with them. As described, I was the beneficiary of this from my father, although it had some negative consequences too. There is also *I'm Okay, You're Okay* going on in families, in which the child is supported and thrives from loving, approving and encouraging parental projections. Parents tell children how lovely they look, how kind they have been, how talented, and so on. We go many extra miles to protect and improve our offspring. All those positives shine through in later life, every bit as much as the consequences of maltreatment and other negatives.[24]

What is more, some of what we achieve as adults can be the consequence of maltreatment being converted from the lead of despair and fear into the gold of creativity and insight. Much great art results from this, John Lennon's acerbic lyrics, Van Gogh's self-portraits, Virginia Woolf's *To The Lighthouse*. But on a more mundane level, just being able to understand that everyday difficulties you may have at home or work are partly caused by mistaking others for a parent who had maltreated you can liberate from feeling persecuted. For example, you may feel your boss is a tyrant and realise you are confusing them with your father. The positives of what our parents gave us, as well as the negatives, can be used to cope with this. Perhaps one parent could be terrorising but perhaps the other was a good listener and sometimes playful. That patch of parental sunlight can be the insightful torch illuminating the darkness in your office predicament.

The ideas presented in this chapter take some absorbing. The next chapter provides a detailed illustration of how the mechanism by which we become like our parents plays out.

SO WHAT? 3 TAKEAWAYS

ONE: How similar are you to your parents. Why?
Here is a simple method for identifying similarities between you and your parents.

Write down five positive and negative traits of your mother. Quite often, because of *Offspring Stockholm Syndrome*, people find it difficult to identify negatives about one or both parents, so you may have to dig deep to identify them. Write the traits down before reading on.

Now write down five positive and negative traits of your father. Again, do it right away, no faffing.

Finally, write down five positive and negative traits of yourself. Do not read on until you have done this!

Take each of the ten points you now have for your parents, and map across to the ones you have written down about yourself. Unless you are very unusual, you will find that there is some overlap between you and both your parents.

Why do you share these traits and not others? As you will see in Chapter 5, part of the reason is the role you were ascribed, or carved for yourself, in the family dynamics. A good deal of the reason will also be the result of teaching, modelling, identification, and maltreatment and love.

To some extent, using the information in this chapter, you will be able to work out the answers. However, for most of us, it's not quite that simple.

While you may not have sufficiently serious problems to require it, therapy can be the best way to discover those answers.

TWO: Believing The Unbelievable: find a therapist who can give you insight into your childhood and provide a different experience from that

Offspring Stockholm Syndrome makes it extremely hard for most of us to *Believe The Unbelievable* truth that our parents did maltreat, as well as love, us. Nearly all of us need some therapy, and in most cases it needs only to be brief and simple. For example, in only sixteen sessions, cognitive analytic therapy can make a profound difference to any specific traits that are troubling you. There are many other kinds of brief therapy that explore the impact of your past and use the relationship with the therapist to give you a different experience, as well as providing practical tips or teaching methods that change the way you think. There is no doubt that yoga and meditation can help to provide daily doses of calm. The therapies of which I have good knowledge and know can be effective include transactional analysis, transpersonal psychology and the Hoffman Process (especially effective for depression). There are many variants and I would not pretend to be an expert about all of them. The key ingredients are a good relationship with the therapist and being prepared to uncover the childhood origins of problems. At the deepest level, as explained in this chapter and exemplified throughout the rest of the book, the relationship with the therapist can provide an alternative experience from the traumatic childhood one, replacing the bad internalised parent with a good one in the form of the therapist. Using thoughts to change feelings through techniques like diagrams or getting you to visualise yourself as behaving differently, are secondary in promoting change.

There is a desperate need for these kinds of therapy to be made available on the NHS for free. Nearly a quarter of Britons are suffering from a mental illness, mostly anxiety or depression, at any one time.[25]

The cost to our economy is enormous (estimated to be £105 billion a year), never mind the personal anguish, and for too long the main treatment was pills. What a tragedy that the first attempt to provide nationwide talking therapy is using the wrong kind: cognitive behavioural therapy (CBT).

The CBT theory is that your thoughts control your feelings. Change your thoughts, change how you feel. In just 6 to 16 sessions, CBT claims to be able to convert you from depressed or anxious, to 'recovered'.[26] You are taught to stop calling yourself fat or ugly or stupid, even if you are. If you keep getting anxious for no reason, perhaps worrying that something awful will happen or that you will make a fool of yourself, CBT teaches you to think the opposite.

The scheme introducing CBT nationwide – entitled the Improving Access to Psychological Therapies (IAPT) programme – was created in 2009 by Professors Richard Layard, an economist, and David Clark, a clinical psychologist at Oxford University. They sold it to the New Labour government as a way to help at least half of sufferers from anxiety or depression to recover.

At first sight, the claims for its success seem quite impressive: it has led to 'recovery' in around 40 per cent of people who complete the treatment.[27] Closer inspection reveals a much less rosy picture. CBT is all about marketing. It is a cheap quick-fix.

In their book *Thrive*,[28] Layard and Clark make no mention of the extensive long-term evidence[29] which shows that, when followed up two years later, depressed or anxious people who had CBT are no more likely to have recovered than those who had no treatment.

Two-thirds of those treated for depression with CBT who had apparently 'recovered', relapsed or sought further help within two years. When the treatment actually ends, the average patient is still depressed (around 30 per cent do not complete the course). The fact is, if given no treatment, most people with depression or anxiety drift in and out of it. After two years, those given CBT have no better mental health than ones who have been untreated.

Working as a psychotherapist I rarely encounter clients who have not been subjected to CBT which failed. The problem is that it makes no attempt to understand the causes of depression and anxiety. Proper therapy – such as psychodynamic therapy – successfully treats the causes, resulting in sustained cure.[30] Major reviews of the evidence,[31] like that by the American psychologist Jonathan Shedler, show that therapies which do explore childhood causes and focus on the relationship with the therapist truly work in the long term. If IAPT had truly been evidence-based, it would have used those therapies.

Given the strength of the evidence that mental illness is largely caused by maltreatment, it is bizarre that practitioners of CBT are explicitly required to steer patients away from their childhood memories. The CBT theory ignores causes, forcefully teaching practitioners to concentrate only on how thoughts are causing symptoms.

Knowing Richard Layard to be well intentioned, and an economist, not a psychologist, I can forgive him. But David Clark is an Oxford University psychology professor. He strongly stresses that CBT is *the* evidence-based, scientific treatment, yet he does not accept that this evidence proves it does not work in the long term (two years or more later). When challenged to produce persuasive supporting evidence in an email correspondence I have had with him and Layard, they did not do so, despite having the resources of two major university departments to draw upon. There is no sound basis for portraying CBT as a cure or as more scientifically supported than other therapies. It is psychodynamic ones that are proven to work, long term.

A few anxieties, such as panic and possibly obsessive compulsive disorder, are sometimes changed long term by CBT but for the great majority, when the gloss wears off, the distress returns. Yet thanks to Clark and Layard, CBT is now largely the only kind of therapy it is possible to obtain from either the Health Service or from private health insurance companies.

Of course these two men aren't exclusively to blame – CBT appeals to politicians and the National Institute for Health and Care Excellence (NICE), because it is quick and therefore cheap. The therapies that are proven to work long term – like psychodynamic therapy – are not so cheap because they require more sessions than 6 to 16.

CBT does have some virtues and has been a wake-up call for some other therapies. It encourages practical steps proven to improve well-being, such as taking exercise, meditation and yoga.

Professor Clark himself is a highly skilled clinician and I do know people who claim that CBT has reduced their depression. But all of them had done it for many years and the relationship with the therapist is what helped, not the change in thinking patterns. Studies prove this:[32] insofar as CBT works, it works when there is a good relationship between the therapist and patient. But the CBT that is available on the NHS is brief by definition and discourages the emotional attachment to the therapist.

For the vast majority of people, CBT is virtually all that is on offer. In its stead we urgently need therapies for everyone – not just those who can afford the alternatives – that treat the childhood causes of depression and anxiety (and all other mental illnesses) through the relationship with the therapist and exploration of childhood.

THREE: Turning I'm Okay, You're Not *Into* I'm Okay, You're Okay

All of us sometimes use *I'm Okay, You're Not* as a way of dealing with unwanted emotions, in our dealings with family, friends and colleagues. By implication, that means all of us sometimes have to cope with it being done to us.

Without the help of intimates or a therapist, it is usually very hard to catch yourself doing it. A simple exercise is to decide to check yourself from criticising your friends and family or insisting that your opinion about a vexed matter is the right one. Instead, observe yourself during that moment and closely examine what is going on. Is it really necessary for your child to eat at the table on this particular evening? Is it quite as certain as you believe that your partner is giving you the cold shoulder? Is that devious colleague really as devious as you suppose?

When you ponder what happened in your childhood in relation to this issue, you may find surprising connections. Perhaps your parents were relentless about making you sit at the table or very lax about it, likewise regarding cold shoulders and deviousness. Of course, it could be that you are right and they are wrong. But it's often not as simple as that.

Equally, when it comes to being on the wrong end of *I'm Okay, You're Not*, it can be hard not to disappear into a vortex of uncertainty, of wondering, 'is it me or is it them?' One helpful tip is that certain kinds of people are much more likely to use this defensive manoeuvre on you than others. As I described in my book, *Office Politics*, people with the triad of psychopathy, narcissism and Machiavellianism are much more likely to use *I'm Okay, You're Not*. If you think you have identified a triadic person in your orbit, then their use of *I'm Okay, You're Not* can be a strong clue.

A simple method can be used to detoxify yourself once you have identified that you have been the object of *I'm Okay, You're Not*. Picture the attribution that the person has assigned to you – 'stupid', 'lazy', 'devious' – and imagine wrapping it up in a paper towel. Now chuck that rubbish in an imaginary bin. Or, picture it as an image, then make it slowly dissolve, and relish the feeling of ridding yourself of their problem. Interestingly, these kinds of techniques are commonly used by CBT to treat mental illness; they are much more suitable for this kind of temporary relief of a problem.

For parents, at the end of Chapter 4 I describe my Love Bombing technique, described in my book of that name. It is remarkably effective at forcing you to stop doing *I'm Okay, You're Not* to your child, although that is not its primary goal.

Likewise, if you have a relative with dementia, many people have found the method described in my book *Contented Dementia* helpful.

Two of the Golden Rules for managing people with dementia are Don't Ask Questions and Never Contradict. In all relationships, obeying these rules for five minutes when with someone who causes you problems can be remarkably revealing. You may be able to catch yourself at having been about to embark on an *I'm Okay, You're Not* mental operation.

Chapter 2

Why was Peaches Geldof so Like her Mother?

On 17 September, 2000, at the age of 41, Paula Yates was found dead in her home, killed by an overdose of heroin. Her three-year-old daughter Tiger Lily was alone in the house when the body was discovered.

Fourteen years later, during the night of 6–7 April 2014, Peaches Geldof, aged 25, Paula's second daughter with Sir Bob Geldof (creator of the global phenomenon, *Live Aid*), also died at her home of a heroin overdose. Peaches' eleven-month-old son was found alone in the house when the body was discovered.

It only serves to heighten the tragedy that this happened to one of the world's great humanitarians. He had lost his own mother when aged five, now he had to endure this awful end to the lives of both his much loved wife and his precious daughter.

Peaches' funeral took place in the same church where she was married, the one where her mother had also been married and had her funeral.

Paula and Peaches had each suffered several drugs overdoses before their fatal ones. The coroners did not offer verdicts of suicide in either case. Neither appears to have deliberately killed themselves but both ingested fatal quantities of heroin while in sole charge of their small child. Both of these women were warm-hearted, intelligent and loved their children.

That they felt driven to use heroin at all, let alone when at home and with their little ones in the next room, indicates a level of anxiety and turmoil almost beyond our imagining.

Shortly before her death, Peaches went so far as to say that Paula was 'living through her' because 'we are just so similar'. Peaches was indeed strikingly similar to her mother in many other respects than the hideous manner of their deaths. There must be physical or psychological mechanisms which explain this. Given that it was not genes, it is possible there were other physical processes, as with my son's football dribbling and me. But there is no question that the particular ways in which Paula related to Peaches, as opposed to her other daughters, played a big part. As a test case of how and why psychological traits pass from parents to children and why traits run in families, it is illuminating.

Both Paula and Peaches' careers were in journalism and television presenting. Both were quick-witted and articulate. Often courting tabloid attention, their personal lives became media stories.

As people, they were febrile, emotionally insecure and self-focused. While they longed to have more stable and admirable characters, neither could sustain that ambition for long. In public, they proffered Barbie Doll personae, posing as pink-wearing, exaggeratedly feminine women, but that was misleading. Both were also hard-headed and could be manipulative, personally as well as professionally. Both lived histrionic lives, filled with sensation-seeking melodrama, yet in moments of reflection, they hankered to be sounder, calmer, more stable. They could be loving, longing to give and receive affection.

They began taking hard drugs in their early teens. As a 12-year old schoolgirl in Malaga, Paula spent two years regularly smoking heroin with a much older boyfriend. Peaches began taking drugs around that age, including heroin. Neither drank alcohol heavily or regularly, except for a brief period at the end of Paula's life.

Paula's sexual misfortunes began when young. In hospital at the age of nine, she was interfered with by a night nurse. She was allowed to regularly share a bed with older boys and men from the age of 12, although she did not lose her virginity until she was 15. It is not clear when Peaches became sexually active, but it does appear that, like her mother, she became prone to promiscuity as an adult.

Both were prone to inventing fairy tales about their lives, which they half-believed. In particular, they longed to have perfect marriages and be perfect mothers, weaving fables to this effect in the media.

Paula's imperfections as a parent were maltreatment of her children and repeated infidelity. She wrote of hoping to give her children a different childhood from the one she had suffered, but she was unable to.

During her two years as a mother, Peaches was far more able to meet the needs of her infants than Paula, but by the time of her death she was finding it exhausting, her children going for weekends to her parents-in-law to give her a break. The strain of not repeating the past was showing at the time of her death.

It so happens that I have considerable knowledge, both first- and second-hand, of their difficult lives. A close friend of mine was the television executive in charge of the music show, *The Tube*, of which Paula was co-presenter. On many occasions, he took me to watch it being produced at the Tyne Tees Television studios, introducing me to Paula in 1985. The next year I worked with her for six months on a television series titled *Sex With Paula* and visited the home in Chelsea where she lived with Bob Geldof.

Ours was a professional relationship but I had many opportunities to observe her during the filming of the series and, on a few occasions, spent time on my own with her. I knew several people who were her intimates until the end of her life, and who were also witnesses to Peaches' life, including her early years. These people have given me detailed information about the kind of people Paula and Peaches were.

There are also publically available sources of information, most notably Paula's autobiography, published in 1995. Peaches wrote about her life in newspapers and magazines.

I have never met or communicated with any of Paula's daughters but from all these sources it has been possible to piece together a picture of the mechanisms by which Peaches became like Paula, much more so than her two sisters and her half-sister.

Some readers may feel it is distasteful to write about Peaches two years after her death. It is a grievously sad story. However, I am confident that what I have to say is true and that it will be of assistance to those who live on after her, if inevitably upsetting in some respects. Both women were prominent public figures, seeking the public eye. Analysing the similarities in their lives and the ways in which Paula unwittingly nurtured those similarities, serves a valuable purpose. Many readers will be able to engage with these women, having felt close to or involved in the stories of their lives through the media. This emotional proximity creates a natural interest in their stories. It is conceivable that by reading my analysis of them, such tragedies will be less probable in the future.

Peaches' childhood

Peaches was born in 1989, the second of three daughters that Paula had with Bob Geldof. Her older sister, Fifi, was born six years earlier; Pixie was 18 months younger.

When Peaches arrived, Paula passed her over to the exclusive and nurturing care of their nanny, Anita Debney, which took place in the basement of their house. Paula was anxious to avoid unsettling Fifi and did not want to disrupt the status quo. It was not until Peaches was aged two that Paula tried to take over the care of her, a disaster that lasted only a month. Peaches could be seen at the window crying every night, unable to be soothed at bedtime. Debney, who had effectively been her full-time mother, was restored to that role, which she continued to occupy throughout Peaches' early years.

Immediately following the one-month separation, Peaches developed eczema, a severe rash. Studies of this psychosomatic reaction[1] show that it could have been an indication of the strength of the attachment to her nanny and the insecurity she felt in her absence. Such prolonged separations from their main carer can be highly traumatic for toddlers.[2] In later life, the eczema would reappear when she was distressed after breaking up with boyfriends.

Peaches became a woman who was terrified of rejection. She was insecure in her relationships with men. With her intimates, she found even a simple parting difficult, had trouble just saying goodbye.

Paula treated Peaches markedly differently from her two sisters. She felt rejected by Peaches and was consequently much more irritable with her, and prone to upsetting her. She wanted to feel that Peaches loved her but if Peaches fell over and was upset, she would go to her nanny for consolation. When she needed medical care, it was Debney who took her to the hospital or doctor. Paula had never had sustained responsive care from her own mother and may have envied Peaches' close relationship with Debney.

Nonetheless, Peaches desperately wanted to feel loved by Paula and identified with her cleverness early on, like a sensible hostage would with a captor. It made her a smart child, quick to understand what was needed. From a young age she realised that to gain her mother's approbation she had to tell Paula what she wanted to hear. This is a good example of how 'quick-wittedness' can come about. Peaches was not born smarter: the particular role she occupied in the family made her use cleverness as a bridge to Paula.

She also sought to connect herself with Paula through exhibitionism. By the time Peaches went to school, other parents saw her as her mother's daughter in that respect. She had Paula's taste for the flamboyantly feminine, with a pink canopied bed surrounded by fairy lights.

The many incidents in which Paula expressed fury at Peaches for being so attached to her nanny were disturbing. But the most serious maltreatment occurred after Paula had fallen in love with Michael Hutchence, the lead singer of the famous band INXS. In 1995, when Peaches was nearly six, Paula separated from Geldof and began living with Hutchence.

Following the separation, the children bounced between the parents for two years, with Debney providing the only continuity of care. The period entailed a state of perpetual motion as they moved between a bewildering variety of residences and countries. Paula, Michael and Bob were constantly travelling, the children followed.

In July 1996 Paula gave birth to Tiger-Lily, her daughter by Hutchence. His gruesome suicide was a terrible shock, in Sydney a year later, understandably destabilising. Since being with Hutchence, Paula had often taken hard drugs or was drunk when in charge of her children. Consequently, a high court order in 1997 that gave Paula and Geldof joint custody of the children, but with them mainly living with Paula, was disastrous for eight-year old Peaches. Debney was granted access every six weeks, effectively parting Peaches from her emotional mother for long periods, Geldof's access was only fortnightly. At this point Fifi was at boarding school but her younger sisters had to spend the majority of their time with an unstable and drug-abusing mother.

Now that Debney was no longer there, a new nanny was employed but she was strict about leaving the home at 6 p.m. on the dot, after which the children were in the exclusive care of Paula. She picked on Peaches without the consolation and protection of Debney. Sometimes Paula would mount charm offensives but then would snap, becoming mean and malevolent when Peaches did not respond. Paula was most incensed when Peaches begged to stay with Geldof. At first, Peaches described the maltreatment to the court welfare officers and pleaded not to have to stay with Paula. When everything she said was passed on via lawyers, she learnt not to tell the truth of what was happening to avoid a Paula tantrum.

Up to the time of her parents' separation, Peaches had never known her mother to drink or take drugs. Following the court order, aged only eight, she frequently witnessed it and objected. Paula took to pouring spirits into Coca-Cola cans or hiding miniatures in her bag. Peaches found it scary and crazy-making that her mother would lie to her about this. Paula would go into a lavatory and come out in an unmistakeably altered mental state. Peaches would know her mother had taken a mood-altering substance. She knew that Paula knew that she knew she had done so, yet was denying it, a state between parent and child which is a prescription for deep confusion and distress, emotionally abusive.

Paula's aggression to Peaches when challenged was sometimes severe. On one occasion, a drunken and furious Paula shoved Peaches out of a moving taxi for doing so. During this time Peaches informed a number of people that she wanted to die, beset by dark moods chronicled in despairing letters.

The Sunday nights at the end of her weekends away from Paula with Geldof or Debney were desperate occasions. Peaches would beg not to be sent back. Apart from the emotional abuse, there was neglect. She did not get fed properly when with her mother, and was not given the correct items of school uniform. She was often left unsupervised and as they got older, from the age of eight, she would wander with Pixie around the King's Road, near where they lived in Chelsea.

Offspring Stockholm Syndrome meant that Peaches was the one to feel she must take responsibility when, on at least three occasions, Paula made suicide attempts. Following an overdose, she came upon Paula's limp body and ran into the street, shouting to passers-by that her mother was dying. On another occasion, Paula climbed out on to the window ledge, about to throw herself off. Peaches talked her out of it, but when her mother came indoors, she threw herself down the stairs, fortunately only suffering minor injuries. On a third occasion, Peaches worked out that Paula had taken an overdose, although Paula denied it. These were traumatic experiences, terrifying for a girl of that age. Pixie was either not involved in these episodes, or peripherally so.

Paula's drug use spiralled after Hutchence's suicide. She became even more promiscuous, with a string of much younger boyfriends. In 1998, Geldof finally obtained a court order giving him custody. However, Peaches and Pixie still spent alternate weeks in the care of Paula, a woman who was disintegrating.

Her death in 2000 created mixed feelings in Peaches. Since Paula had been an emotionally and physically abusive presence for five years, it was a huge relief to no longer be forced to spend time in her company. At the same time, it was a terrible shock and there was a suppressed sense of an irreplaceable loss.

True to the intergenerational transmission of trauma, Paula had herself been maltreated. Jess Yates, her father, experienced severe mood swings, which sometimes made his a scary presence. Paula claimed that her mother was neglectful and unresponsive.

On many occasions, both Paula and Peaches publicly declared their desire to avoid repeating the maltreatment they had suffered. Paula wrote that 'I think about my own childhood and I want theirs to be different'. Having known Paula, I believe that her incapacity to fulfil this wish was due to her lack of insight. Yes, she was clever enough to realise that the maltreatment she had experienced in her childhood had affected her. But she was unable to use this knowledge to alter the trajectory of her parenting through the moment-by-moment self-awareness that insight can confer. What therapy she had, failed. She was unable to believe the unbelievable about her childhood, rather than merely knowing some of it. Knowing something intellectually and feeling it are not the same thing.

A stable, emotionally warm relationship with a therapist would have given her a different experience, a new platform upon which to build new patterns. It seems that none of her therapists were able to establish that; perhaps she was incapable of such an attachment. Although she had brief periods in and out of mental hospitals and addiction centres, these institutions rarely provide therapy which deals with causes. Authority figures, like psychiatrists (doctors specialising in using largely physical methods, like drugs, to treat mental illness), force vulnerable patients and addicts to accept the story that they have an incurable, genetically caused illness that can only be managed through pills or cognitive tricks. There is strong evidence that patients of doctors who are persuaded they cannot be cured of their 'illness' are less likely to recover than ones who do not buy that fiction (see Appendix 4).[3] While in the case of addiction,[4] acceptance that their compulsion is beyond their control can be very helpful in the short term (the focus being on not enacting the addictive behaviour), only insight into the true childhood causes can bring about profound change or even complete cure.[5] Although Paula was treated by many private clinicians none of them was able to address the true causes which lay at the root of her problems. Lacking insight, Paula never learnt how to turn the wheel before the car crashed into the wall, or, as John Lennon famously put it, she didn't notice that the lights had changed. To be able to register the red lights in your life and stop, you have to understand the past in your present.

In the case of Paula, one legacy of her childhood maltreatment was severe emotional abuse for Peaches. That legacy was played out in Peaches' life in ways that closely mimicked Paula's.

Peaches' teenage years and adulthood

By the time she was 12 years old, Peaches had been exposed to her mother's highly sexualised persona and had adopted some features of it, in her clothing and self-presentation. Paula had always offered that as a model to her daughters and Peaches identified with it the most strongly. The emotional abuse she suffered from Paula when small, combined with the severe maltreatment from when she was eight until she was eleven, increased the risk of an unstable adulthood – emotional abuse is the strongest predictor of severe mental illness.[6]

Only because she had had the security supplied by Anita Debney was she not much more disturbed. Severe maltreatment of all kinds is very common in the childhoods of people with personality disorder,[7] which both Paula and Peaches suffered from. It entails an excessive self-focus, me-me-me narcissism, grandiosity, febrile moods and a tendency to fantastical ideas. Such people can be highly entertaining and, having felt powerless, humiliated or worthless when young, in their eagerness to regain control or the esteem of others they may seek and obtain success. As we shall see in more detail in Chapter 7, 'talent' is not inborn. As well as sometimes growing out of loving and authoritative nurture – self-motivated enjoyment of learning and achievement – it is often the result of adversity. For example, one in three exceptional achievers lost a parent before the age of 15,[8] as did Bob Geldof. In her early career, Peaches certainly showed promise of high achievement.

From a remarkably young age, 14 to 17, she was embraced by national newspapers as a voice of her generation, with a column in the *Daily Telegraph* and articles in the *Guardian*. She made several television programmes and modelled, becoming the face of a fashion brand. Like so many personality disordered and well-known people,[9] she basked in public attention, the feeling that she was special. Like Paula, her sexual relationships soon became regular tabloid fodder and there were public appearances in which she appeared to have taken drugs. It is common for the emotionally abused to use substances as a form of self-medication to ease their distress.[10] Heroin contained particular appeal for Peaches, she described it to her intimates as 'a means of removing the pain' by taking her to 'a floaty, warm place'.

When she was 17, Peaches disappeared to America and Geldof realised Peaches was in danger of destroying herself, as her mother had. He instituted an 'intervention' at a drugs rehabilitation unit, which he and Pixie participated in, to no avail. On running away from it, Peaches had a period of wayward, chaotic drug-taking and sexual incontinence, eventually marrying Max Drummey, an indie rock musician, at the age of 18. This was never a stable relationship and her substance abuse was only halted for a time by an affair with the film director Eli Roth, who was 17 years older than her. Having suffered an ectopic pregnancy during that relationship, she realised how much she wanted to be a mother. She also believed this was never going to happen, partly because the doctors had warned her that she was unlikely ever to conceive again. The relationship ended when she slipped back into drug-taking and promiscuity.

Like Paula in her last few years, to a large extent she simply did not seem to care what happened to her and courted sexual aggression from men. By now, she had taken so many drugs and had had so many reckless relationships that she felt herself to be strangely invincible, that nothing could hurt her. However, on returning to England in her early twenties, she suddenly went in a different direction, albeit only for a year. She met Tom Cohen, a rock musician whom she later married, becoming the devoted mother of their two sons.

Given that she had been told she was likely to be infertile, the pregnancy came as a big surprise and it refreshed the relationship with Cohen, which was already flagging because he was the kind of gentle, loving man with whom she felt uncomfortable. Becoming a mother led to the only settled period in her adult life, during which she was prescribed methadone in increasingly low doses to wean her off heroin. It is likely that the main reason she overdosed fatally was because her body was unaccustomed to heroin and the drugs she took on the night of her death were of exceptional purity. She had told friends that she simply did not believe she could buy illegal drugs in England that were strong enough to kill her.

When she died, Peaches' relationship with Cohen was faltering. Like her mother, Peaches never managed to sustain interest in one man for long. It seems likely that, had she lived, she would have put her sons through similar instability to that inflicted on her by Paula, fuelled by her drug use and difficulty in remaining in a stable relationship.

Why was Peaches' death so similar to Paula's?

Although neither appear to have deliberately killed themselves, their deaths were the result of strong self-destructive impulses. Repeated overdoses are not necessarily attempts to die but they indicate a wilful lack of concern about living.[11] Insofar as they are akin to suicide and since it runs in families, it is not extraordinary that one of Paula's children died in the same way.

A study of the whole Swedish population over the last 30 years shows that suicide is three times commoner among children whose parents died that way.[12] We know this was not the result of genes because suicide rates were not elevated in children who lost parents through accidents or illness. It is parental *suicidal* death that plants the idea of repeating it, it is contagious.

We know that from suicidal clusters identified in groups of doctors, police and farmers.[13] When one member of a profession kills themselves, it increases the likelihood of others who knew them doing so. Contagion is also rife in schools and universities: a student suicide increases the risk of further ones in an institution.[14] When celebrities or characters in television fictions kill themselves,[15] the vulnerable are put at risk. Fans of the same gender and age do it in greater numbers in the succeeding months,[16] suggesting an identification.

In Paula's case, she attempted to imitate Hutchence's manner of death. A number of independent witnesses reported that she was suicidal after it. Heavily drugged, he had hung himself from a door. Only months afterwards, a visiting friend came upon Paula unconscious, also hanging from a door. It illustrates the precision of the contagion and that appears to have been crucial in the case of Peaches.

Studies show that if the mother rather than the father kills themselves, offspring suicide is twice as likely, but more so for the daughter than the son.[17] The daughter of a suicidal mother is twice as likely as her brother to do it than if her father kills himself.[18] Risk for sons is also increased by maternal rather than paternal suicide, but not as much. This fact is powerful evidence that daughters identify more with maternal suicide than sons.

On top of all this, women who have been sexually abused are 13 times more likely to attempt suicide.[19] Sexual abuse – suffered by Paula – increases the likelihood of injection of drugs, rather than other methods.[20] Injection greatly increases the danger of overdose. Both Paula and Peaches tended to inject rather than smoke the drug, putting themselves at greater risk (although on the night of Paula's death, she had smoked it). It may be seen, then, that Paula's overdose in itself put Peaches at risk of dying in the same way.

Peaches' sisters were also put at risk by the suicide, so it does not in itself explain why Peaches died in this way and her sisters did not. Apart from the fact that Paula maltreated her more and that Peaches witnessed three of Paula's suicide attempts, perhaps an important difference was that she was unable to properly mourn Paula. In 2012, she told a journalist that 'I remember the day my mother died, and it's still hard to talk about it. I just blocked it out. I went to school the next day because my father's mentality was "keep calm and carry on". So we all went to school and tried to act as if nothing had happened. But it had happened. I didn't grieve. I didn't cry at her funeral. I couldn't express anything because I was just numb to it all. I didn't start grieving for my mother properly until I was maybe 16.'

Alas, those who forget the past are condemned to repeat it. In Peaches' case, she was extremely vulnerable, with very mixed feelings about her mother. From the ages of eight to eleven, she was increasingly terrified that her mother would kill herself. It seems likely that the idea of death by self-destruction was both modelled and led to an identification with a self-destructive, substance-abusing maternal figure. It is possible that Peaches hoped to be reunited with her mother through death.

Peaches only began to mourn her at 16, which was the age at which she became very similar to the self-destructive Paula, taking plentiful drugs and becoming promiscuous in America. Only when she returned to her real emotional mother, Anita Debney, did she manage not to be like Paula. During the first year of her relationship with Tom Cohen, and following the arrival of her first child, at last she ceased to resemble her. Having weaned herself off heroin, and as a result of providing love to her son, she realised that there was more to life than being in the public eye, and no longer courted publicity for the exhibitionist reasons Paula had.

The trouble seems to have been that the identification with Paula was too strong. The scale of the maltreatment had been so great that the urge to repeat it in the hope of a different outcome took hold. The identification and the maltreatment reasserted themselves. She told those close to her that her husband was not enough for her, just as Paula claimed she felt about Geldof. She felt restless and in need of stimulation, eventually returning to heroin, as did her mother.

Only she knew what was in her mind on the night of 6 April 2014. She left no letters, made no other communications to anyone about it, perhaps unconscious that it was about to happen. She went home from a party, and was in sole charge of her youngest son. How she could have rationalised taking heroin in those circumstances, given what her mother had done, is crucial. At some level, we have to assume she felt very much like Paula and indeed, she truly was. If taking heroin when in the role of mother made sense, it made sense to the Paula in her.

The fact of her equation with her mother was spelt out in one of the last interviews she gave shortly before her death.[21] She said she felt Paula was *'living through me all the time because we are just so similar'*. Perhaps part of Paula 'living through me' included dying in those particular circumstances – death by overdose while in charge of a small child was part of who Paula had been. By dying in this way, more or less unconsciously, perhaps she hoped to be reunited with her.

Why was Peaches more like her mother than her sisters?
It may seem strange that, considering she was singled out for the worst maltreatment, Peaches was so much more like her mother than her sisters. Logic might dictate that having something horrible done to you would make you avoid it in yourself and others. In fact, it was precisely because she was singled out that the similarities were greatest. This worked in two main ways: *Offspring Stockholm Syndrome* and identification resulting from maltreatment. When children are disturbed by their parents' disturbance, it becomes part of who they are, just as the converse can occur: witnessing calmness and emotional health in parents often nurtures it in children.

Pixie also was exposed to Paula's various disturbances, but she did not bear the full brunt of them. Above all, Peaches experienced different care from her sisters. It was she who tried, as so many children do, to prevent her mother from drinking and from killing herself. It was Peaches, not Pixie, who was pushed out of moving taxis for doing so. Meanwhile, Fifi was away at boarding school during the period when Paula was most disturbed. In later life, Fifi was to report suffering from depression, a quite different reaction to childhood trauma from Peaches' delinquency and chaos.[22]

That Paula's daughters took after her in different ways and to different degrees is typical of the way in which siblings are made different by their family's dynamics and the differing exposure they have to positive and negative features of their parents. I believe this is so powerful that if Fifi or Pixie had been swapped with Peaches at conception, they might have turned out like her, quite possibly including the manner of her death. The particular kind and extent of the maltreatment Peaches endured made her different.

Just as genes do not explain psychological similarities between parents and children, so genes are not the reason siblings are different from each other. As explained in the next chapter, the Human Genome Project is proving this.

SO WHAT? – 3 TAKEAWAYS

ONE: Insight turns the lead of maltreatment into the gold of emotional health – but the more maltreatment, the harder won the insight

Paula's life became a nightmare soon after she split with Geldof. Although she had had affairs before, her catastrophic relationship with Hutchence could be argued to have been the cause of her death. However, that would be to ignore the extent of her disturbance and the lack of progress she had made in understanding it. She had learnt little from her experience and exactly the same was true of Peaches. Both imbibed that fatal cocktail of childhood experience that sometimes makes it almost impossible to avoid disaster.

There is good evidence that premature death among the famous is linked to the extent and kind of childhood maltreatment.[23] Overall, more rock and pop stars die prematurely compared with the general population. One study examined a sample of 1,210 musicians voted as the creators of the most popular albums in America or Europe since the 1950s, with a minimum of five years of fame: 9 per cent died prematurely.[24]

The crucial finding was that Adverse Childhood Experiences (ACE – which includes experiences like parental divorce or maltreatments like emotional neglect or abuse) were the main cause of premature death. A key factor was that ACEs increase substance abuse. Twice as many of the stars who died from substance abuse had at least one ACE compared with those who died of other causes. Under a third of those who died from substance abuse had no ACEs, whereas 80 per cent had two or more.

This is exactly what studies of the general population would predict. Having four or more ACEs makes you seven times more liable to abuse alcohol and twelve times more likely to attempt suicide.[25] The number of ACEs has also been shown to be a major cause of personality disorders like narcissism, which, in turn, have been proven to be more common among both fame-seekers and the famous.[26]

The problem for people like Peaches and Paula, and the stars who die of overdoses, is that the extent and nature of their childhood maltreatment makes it much harder for them to gain insight. If you had such a childhood you will be that much less able to recall it because it was so upsetting[27] – we prefer not to remember horrible things. You need to recognise that is so and realise how hard it will be to change. You also need to grasp that you will have a persistent tendency to try to repeat the trauma in the hope that this time, it will turn out better. It will probably take several years of work with a therapist, one who can give you a different experience of security. One of your biggest problems is likely to be your fear of such dependence (because depending on your parents was so scary) and your defensive belief that you are special and different, that the normal rules do not apply to you (the defence you used to avoid feeling worthless, invisible and powerless). You have to overcome that and find a therapist who can be the mummy and daddy you never had.

Natalie, a client of mine, was 26 when her mother died in a car accident. Her father was distraught and my client maintained a suicide watch on him, moving into his house. One day she returned from work to find he had shot himself.

However good their early years, for obvious reasons all offspring are liable to be severely distressed by parental suicide.[28] Prior maltreatment and adversity increase the risk of irreversible distress.[29] Natalie had been interfered with by an uncle and subsequently raped when she was 11 by a stranger, similar to the abuses that befell Paula as a girl. Although now married, like Paula, Natalie had been sexually promiscuous when young and she still was prone to occasional lesbian adventures, although with the consent of her understanding husband. Part of the legacy of her sexual abuse was a tendency towards sexual sado-masochism. Even without the fatal calamities she would have been a troubled woman.

Her mother had been a cold, hypercritical academic but Natalie had been close to her warm and imaginative father, also an academic, which made his loss all the more intolerable. He left her a suicide note apologising for having failed her following the death of his wife.

She was furious with him for the manner and fact of his death, suffering horrific hallucinations of the gruesome scene he had inflicted on her and unable to sleep, having only managed two to three hours of unconsciousness per night since his death. She developed cleaning rituals around her house in attempts to reduce her anxiety and maintain a sense of control. She sometimes cut herself for the same reasons. She kept herself going by continuing her job as a nurse, although she had to be supervised by a psychiatrist as a condition of working (he used CBT and she characterised him as The Moron).

Although a nurse by profession, Natalie was a prodigiously talented woman, producing poetry, writing and performing as a guitarist, and was a remarkably able artist who was obsessed with Vincent Van Gogh, who famously killed himself. She had an encyclopaedic knowledge of popular culture, using her insomnia to read, watch films and television programmes. She was friends with several famous men and women from the arts, and would have been capable of similar achievement. She was not narcissistic, having no desire to make herself feel superior through fame and wealth. Like her hero Van Gogh, who was unrecognised in his lifetime, she wanted to be a hidden gem.

She watched and read the Harry Potter films and books repeatedly. Since Potter is an orphan, she strongly identified with him and found solace in the devices that J.K. Rowling provides for him to see his beloved parents (the portraits that come alive). She was also reassured by Potter's feeling that they are watching over him and that they died in order for him to be able to live.

The period preceding the first anniversary of her father's death was precarious. Natalie felt strong impulses to kill herself, partly to join her parents, partly to punish them. It is rare in cases of suicide that there is not the angry statement: 'Now, you bastards, look what you've made me do. Now you know how I feel', a form of *I'm Okay, You're Not*. He had set her the task of coping with loss better than he had been able to.

She formed a strong attachment to me. I was at pains to acknowledge her intellect, for she was considerably quicker-witted than me and much better informed on many cultural matters. The therapy was only possible for her if she did not think of it as such, she needed to feel we were friends, rather than in a professional relationship. We managed to do this while keeping to the boundaries of what was appropriate. As the anniversary approached we had daily contact by telephone, when there were no sessions scheduled.

Through this intense bond she was able to survive the anniversary (always a painful time during mourning) and discovered seams of self-reliance and stoicism with which to keep on going. She was a difficult spouse, not least because of her sleeping habits, and eventually her husband moved out (they had no children). What sustained her was the love she had had from her father in childhood, a profound link. Having transferred it to me, she could keep it alive.

Today, by no means can she be said to be 'cured' of her trauma, she still has several symptoms of post traumatic stress disorder. But she found a basis for continuing to stay alive, at first working with impressive devotion and skill in a hospital accident and emergency department. Dealing with the physical and emotional damage caused by accidents, like the one that killed her mother, and the anxiety created by emergencies, like the one her father faced and then inflicted on her, was her way of controlling what had happened to her. She became conscious that, in trying to minimise this damage, she was repeating her trauma in the hope that it would turn out differently. But as the therapy uncovered the childhood experiences that had made her particularly vulnerable, she was able to move to obstetrics, a less disturbing specialty. The urge to repeat the trauma diminished and, through feeling cared for by me, she carved out a relatively emotionally healthy life for herself, helping babies to flourish.

It is likely that Peaches had PTSD. Had she formed a sufficiently intense relationship with a therapist, perhaps she also could have survived.

Of course, these are extreme cases. But most of us sometimes use 'drugs of solace',[30] from nicotine to alcohol to excessive eating, to make ourselves feel better. There are a host of other ways we can distract ourselves from our distress, from workaholia to obsessive hobbies. In dealing with these unwanted habits, what applies to the extremes applies to us all: we can only rid ourselves of self-destructive patterns by gaining insight into their childhood roots. While self-help books and cognitive tricks may give us temporary relief, sooner or later the underlying problem will recur. Whack-a-mole responses do not work: we have to deal with the causes.

TWO: Tease out toxic identifications with parents
Peaches' demise resulted from strong identification with Paula. This is never easy to recognise and overcome.

If you go back to TAKEAWAY ONE at the end of Chapter 1, you will recall that the exercise showed similarities between you and your parents. Consider again some of the negatives you share.

Ask yourself if you were taught this similarity, whether you modelled it or whether it was an identification. For example, my father used to enjoy saying, 'rules are made to be broken', he *taught* me that. I am conscious of it, I have had to learn that, although there may be wisdom in the dictum, it has to be applied with great care. I have choice about that one.

Then, my mother modelled swearing. From as young as I can remember, when frustrated she would start with 'fuck it'. As the annoyance grew, this would be repeated and if the problem did not go away, she would reach a crescendo with 'fucking bloody hell'. Again, I know about this, I have to watch my swearing.

Much trickier are identifications. In therapy, I came to understand that my parents made me into a naughty boy by a mixture of teaching ('rules are made to be broken') and modelling (my dad's dodgy driving). Having become the bad boy, I identified with their perception of me as that. It was a great relief when I gained the insight that the adult me is not necessarily bad, that I do not have to walk around all day with an uneasy feeling that I am bad and in danger of being proven to be so (that is an insight I thank the Hoffman Process for providing – see the Internet for further information).

R.D. Laing wrote that 'we are the veils that veil us from ourselves'.[31] The struggle is to grasp that the Oliver who is considering the question of whether he is bad is himself infected with this self-perception. Only by reaching a level beyond the child and parent can we understand, from the detached adult position, that we have identified with something our parents made us, or one of their traits.

It is most likely to be achieved through the help of a third party, probably a friend, a partner or, if necessary, a good therapist. The lesson of Peaches' life for all of us is that we simply cannot afford to live without insight. While few of us are at risk of her ultimate fate, none of us is free from negative identifications that damage our relationships, and impede our work and play. It is imperative for us to be free of them.

THREE: Minimise Offspring Stockholm Syndrome *in your children*

Paula placed Peaches in a position where she felt a strong need to protect her mother and to repeat her mistakes, compulsively. As parents, it behoves us to do our best not to do that to our children.

Of course, it comes with the territory of being a child that *Offspring Stockholm Syndrome* will occur. In many ways, it works well for both sides. One of the joys of being a parent is the unquestioning admiration and love we get from our children, encouraging parents to be nice to them. For the child, *Offspring Stockholm Syndrome* provides security and identity.

But we need to remember that we are the adults and not exploit our child's vulnerability. If we are sad or angry or flat, we must do our best not to make that emotion something the child feels they have to deal with. We need to look after them, not the other way around.

I know, it's easier said than done. It's impossible for a parent to completely conceal distress when things go wrong. All of us lose our temper. But what we can do is explain to children that they do not have to feel responsible for our emotions.

The challenge for parents is to really deliver the childhood that Paula wanted for her daughters. We must do our best to provide a safe and loving captivity for our hostages. Along with the gold dust of creativity and playfulness, it is out of satisfying our children's need for dependence that their independence is born.

Chapter 3

Not in Your Genes

Wyatt and Jonas Maines are genetically identical twins. Their faces look exactly the same but in one crucial psychological respect, they are as different as can be: Wyatt wants to be a girl.

When small, he liked pink tutus, beads and had a fascination with mermaids. For his fourth birthday, he demanded a Barbie birthday cake. On Halloween, he wanted to be a princess.

Jonas, on the other hand, wanted to be Buzz Lightyear. Jonas loved Spiderman, pirates and swords, he had no thoughts of being a girl, he was stereotypically boyish.

In his early teens, Wyatt renamed himself Nicole. He had a transgender hormone treatment to prevent the development of male secondary sexual characteristics – facial hair and so on. Nicole hoped to have an operation to remove his penis. He felt he was a girl in a boy's body.

Whatever else might explain Wyatt's wish to be a girl, it cannot be genes. His DNA has identical sequences to those of his brother. If his transgender tendency was caused genetically, Jonas would also have it, just as they share eye colour and facial shape.

This is an anecdote and, in itself, proves nothing. People will pick and choose the information that suits their opinion in the nature–nurture debate. In theory, only scientific evidence can alter it. Most of us probably like to think we will change our views in the face of strong evidence based on properly conducted studies.

In the next couple of pages, I will summarise as dispassionately as I can the evidence regarding the role of genes in explaining differences in our psychology established by the Human Genome Project (HGP), the name of the scientific programme that mapped all our genes. What follows is universally accepted by scientists of virtually all complexions. I shall keep the account very short and put it as simply as possible. Those who wish for more detail should read Appendix 1, which contains a peer-reviewed, published scientific paper I wrote. Those who want still more evidence should consult my scientific monograph on the subject, *It's The Environment, Stupid!*

Remember, what you are about to read is the view of the scientific community, it is not my interpretation of it.

The consensus view of the findings of the Human Genome Project (HGP)

In 2000, a worldwide media fanfare trumpeted the initial findings of the Human Genome Project (henceforth, HGP). It was claimed we had around 35,000 genes. It has since been established that the true number is just 23,000, only a few thousand more than the common fruit fly. The expectation had been at least 100,000.

Right away, Craig Venter, one of the two lead researchers of the HGP, predicted that the fact that we had so few genes would mean that there were not enough to explain why we differ as individuals, psychologically. He suggested that so few genes would only be enough to ensure we had basic human kit, like human noses, eyes, limbs and so on, not monkeys' or cows'. He stated that the small number of genes discovered by the HGP proved that, as regards our psychology, 'the wonderful diversity of the human species is not hard-wired in our genetic code. Our environments are critical'.[1]

Venter's prediction turned out to be uncannily accurate but at that time it was not accepted by his professional peers. They began seeking the genes for intelligence, mental illnesses and personality which they had been predicting for decades would be identified by HGP methods.

Within only four years it was accepted by almost all scientists that individual 'genes for' psychological traits of any kind did not exist. While some specific genetic abnormalities exist in humans for a few rare disorders, causing particular traits like Huntingdon's chorea or Down's syndrome, it was established to everyone's satisfaction that no one gene existed which causes differences in any common psychological characteristics, like proneness to cleverness or depression.[2]

Within a remarkably short period, the prediction that there were genes for depression, intelligence or homosexuality was dropped, almost as if it had never been made. The general public have still not been told this truth by the media. The gene scientists (known as molecular geneticists) were not in the least dispirited. With the same supreme certainty with which they had peddled single genes, they now asserted that psychological traits were caused by dozens, even hundreds or thousands, of tiny variants in genes (or DNA, the code). It was simply a question of developing faster techniques for sequencing the genes of very large samples of people. Resources were poured into the project and to date, about $8 billion has been spent on the HGP. Large numbers of potential DNA locations were examined in huge samples.

As the 2000s came to an end, after many false dawns, these studies gradually identified a few differences in DNA that were reliably associated with particular traits. These were mostly for rare mental illnesses, like schizophrenia. But there was a problem, one that began to seriously worry the researchers.

The trouble was that the variants in DNA explained virtually nothing. When their effect was added together, the amount of heritability – the role that genes play in causing the presence of a trait – was so small as to be barely worth mentioning, less than 5 per cent. It is a fact that there has not been a single study, not one, which finds replicated DNA variants that explain significant heritability of any psychological traits, with the possible exception of autism. That may sound unbelievable, but it is the undisputed truth. In 2010, some of the leading molecular geneticists wrote that

'It seems highly unlikely that most of the genes responsible for any complex traits (i.e., like IQ, schizophrenia or depression) will be identified in the foreseeable future'.[3]

Instead of concluding that genes simply do not explain much, the researchers called the absence of findings 'Missing Heritability' or 'the DNA Deficit'. This was because of the results of studies of identical twins. Prior to the HGP, they (along with studies of adoptees) had been the scientific basis for assuming that genes played a significant role in causing traits. Twin studies had produced heritability estimates of 50 per cent or more for some traits, like intelligence, severe depression and schizophrenia.[4] Because these estimates were widely accepted as correct, the scientists dubbed the yawning gulf between the estimates from HGP studies and those of twins, a 'Missing Heritability'.[5]

However, some scientists soon began to doubt that the heritability was missing, suggesting it was simply not there, that the HGP was proving an unforeseen importance for the role of nurture and that twin studies were wrong. This was the potential implication of a 2010 editorial in a key scientific journal, entitled *It's The Environment, Stupid!*

Coming to the present day, the number of scientists who suspect that genetic inheritance of psychological traits is non-existent rather than missing is multiplying, because the HGP studies continue to find minimal heritability. To take just one example, a 2014 study examined the genes of 150,000 people, of whom 36,989 had been diagnosed with schizophrenia.[6] This is a vast sample. The study identified 108 genetic locations where the DNA sequence in people with schizophrenia tended to be different from those without it. Taken together, the total heritability which these differences in DNA sequence explained was a paltry 3.4 per cent: 96.6 per cent of why schizophrenia was present was not caused by genes, if this study was to be believed.

In the case of severe depression, not even these kinds of findings have emerged.[7] No different variants have been identified by surveys across the genome comparing the depressed and the non-depressed.

What I am stating is undisputed: it is accepted by almost everyone in the field that there is an enormous Missing Heritability problem. I could quote several hundred scientific papers in which it is asserted that the HGP has been unable to explain more than a tiny part of the heritability of any psychological traits.[8] Instead of boring you with that, let me cite what Britain's leading gene psychologist, Professor Robert Plomin, told *The Guardian* newspaper in February, 2014.[9]

Plomin is one of the most distinguished scientists in this field, a man whom I have interviewed when making television documentaries, and with whom I have conversed at length about the nature–nurture debate on a number of occasions. I can vouch for his love of science and of the truth. Asked about the current evidence for genes that explain psychological traits, he said 'I've been looking for these genes for 15 years and I don't have any'. Plomin is the most respected authority on the subject in Britain. I repeat, he said 'I've been looking for these genes for 15 years *and I don't have any*' (my emphasis).

Beyond genes

If what you have just read is true, how come you have never been informed of it by the media? Consider the example of the reporting of the schizophrenia study, described above.

It was heralded on the BBC Radio 4 *Today* programme as 'a huge breakthrough'.[10] Taken at face value, it could be suggested that the study proved that 96.6 per cent of the difference between schizophrenics and non-schizophrenics is not caused by genes. If the study was a huge breakthrough, it was because it proved that schizophrenia is almost completely not genetically caused (only 3.4 per cent), the exact opposite of the way in which it was portrayed by the BBC.

This is typical of how the media has reported the HGP story and explains why you are unaware of the true findings. On numerous occasions, studies find a handful of DNA differences between one group and another. What is never mentioned in the media reports of them is that the DNA variants actually explain almost none of the reasons why some people have the trait and not others. If you go to my website you can hear a good example of this. In 2010, I appeared on a BBC Radio 4 *Today* programme item reporting supposedly strong evidence that Attention Deficit Hyperactivity Disorder (ADHD) is caused by genes,[11] when, if anything, it proved the opposite – that at least 85 per cent of ADHD is not genetic. In fact, since then it has been proven that only 1–3% of ADHD is explained by genetic variants.[12] You can also hear an item on the BBC Radio 4 *Feedback* programme in 2013 where I point out that the *Today* programme did something similar in another of their reports.[13] It is guilty of serial offending.

Of course, if you are a genetically inclined person with an enquiring mind, that is not the end of the story. You may be thinking, 'Okay, so they haven't found the genes yet, but that doesn't mean they never will, they just need to keep looking'.

It is conceivable that you are right. But, anecdotally speaking, I have talked to many molecular geneticists, and off the record they freely admit that it is extremely unlikely that the genetic variants will be found. The reason they say this is the simple fact that they have already looked everywhere that the genes plausibly might be found. Some argue that there are complicated statistical reasons why thousands of tiny variations will never be identified, others that they simply do not exist.

The general reader will not be interested in the details of the places where they are still looking (see Appendix 1 for that) but let me provide one brief example. Until recently, it was assumed that the vast majority of our genes are 'junk' because they seem to have no purpose. They were dismissed as genes that had once played a role but which had been superseded by evolution and had not yet ceased to be part of our genome.

Confronted with the HGP findings and the prospect of genes playing virtually no role in explaining why we are like we are, out of sheer desperation, some scientists are now trying to reclassify the junk ones as being important after all.[14] Again, off the record, very few scientists really believe the junk will turn out to be of much or any significance. This is because for a gene to have direct effects on what we are like, they must code for proteins, which only 2 per cent do; junk genes do not.

There are other theories that some readers may have heard of, like epigenetics or gene-environment interactions, but I refer them to the scientific evidence in Appendix 1 if they wish to pursue them further. The common sense idea that we are the product of 'a bit of both' of nature and nurture is not stacking up (see Chapter 6 for exemplification of this in regard to 'difficult' children).

Most readers' assumption that genes have been proven to be important will have been fostered by a single study of identical twins that were supposedly reared apart, widely covered in television documentaries, newspaper articles and books (see Appendix 3). This study was headed by Thomas Bouchard and done in Minnesota. It seemed to provide incontrovertible stories of identical twins who had not met since shortly after their birth. Despite being raised by different, non-biological parents they appeared to have astonishing similarities, ones that seemingly could only be explained by their identical genes since they had been raised apart.

A famous example was the Jim Twins. Both married a girl called Linda, divorced, then married one called Betty. Both named their first-born sons James Allan, both had had a dog named Toy when they were children. So it went on, but this study and its findings are now discredited by the findings of the HGP. There have also long been major doubts about its reliability (see Appendix 3).

Perhaps the most important is that it is simply untrue that all these twins were separated at or near birth. Many of them were in contact for considerable parts of their lives. On average, they had had contact with each other for over two years before being studied, in one case for 23 years. That makes it possible that nurture could have made them more similar, especially in the early years.

Another serious problem is that all the twins in the study volunteered for it and in some cases, made substantial sums of money out of their alleged similarities through selling stories about them to the media. There was fame and money to be made from claiming they had a dog with the same name and so forth. Some admit to having lied about their similarity, in one instance claiming falsely that both had always wanted to be opera singers. What is more, the study is under suspicion from scientific peers since the researchers refuse to allow independent scrutiny of their data. If the HGP proves that DNA is unimportant, the study will have to be rejected as wholly bogus.

Other readers may have heard of the hundreds of studies of twins reared together. The Human Genome Project evidence seems to be incontrovertible proof that these are not measuring heritability. Quite simply, the greater similarity of identical compared with non-identical twins is probably caused by greater similarity of nurture, not identical genes. This is because, *as evry fule kno*, they look so similar and are treated much more similarly than non-identical twins, who parents, teachers and others who come into contact with them can tell apart (see Appendix 2). Similarity of nurture has been mistaken for genetic heredity.

Studies clearly show that identical twins are treated much more similarly than non-identical twins. For example, it has been proven beyond doubt that schizophrenia is at least partly caused by childhood maltreatment.[15] When the nurture of identical and non-identical twins is studied, the identical pairs are significantly more likely to have both been maltreated in ways that cause schizophrenia, such as sexual or emotional abuse.[16] For example, the ones who become schizophrenic are almost twice as likely to have both been emotionally abused than non-identical twins. We can be sure from the HGP that this is because they look more similar, not that their personalities are made more similar by genes, causing them to provoke emotional abuse (it is hard to believe children ever do so). Another very telling fact is that where one identical twin is sexually abused but not the other, the abused one is much more likely to develop problems in adulthood.[17] Much the same has been proven for ADHD. It is more likely to be found in the twin where parental engagement is lowest.[18]

To me, the really intriguing question is what it would take for geneticists to accept that the heritability is not missing, it is largely or wholly nonexistent. To use a simple analogy, think of that common situation where you get home from work and cannot find your mobile phone. You are absolutely positive you had it with you when you left work. After a cursory glance around the kitchen and a patting of your pockets, you reach for the landline phone and dial your number. Nothing happens, not a squeak. Darn, you must have let the battery go flat, although you could swear the damn thing was charged. You look in your bag, your coat and the car. Still no phone. The rest of the family is enlisted in the search. Children who sometimes nick the phone to play Minecraft or Clash of the Clans are disbelieved when they claim not to have taken it and are sent to search their rooms. With increasing frustration, ever more improbable locations are investigated, behind cushions on sofas, inside ironing cupboards, even down recently flushed toilets. What will it take for you to accept the null hypothesis of your theory that you had it with you when you came home, namely, that you did not have it and probably left it in the office?

This is the stage the gene-hunters are at. They are reaching the point where they are having to countenance improbable theories, ones they would have scoffed at and dismissed with derision before the HGP got underway (that would have been the response if it had been suggested junk genes are not junk). It is a bit as if the mobile phone searcher, rather than rejecting their theory that they brought it home, is saying 'you know how I have always ruled out the idea of ghosts? Well, you have to keep an open mind. It's always possible, in theory, that a ghost has borrowed my phone to make a call and it will reappear before long'.

Some scientists still maintain that if they are allowed to look at ever-greater samples with ever more hi-tech machines they will obtain results that close the gap with the findings of twin studies. But respected journals are finally now beginning to admit that this is either a very distant possibility or that, however big the samples and however advanced the technology, they have pretty much found everything there is to find.[19] It very much looks as if the findings of twin studies will have to be accepted as false (see Appendices 2 and 3) and other pathways explored.

That will not stop some people from keeping the faith. The extent to which even scientists will still do so is illustrated by a telling final statement in the newspaper article in which Robert Plomin was interviewed. At the end he was asked what he would think if the genes he is looking for are never found. He replied that 'I will still believe that [genetic] heritability is true'. That is faith, not science.

In a few years' time the technology will enable every single part of each person's genome to be examined (known as whole-genome sequencing). At that point, it will be possible for huge samples of people to be compared right across the 3 billion base pairs that each of us has on our genes. Once those results are published, I predict that there will be nowhere for the gene-believers to hide.

I have already offered my view of what the true explanation is for the transmission of traits from parent to child – mainly, its patterns of parenting. But another question arises. If it's not genes, then what explains why siblings in families are different or similar? My answer is divided into the two chapters which follow.

SO WHAT? 3 TAKEAWAYS

ONE: Identify what you believe is genetic about yourself
and think again

We all have our theories about why we are as we are. Identify a psychological trait in yourself that you assume to be largely or completely genetic. It might be your inability at crosswords or something much more significant, like your obsessive tendencies. Now put your beliefs about nature–nurture to one side for a moment and consider this: just believing that your trait is not fixed makes it more likely to change.

I am not suggesting that change is easy. For example, your conviction about the geneticism of your trait is itself a belief that will not be easy to shift (held by one or both your parents...?). For now, let us stick with the evidence that merely believing something is fixed means it is more likely to stay that way.

TWO: Grasp that change is made possible just by assuming traits are not fixed by genes

The most startling and practical implication of genes playing virtually no role in our individuality is that, simply by believing this, big changes are sometimes possible. There is a lot of evidence for this, some of it reviewed in Appendix 4. The findings can be summarised in the following injunctions:

⟩ *Beware of 'The Little Devil' attribution to your offspring.* Assuming there is a fixed difficultness in a baby, toddler and child has been shown to greatly increase the risk of becoming authoritarian to the point of abusive. Greater harshness results, with higher rates of depression in the parent, because they feel helpless in the face of an intransigent, unchangeable 'demon'. Lack of empathy with the child is fuelled by assuming they are wilfully being bad – not sleeping, eating or otherwise behaving in desired fashions.

⟩ *Conversely, by seeing your child as malleable, they are more likely to change.* For example, there are studies showing that when a child is taught that its ability in math is changeable, it is more likely to improve. In particular, the more the child believed initially that its inability was fixed, the greater their maths improved when taught that ability is malleable.

⟩ *Perceiving mental illness in yourself or others as fixed increases the likelihood of it continuing or recurring.* This applies to the mentally ill but also to their parents and professionals. By not assuming that it is a genetic destiny, change for the better is more likely.

Overall, you can see that much may be possible just by letting go of geneticism as an idea. However, we must not get carried away . . .

THREE: The limits of what is possible

I once had a friend who was addicted to heroin. A compelling and intelligent woman, she was much loved by those who knew her. She fought hard to overcome her addiction and a succession of boyfriends did their best to support her. In the end, it was to no avail, and she ended her life with an overdose in her late twenties.

In retrospect, it is clear that she always managed to keep a secret part of herself concealed. She was capable of real intimacy but she felt a compulsion to betray the faith and love she was shown. The origins of that lay in the details of her childhood. The crucial bit of her life's script was that she could only feel safe and real if she pretended to trust others, however reliable they were. That destructive pretence killed her by concealment of drug use. The suicide was revenge on her parents and sexually abusive brother, two fingers to them. But in the process, she betrayed those who really did love her.

As we shall see in the coming chapters, our early years profoundly affect the physical content of our brains, the baseline chemicals and pattern of brainwaves. With some traits, in some cases, just believing something is not fixed by genes is enough to achieve change. But for many others, it is not enough.

While therapy, the love of a good partner and all sorts of other benign experiences can shift these more intractable traits, it may be that there are some which nothing can change. For example, years of therapy transformed another ex-heroin addict in many respects but despite all that, today he still only gets three or four hours of sleep a night. It is possible that the sexual abuse he suffered as a child means that certain key parts of his brain are underdeveloped and that this is unchangeable.[20]

This is an extreme case, but even for the rest of us in the normal range of problems, there are likely to be some traits we have to accept will never be eradicated. In my own case, for example, I am addicted to nicotine. I have tried everything to rid myself of it, nothing has worked. Both my parents were heavy smokers throughout my childhood, including when my mother was pregnant with me. It is possible that my body has been irreversibly made into one that cannot cope without nicotine. It's something I accept and the price I pay is a life using cigarette substitutes, like the gum I am chewing at this moment.

Interestingly, one of my sisters also has multiple sclerosis and finds nicotine soothing, whereas my other two sisters are free from it. It so happens that the two of us who are nicotine addicts were not breastfed whereas the other two were. Exactly how that might translate into multiple sclerosis and nicotine addiction remains to be discovered, if there are any links. It could be there is a physical mechanism involved (though, logically, breastfeeding by a heavy smoker ought to increase, not reduce, the risk of addiction) or it could be that we bonded less with our mother as infants because she did not breastfeed us, making us more needy: people who have suffered childhood maltreatment are three times more likely to smoke than ones who suffered none.[21]

Whatever the cause, this is not the end of the world, I can live with it. By getting to know ourselves well enough to understand what is unchangeable, we can devote more energy to what can be altered.

Chapter 4

Maltreatment and Love (Why Siblings are so Different, Pt 1)

Recently, I received this email from a mother.

I'm writing about my five-year-old girl. Unfortunately for her, the hugging has mostly gone to her three-year-old brother. I can easily see I've been a very different parent to both of them, and I can definitely see the impact it has had: my hugged son is the quietly confident type whereas she is much more fearful.

My 'crimes' to her include doing controlled crying at about six months of age for around three weeks (I know!!). I put her in childcare on my return to work at 11 months of age for three days a week for around four months. She took it really badly, lost a lot of weight and I ended up taking her out and getting two nannies. One did one day and the other two days, but they remained with her till after she was three.

As a toddler and young child she had very strong temper tantrums that perhaps I could have handled better. Throw into the mix a relocation to my home country for one year, and the birth of my son when she was two and a half (he was premature and required a load of attention).

So the heart of the matter is that I'm concerned for her. She is a lovely little girl and is doing really well at school, but she is very fearful about many things: darkness; trying out new foods is a big no; she still requires one of us to put her down to sleep every night and she is genuinely terrified of being by herself in the room at night; she still sucks her thumb to sleep and during the day if tired or distressed. Also, I've noticed that when she relates to her peers she tends to be extremely compliant and relatively lacking in personal confidence. It might sound petty, but I find the comparison with my son heartbreaking (I understand comparing isn't ideal . . .).

There is nothing remotely unusual about this story, it's the norm, not the exception. Siblings receive different amounts of both maltreatment and love – just think about you and your siblings, or the different care your offspring received. The five-year-old daughter endured erratic care of varying quality whereas the son was hugged with sensitive and loving care, and looked after by the same carers throughout. At age five, the daughter was insecure, fearful and compliant with peers, whereas the son was quietly confident: in some ways it is truly as simple as input and output, cause and effect.

Good early care has as benign consequences as unresponsive care is damaging[1] and siblings get a significantly different deal from each parent.[2] Overall, many traits do run in families, but they do not do so nearly as much as we often imagine.[3]

So different is the care offspring receive that they are often as unlike each other as unrelated peers. If one sibling has an extrovert personality, there is an 85 per cent likelihood that another **will not do so**. If one has a particular mental illness, like depression or anxiety, 90 per cent of its siblings **will not do so**. If you are highly intelligent, there is a strong likelihood your siblings **will not be**. The crucial fact is this: whether people are the same is much more strongly predicted by the kind of nurture they have had than whether they are from the same family. The sexually abused from different families have more in common than one sibling who was abused and one who was not. Unrelated favoured children have more in common than their disfavoured siblings. If one identical twin was sexually abused or bullied but not the other, it is more like an unrelated fellow victim of maltreatment than its genetic identikit.

Insofar as siblings are similar, the question of why is much less complicated than that of their differences. In all families, to some degree, there are similarities in the treatment provided.[4] Family cultures rub off. In my childhood home, for example, both my parents had trained as psychoanalysts. The reader can easily imagine the kind of intense debates that ensued around our dinner table, nurture versus nature being at the top of the list. As adults, all four of us have had therapy of some kind and have done trainings as therapists. My three sisters and I inherited an interest in these matters as a result of our upbringing. Genes have nothing whatever to do with the fact that, when gathered together, we still debate the role of genes in causing us. The same is true of many families of engineers or lawyers regarding issues in engineering or law.

That genes play little or no role in making siblings' psychology similar is easy to grasp. Although studies of twins seem to suggest that children's similarity is almost completely caused by genes, the HGP has disproved this: the twin method simply confused genetic heritability with shared nurture (see Appendices 1 and 2 – identical twins get treated more similarly, that is why they are more similar). Most people can see that if you are brought up in a family that is broadly conservative or left wing in its politics, it's no puzzle that the children tend to be similar in their views.[5] You do not have to posit genes as the reason why middle-class children read more than ones from low-income families and why their scores on intelligence tests are higher.[6] All the children are liable to be exposed to these parental influences and affected accordingly.

People often say 'We came from the same family, we were brought up the same, but look how different we all are – surely that has to be genes?' It's the differences between siblings that are more difficult for many people to accept as not being genetic. But you were not brought up the same. You had the same parents yet each child was related to differently. The specific reasons why children are different are summarised as follows:

⟩ The baggage parents bring from their own childhood *to this particular child*.

⟩ The state of the relationship between the partners (where there are two parents present) at birth and how that plays out in relation *to this particular child*.

⟩ The form and content of the maltreatment or love for *this particular child*.

⟩ The extent to which there is favouritism for *this particular child*.

⟩ The extent to which there is stigmatisation of *this particular child* – stigmatising usually happens when the parents use the child as a dustbin for unwanted feelings, *I'm Okay, You're Not*.

⟩ The place *this particular child* comes in the family, their birth order.

⟩ *This particular child's* gender.

⟩ The way that sibling rivalry panned out (there is always some) for *this particular child*.

It is rare that any of these reasons is the only one, most tend to be present as causes of sibling differences, to varying degrees. The form and content of the maltreatment and love that the particular child receives is the subject of this chapter. I will particularly focus on the way care in the early years affects whether or not a child develops into a mentally healthy adult. The next chapter addresses the way that the child's role in the family drama affects them – things like birth order, gender, favouritism, stigmatism and sibling rivalry.

Differential maltreatment and love as causes
of sibiling difference

Here is another mother's account of her two children, particularly her troubled son, and her view of how unique nurture caused his difficulties. In what follows, I shall use it to illustrate the evidence.

Our family is at an impasse: angry parents and angry son (aged five), with an angry two-year-old sister not far behind, although she has had a better time of it. Often I find myself hiding away crying with shame, anger and a lot of self-loathing asking myself 'How the hell did we get here?'

My five-year-old is a gorgeous, funny, clever, vivacious, articulate boy with a propensity for screaming so loudly that I can hear him halfway down the hill from school! Generally, he is incredibly well behaved at school, and very bright and engaging. His most recent report ranks him particularly highly in maths. He is brave when he wants to be. He just performed a dance to music he helped compose, on his own in front of 250 pupils and their teachers. His father and I were hiding watching him, gleefully grabbing each other and tears brimming as we watched our amazing son do this. He spoke confidently to the audience and, though embarrassed, he did it.

So why were we hiding? Because if he saw us, or me, to be more truthful, we expected tears, refusal to do the dance, or meltdown.

If confronted with things, he rebels and either pulls faces at me, grunts at me, shouts the usual 'no' and 'it's unfair' too loudly, screaming at the top of his lungs. Sometimes I can cope with this but it is getting harder and harder. I find myself bitching back, making ridiculous comments and generally behaving like a child myself. Plus I have noticed this week I am absolutely undermining him by saying all of this on repeat to my husband in front of my son, when venting. It is a circle of horror.

His was a very difficult pregnancy, he ended up high risk, premature. Brave, brilliant boy. Sadly my experience was awful.

I developed what was later diagnosed as severe postnatal depression (PND), pretty much within 48 hours. I was badgered by neonatal nurses to breastfeed and they rounded on my husband too. I felt like a prisoner. Those months were hell.

There was no real support from the health visitor who informed us that our son wasn't just our child, 'he was everyone's child'. I got some medical support and was given drugs, which I didn't take because I already felt out of control. I fought for two years to be rid of the PND, all drug free, but my God the family suffered. My husband was a rock but he was emotionally battered by the end. My relationship with our son was tenuous, it took me nearly two years to express love. I am proud that I survived and it's all down to determination, control freak stuff and 'don't let the bastards get you down'. But.

Our son can't switch off that temper response. His fear factor on some things is disproportionate, for example, screeching because he won't jump in the swimming pool with his classmates, despite being able to do it previously . . . until I told him he didn't have to swim if he didn't want to. That it was okay. Guess what? He did it, no fuss. Light bulb moment, not connected until I read your book [called *Love Bombing* (LB), described at the end of this chapter, it suggests giving the child intense, focused periods of being in total control and of feeling loved].

We are in the school holidays and it has been the week from hell. I have tried so hard to be calm but it all boiled over tonight. I ended up telling them both how awful they were and to shut up, meanwhile scaring the crap out of my kids. I am turning into the mother I hate to see and I see my son turning into the kid who reacts to that mother.

I know that on the LB I must let go, which I am going to try my absolute hardest to do. I am so up for this. But with all the naughty steps, marbles, ladders of certain doom, stickers and all that crap being disasters, I am left with working out how to deal with two children whose screaming fits leave me insane. All the time inside I am crying and wanting out, while trying so hard to keep cool . . .

...Our son enters Year 2 as one of the youngest in September and his outrageous screeching tantrums have to stop. For his sake.

Over the years I have had several hundred letters like this. It was extreme in that I subsequently learnt that the mother was psychotic (a total loss of coherence) during her period of PND. But even without that, in a great many cases, parents lose their temper with their children, becoming like them, having temper tantrums too. In what follows, I will analyse how maltreatment makes us unique, using the example of the five-year-old son in the above case. I will refer to the mother as Jill and the son, George.

The real causes of mental illness

The Traumagenic Model of mental illness, or versions thereof, is becomingly increasingly accepted.[7] It proposes that excess stress chemicals caused by early maltreatment – and not a vulnerability caused by genes – create a heightened sensitivity to threat. The child's brain becomes adapted to expect adversity and distressing experiences. Primed in this way, it requires less adversity for the adult to be tipped into mental illness, up to and including psychosis (complete incoherence, disintegration of the self).

When such vulnerable people lose their job, are spurned by a lover or get into debt, they are more likely to become delusional, experiencing sight or sound hallucinations, or have paranoid ideas, such as that strangers are out to get them.[8] In milder cases, this is just the husband who wrongly believes his wife is having an affair, or the employee who thinks her boss is persecutory when that is not so. All of us sometimes get a bit paranoid or have incorrect ideas about the intentions of others,[9] with those tendencies usually having their roots in childhood maltreatment.[10]

The hormone cortisol plays a key role in priming us to overreact.[11] Although other hormones are also important, I shall mainly focus on this one in what follows. Cortisol is secreted to activate the brain's 'fight or flight' system when you are confronted by threat. If you are frequently placed in stressful circumstances you may be jammed permanently in 'fight or flight' mode: even where there is no threat, your brain expects it. Mostly, this results in high levels of cortisol which, over the years, not only reduces your life expectancy, but also makes you into a gibbering wreck – anxious, depressed, irritable, prone to inattention and frantic fire-fighting in all departments of your life. Your heart races, your palms sweat, your irises widen. It takes only the smallest stimulus for you to overreact, one that would not normally seem stressful.

Alternatively, in some cases, having the fight–flight system jammed at 'on' means your system closes down and cortisol levels are abnormally low, blunted. You are so used to feeling threatened that a three-headed purple Martian could appear in your sitting room and you would say 'Hey dude, how's it going?'. In some cases, that is the psychopath, a cold, ruthless and remote person who is unaffected by normal risks.

A large body of evidence now proves that your baseline cortisol level is set by early childhood care, sometimes with lifelong consequences.[12] It is the thermostatic setting to which you return when a threat has passed. Unresponsive, erratic or abusive care becomes electro-chemically enshrined as abnormally high or low baselines.

Despite this evidence of the role of nurture in setting cortisol levels, scientific papers consistently begin with the assertion that mental illnesses are caused to a large degree by genes. Amongst children, attention deficit hyperactive disorder (ADHD) and autistic spectrum disorder (ASD) are widely and increasingly diagnosed. ADHD entails difficulties in concentrating, the mind racing from one thing to another, and speeded up behaviour. ASD is an incapacity to relate to others, or to realise others have minds, often accompanied by ritualised behaviour and obsessive compulsions. ADHD and ASD are close relatives: people diagnosed with one of these disorders will have at least half of the symptoms of the other disorder in common.[13] That they overlap so much casts doubt on the idea that these 'illnesses' really exist as the discrete, identifiable disease entities they are made out to be. The symptoms are also found in antisocial behaviour, since whizzy people (ADHD), or ones who are not very aware of other people (ASD), inevitably tend to be perceived as badly behaved.

Scientific papers discussing these illnesses almost invariably begin by claiming that these problems are 'substantially genetic' in origin, citing twin studies as their source.[14] This is despite the fact that the much more reliable evidence of direct studies of genes from the Human Genome Project show that, for example, in the case of ADHD, only 1–3 per cent is explicable by genes[15] – put the other way round, the HGP proves 97–99 per cent of the cause is not genetic. In what follows, I will particularly focus on ADHD and ASD in illustrating how differential care and prenatal experience are often crucial, not genes.

Rather than sticking an unreliable psychiatric label on George (the five-year-old boy in the example above), one way of looking at him is that he suffers from emotional dysregulation caused by his early experiences. He has a febrile incapacity to control himself, so that emotions flood him and he loses the capacity to control them with his thoughts. This is normal in toddlers while they are learning to find the 'pause button', the bit of their mind that can take charge, detach, relax, get into a position of choice. In George's case, despite being fine at school, when at home, he often cannot find his pause button. If levels of the hormone cortisol were measured, his would be either too high or low. Although aged five, his development in certain respects is arrested and he behaves like a toddler. Without restorative nurture which resets his emotional thermostat, this could lead to an adult with arrested development too – the kind of person for whom the word 'childish' springs to mind when they are frustrated, who easily becomes ratty, furiously angry, self-focused. The problem started before his birth.

The effect of prenatal experience

Your electrochemical thermostat is partly set prenatally. Several different groups of children have been followed from before birth into late childhood. Mothers who are stressed or anxious during the last three months of pregnancy are significantly more likely to have children at ages seven to ten with ADHD, behavioural problems (like temper tantrums) and anxiety.[16] These are all signs of dysregulated (too high or low) cortisol. The effects of prenatal stress are still influential even after other known post-natal causes of these childhood disturbances (like maternal depression, inadequate substitute day care and marital disharmony) are taken into account.

Perhaps most tellingly, when siblings are compared, if the mother was stressed during one of the pregnancies but not the other, stress increases the likelihood of ADHD in the one whose mother was pre-natally stressed:[17] it is becoming increasingly clear that ADHD is not a genetically inherited problem and that prenatal influences are a signifi-cant cause. ADHD is primarily a way of expressing anxiety, really a long-winded label for being a very jumpy or easily bored person, someone with dysregulated cortisol.

Prenatal problems predict other problems too. When pregnant moth-ers are anxious or depressed, or using alcohol or tobacco, even after other key factors are allowed for, their 11- to 12-year-old children are signifi-cantly more likely to suffer from personality disorder[18] – a self-focused, me-me-me incapacity to relate to others, with febrile mood shifts and an incapacity to cope with normal social rules.

Prenatal factors other than stress also have a considerable influence on how we turn out. For example, birth weight has a significant effect.[19] A study of twins found that for every kilogram less at birth, children were that much more likely to have ADHD in later life. Despite identical genes, birth weight played an important role. This is true for non-identical twins as well.

Even extreme problems, like ASD (Autism Spectrum Disorder), seem to be affected by fetal experience. For example, raised levels of the hor-mone serotonin during pregnancy may play a role. It is possible that the large number of serotonin-raising antidepressants[20] being prescribed to pregnant women could be causing increased amounts of autism.[21]

Another possible factor is the kind of birth itself. There are 13 studies[22] which, taken together, suggest a one-quarter increase in the risk of ASD in offspring of mothers who had Caesarean births. Because such operations have become more common in recent years in some developed nations, it is possible that has increased the amount of ASD.

Interestingly, whatever ASD's causes, there is undeniable proof that, once it has been diagnosed, it is not an inevitable genetic destiny. One study identified 34 people in later childhood or early adulthood,[23] who had no symptoms of autism, despite having been fully diagnosed as autistic when under five. Great care was taken in that study to check that the original diagnosis was not mistaken. Since the children had completely recovered, the problem could not have been caused by genes. If introduced early on, the right kind of support for carers significantly reduces the long-term symptoms:[24] providing the right kind of parental nurture reduces the symptoms, even if not wholly eradicating them.

George's problems also were multiplied because he was born five weeks early, with a very low birth weight. Prematurity is a predictor of a host of problems in babies, which increases the risk of subsequent mental illness.[25] For instance, a very preterm newborn is two and half to four times more likely than one born full term to develop ADHD in later childhood.[26] Preterm children are also considerably more at risk of anxiety and depression, which is liable to persist into early adulthood.

Apart from its direct effect on brain development, a key reason prematurity causes problems is that it is harder for mothers to tune into babies who are difficult,[27] mothers like Jill, who had severe postnatal depression.

The crucial importance of the early years

Responsive sensitivity to the infant's signals is now well established as the foundation of emotional health:[28] the essential building block for developing secure attachments, the capacity to function well in school and society, and to be a playful, contented, satiable person. John Bowlby, possibly the most significant psychologist of the second half of the twentieth century, once observed that love is as vital to the development of an infant as vitamins. Another important thinker from that era, Donald Winnicott, wrote that 'there is no such thing as a baby'. He meant that babies only gain a sense of who they are from being related to.

Bowlby and Winnicott have been proved right since making these claims in the 1950s. Numerous studies have shown that unresponsive care in early infancy, not genes, is the primary cause of vulnerability to extreme mental illness.[29] A review of the 23 best studies found that postnatal early maltreatment increased the likelihood of later mental illness.[30]

The evidence for this dates back to pioneering observations by René Spitz in the 1940s.[31] He observed that infants separated from their parents and placed in institutions became withdrawn and incapable of relating normally. Indeed, there was a much higher likelihood of the babies actually dying in the wards of institutions where there was no personalised care.

The vital role of responsive care is supported by 39 documented cases of children who were either raised by wild animals or given no care from humans beyond the supply of food.[32] Language development was nonexistent, there were no social skills. Since then, it has been proven definitively that institutionalised children – who usually get very little responsive care from a familiar carer – have elevated risk of all mental illnesses.[33] For example, they are at much greater risk of ASD (five to six times more) and of ADHD.[34]

About half of institutionalised boys and one third of girls become adults with personality disorders, usually displaying a me-me-me self-focus, megalomania, febrile mood swings and unstable relationships. The personality disordered are much more likely to be highly promiscuous, sexually and socially. The lack of individual care that institutionalised children get makes them prone to 'indiscriminate friendliness'.[35] They will move towards anyone who might provide care or nurture, and want to be everyone's friend. As institutionalised girls enter puberty, they are liable to use their nubility as a way of getting men to pay attention to them, hoping to be able to exchange sex for love, or failing that, for money – much higher proportions of children in local authority care become prostitutes.

Within institutions, children who receive more individual care are more discriminating about who they approach and welcome. Less maltreatment in infancy prior to institutionalisation reduces indiscriminacy. For the neglected, the indiscriminate friendliness can evolve into the charm and social indiscriminacy of people on the psychopathic spectrum – a cold, calculating and callous use of others, since no one can be trusted to meet your needs. Psychopathy has its roots in maltreatment, not genes.[36]

Forty per cent of the British prison population spent time in institutional care during their childhoods.[37] Nearly all such cases were taken into care because their parents maltreated them. Eighty per cent of the prison population have at least one mental illness,[38] most have more than one, in many cases antisocial personality disorder (akin to psychopathy). Small wonder that there are strong links between criminality, mental illness and child maltreatment.

Of course, not all personality disorders (of which psychopathy is a subdivision) are caused by prenatal and early infantile deprivation, but they (and not genes) create the vulnerability.[39] Subsequent maltreatment plays an important part too, with sexual and physical abuse well proven to be predictors.[40] Interestingly, where one identical twin is sexually abused but not the other, the abused one is much more likely to develop problems in adulthood, including personality disorder.[41] This is strong evidence that sexual abuse is a direct cause and that genes are not – identical twins treated differently have different outcomes.

Beyond later maltreatment, social forces play a significant role in causing personality disorder. There are huge variations in the amount between nations,[42] with America having over 50 times more impulsivity disorder, for example, than Japan.[43] Whereas the individualistic American culture encourages both psychopathy and narcissism, Asian cultures tend to limit them.[44] So its not just childhood experience which matters, its also important whether the kind of society you live in fosters or suppresses potential problems.

The impact of early care on cortisol regulation

If later experience can be significant, care in early infancy is critical because the brain is rapidly increasing in size and numbers of neuronal connections. Care at that age profoundly affects the brain's actual size, and its patterns of chemicals and of electrical waves. In accord with the Traumagenic Model of mental illness, reviews of the evidence show that, stressed by unresponsive care,[45] high levels of cortisol impair brain growth. They also cause abnormal patterns of brainwaves. The problems endure into adult life.

At 15 months, if a child had unresponsive earlier care,[46] they are liable to be insecure, showing up in decreased activity in the brain's left frontal lobe. In middle childhood, children who were previously in institutions for long periods have key parts of their brains that have not grown properly.[47] This means they do not make proper eye contact when with people and have other relational problems.[48]

These abnormal brain patterns persist into later life. If the child is insecure at 18 months old,[49] the brainwave patterns are still liable to be abnormal 20 years later, reducing the capacity to process positive experiences. Likewise, insecurity at 18 months is proven to affect the size of key parts of the brain at age 22.[50] Unresponsive care before age two has been demonstrated to predict dissociation[51] (feeling emotionally absent, confused) and personality disorder.[52] When mothers are asked at the time of the birth if their child was wanted, if the answer is negative the child is more likely to become an insecure adult and to suffer a variety of severe problems, including schizophrenia.[53]

Many aspects of postnatal maternal care have been shown to adversely affect the child's cortisol reactivity. For example, the speed with which a baby's cortisol levels settle down after being bathed depends on how sensitively the mother responded during this mildly stressful, everyday experience.[54] Cortisol levels of toddlers can be adversely affected by being left with strangers in groups of other toddlers,[55] such as in inadequate group day care. In one study of 18 month olds,[56] cortisol levels doubled during their first week in group day care, compared with levels at home before experiencing any day care. The problem still persisted three months after entering day care. This is one of ten studies[57] which have found dysregulated cortisol in under-three-year-olds in day care, compared with levels at home: whilst under three, we need responsive care from a familiar adult who does not keep changing and is not distracted by having to care for numerous other small children.[58]

Children of disharmonious parents are more likely to display symptoms of what are known as 'externalising' problems,[59] like screaming and shouting, fighting, disobedience and delinquency. How distressed the child is and precisely how that distress is expressed,[60] has been proven to relate to how their cortisol systems function. The variations in distress are caused by early care. For example, a study of 1,100 mothers and babies[61] measured maternal sensitivity to the infant at 7, 15 and 24 months of age. At each age the babies were exposed to briefly stressful challenges. At seven months, the infants were given an attractive toy to play with for 30 seconds. The experimenter then placed the toy just beyond the poor little mite's reach, behind a clear plastic container. Similar challenges were carried out at 15 and 24 months.

Swabs of saliva were taken from the child before and after the challenges on each occasion to measure cortisol levels. This identified how stressed the child was at the outset and how quickly it recovered from being challenged, its reactivity.

In addition, the amount of physical violence between parents was measured for the previous twelve months at each assessment. Other factors that might affect the child, like parental depression, were also assessed.

Exposure to parental violence did not affect how reactive the child was to the challenge at either 7 or 15 months, but it did at age two. The accumulation of exposure to violence primed the child to become reactive: the more they had been exposed at all three ages, the more their cortisol levels jumped when challenged at age two, and the longer it took for them to settle down afterwards.

But the most interesting finding was that maternal sensitivity at seven months was crucial. Children whose mothers were sensitive then but who had witnessed high levels of violence were still calm when challenged at age two. The good early care meant their cortisol levels were indistinguishable from babies who had had no exposure to parental violence. High maternal responsiveness at 15 months and aged two did not have the same protective effect. If the 7-month care had not been responsive, then even if subsequent care was, the toddler was highly reactive if there had been parental violence.

George's mother reports how she and her husband became sucked into a 'circle of horror'. In George's case, he had already been born with dysregulated cortisol, perturbed by being preterm, and his mother's psychotic depression during his first two years. Primed by this and by repeated experiences of witnessing parental discord, only a little screaming and shouting between his parents was enough to make his temper tantrums worse. This is what the Traumagenic Model of mental illness predicts, his prior experience priming him to be hypersensitive.

Because our brains are still developing, the earlier the maltreatment, the more severe the damage.[62] For instance, in a study of 800 children,[63] maltreatment before the age of three was more disturbing than aged three to five, which was, in turn, more damaging than aged five to nine. In George's case, had he only been maltreated from when he turned five and his parents only been arguing since that age, it is highly probable his disturbance would have been considerably less. With a calmer baseline state, he would have been better equipped to cope with later maltreatment. Resilience, insofar as it exists, is the product of having felt loved or secure for a sustained period.

How differential maltreatment makes us into different adults

All of us are maltreated to some degree, it is impossible for any carer to always meet a baby's needs perfectly or to never snap at their toddler when in a bad mood. The degree of maltreatment and its specific form profoundly influences our different personalities, abilities and emotional health. The maltreatment is likely to take different forms, at different ages, resulting in our unique kinks. Equally, good experiences coming from both parents will vary in what they are like and the age at which they occur. This can be as simple as the fact that a father may be very close to his daughter in the early years, less so later on, perhaps because their interests differ. The same may be true of a mother and son.

There is strong evidence that if parents train their children in specific skills,[64] like learning of musical instruments or second languages, the consequence is measurably different brain patterns. This is hardly surprising. My son and I have spent many hours practising his soccer skills in the garden. It would be odd if that did not show up in some way in his brainwave patterns and in the size of relevant parts of his brain. Since I have not done this with my daughter, it has probably resulted in a measurable difference in their brains in this respect, their differing skillsets expressing it (her dancing and skill in drawing and painting).

By the same token, negative experiences differently affect how offspring turn out. There are numerous studies of identical twins showing that it is the different ways that they are treated that explain why they are different.[65] For example, ADHD is more likely to be found in the twin where parental engagement is lowest.[66]

Studies of adoptees are particularly revealing of the long-term damage caused by early maltreatment. Large samples of children who were institutionalised as a result of being orphaned or maltreated and then subsequently adopted,[67] have been followed into the teenage years and beyond. Common problems identified are aggression, indiscriminate friendliness (looking for love from strangers) and insecurity in relationships.

Institutionalised children are five to six times more likely than normal to be diagnosed with autistic symptoms.[68] There is also reduced intelligence and academic performance. Institutionalisation and prior maltreatment adversely affect their brain development and cortisol levels.

The long-term outcome is partly affected by the kind and amount of damage occurring before the child is taken away from the abusive parents. The longer the child spends in an institution, the worse the outcome. The kind of institution matters, less individual attention is more damaging. The later the child is adopted and the worse the quality of care in the adoptive home, the more harmful. It has been shown that lengthy institutionalisation[69] directly affects brain growth and cortisol levels.[70]

Studies of early deprivation where the child is raised at home reveal the same effects. If a mother gets depressed,[71] the longer she is afflicted and the more profound the depression, the greater the harm. The mother's responsiveness is impaired and that is proven to increase risk of insecurity and depression in the child. It can lead to atypical brain development.[72] The younger a child is when the depression begins, the greater the long-term damage.[73]

In George's case, it was not until he was aged two that his mother recovered fully from her psychotic depression. Having ceased to be depressed, the early lack of responsiveness will have still played a big part in his problems as a five-year-old.

There are numerous studies showing that the more severe childhood maltreatment is, the worse the subsequent outcome.[74] Severity refers to how frequently a child was maltreated and how extreme it was. In the case of sexual abuse,[75] the more repetitive, the more penetrative and the closer the blood relation of the abuser to the abused, the more harm. The same is true of emotional and physical abuse.

For example, while working in a mental hospital, I had a client who lived in a permanent state of fear, often unable to sleep and found wandering the corridors at night in a confused state. He was the second of four children. It turned out that his father had been badly abused and was terrifying, prone to unpredictable outbursts of rage. Fortunately for my client, he was never hit by his father and he spent a good deal of his childhood living with his aunt. His two sisters were also never hit and buttressed by a close relationship with their mother but one of his siblings was not so lucky. His older brother was frequently beaten, as well as being whacked without warning.

Although severely anxious, it was possible to help my patient to disentangle himself from his father, towards whom he felt considerable sympathy – *Offspring Stockholm Syndrome* – as well as anger. Once the therapy enabled him to grasp that his father's disturbing behaviour was a consequence of abuse, he felt great relief because he had always felt responsible for his dad's distress.

His sisters married gentle, loving men and, although anxious women, had managed to carve out lives in which they felt relatively safe. His older brother was most disturbed, the one who had borne the full brunt of their father's distress: the more maltreatment and the more extreme, the worse the outcome. He had grown into a paranoid man, who mostly kept to himself. At times, he would go to the pub and get very drunk, picking fights with strangers in the street on the way home.

The most common comment preceding a city centre violent crime is 'What are you looking at?'[76] In most cases, the person to whom this is addressed was not 'looking' at anything, and did not intend any slight. But the questioner, disinhibited by alcohol, his mental connections loosened, believes there is malice in the innocent look. Threatened, he launches an attack: much violence is committed out of a delusional need for self-defence (how true is that of international conflicts?).

That was the pattern of the older brother and when particularly distressed and drunk on one evening, he kicked a man to death. Witnesses overheard him calling the man the name of his father: in his mind he was attacking his childhood tormentor. Nonetheless, psychiatrists passed him as fit for trial and he received a life sentence. He joined the 80 per cent of prisoners who qualify for a diagnosis of at least one mental illness[77] (the old debate about criminals is long since resolved, mad not bad, if mad is the word; it somewhat contradicts Margaret Thatcher's notorious and offensive comment on criminal psychology: 'The criminal and only the criminal is to blame').

Had my client been firstborn in the family, I have little doubt that extreme violence would have been his fate too. Instead, he suffered from a severe anxiety disorder, as well as identifying with his father's trauma. Such is the differential effect of different exposure to different kinds and extents of maltreatment.

Multiple combinations of maltreatment are more harmful[78] than a single kind but where one kind is found, there are usually others. If there is physical abuse, for example, it is very often combined with emotional abuse or neglect and other maltreatments, likewise sexual abuse. In the case just described, it emerged that their mother had suffered postnatal depression during the first year of the older brother's life. She had recovered by the time my patient was born. It is likely that the older brother was made more vulnerable to the abuse he suffered from his father by his mother's depression.

Overall, when adults are asked to look back upon their childhoods, the amount of maltreatment they recall strongly predicts how mentally ill they are. A comprehensive study of Adverse Childhood Events (ACE)[79] in 17,000 middle-class Americans asked them to score themselves on eight categories of childhood maltreatment (like sexual, physical and emotional abuse). A total ACE score is the number of categories of maltreatment a person believes applied to them in their childhood.

One third of the sample scored 0 – recalled no events and therefore had no categories of maltreatment (this is likely to be an underestimate since a significant proportion of adults repress the fact that they were maltreated, partly out of *Offspring Stockholm Syndrome*, partly because they find it painful to recall it). That left two-thirds of the sample having suffered at least one ACE. Of the whole sample, one in six had more than four ACEs.

Regarding depression, 80 per cent had at least one ACE. The greater the number of ACEs, the greater the likelihood of all kinds of mental illness. This is true of hallucinations and dissociation (feeling remote from yourself and others) and damaging lifestyle behaviours, like smoking, drinking, obesity, drug use and sexual promiscuity. Over half of suicide attempts are attributable to ACEs. A person who has five or more ACEs[80] is up to 193 times more likely to be psychotic (disintegration of the self) than one who has none.

So what are the prospects for George, compared with his sister, who received far better early care? Jill has battled heroically to alter the pattern of care he is receiving and to reverse the damage done by his early experience. In my book *Love Bombing* I describe many examples of mothers who transformed the behaviour of their children, including ones as old as 12 (see TAKEAWAY 3, below). There is even a case of a child diagnosed as autistic whose symptoms were greatly reduced through the Love Bombing technique. It is possible to reset the emotional thermostat but it is not easy. Since receiving her first email, I am glad to say Jill has used Love Bombing to largely eradicate George's tantrums. But the prospects for a boy like George whose mother did not change the pattern of care would not be good.

Dozens of studies have shown[81] that infants and toddlers of depressed mothers have different patterns of brainwaves from those of non-depressed mothers. This is hardly surprising, since one might expect that if your parent is consistently irritable and unresponsive, as many depressed ones are, it would be mirrored by offspring brain patterns. The impact of maltreatment on brainwaves endures into adulthood. For example, adults who were traumatised as children have decreased activity[82] in the parts of the brain which enable thought and the capacity to take action. Trauma makes the child freeze, becoming an emotionally frozen adult.

Although adults who have been traumatised as children may be highly effective parents, partners or professionals overall, they may have another side to them where they become helpless and needy, feeling that they are stupid and ineffective, having to ask others what to do, even looking to them for guidance as who to be. They are paralysed, and feel like zombies at such moments. It is because they are having a primitive re-experience of being ignored, unloved, attacked or whatever the early trauma was. This is but one of many findings which suggest that patterns of maltreatment cause the brain to adapt to them.

Multiple studies have identified abnormal reductions[83] or enlargements in the size of key parts of the brain in the abused and neglected. Compared with non-maltreated people, the maltreated have 5–16 per cent less volume in those parts. Cortisol reactivity is a major reason why. Stress chemicals can cause the loss of neurones[84] (the cells out of which the brain is made up) or lack of growth of them. However, fascinatingly, this does not mean that the brain is the same in all contexts.

It is an interesting fact that George was well behaved and talented at school. Brain chemistry varies according to who we are with and our social contexts. When with a parent who has been abusive, priming means the child is constantly fearful of that maltreatment. Away from the parent, the child can be someone wholly different – the George performing on a stage to a high standard. He was also exceptional in some skills at school, and able to regulate his emotions very effectively when there. That may well have been because he used maths and other areas of achievement as a way of making himself feel good. That he was almost a different person is undeniable proof that his brain was not damaged in all contexts, and therefore not a fixed biogenic destiny. The destructive patterns were only activated when with his family. He was jealous of his sister, scared of his mother and disturbed by his parents' disharmony. As we shall see in Chapter 7, exceptional achievement is often a response to child maltreatment.

The medical model of mental illness is challenged by George's story and the millions of others like it. It is simply not true that he was born with a genetically inherited brain disorder. Rather, his brain was affected by his early years and subsequent care in such a way that he could not regulate his emotions when with his family, because he was awash with cortisol.

At school, his electrochemistry was quite different: he was an obedient and disciplined student, a talented performer. If his brain was genetically programmed to malfunction, that would occur in all contexts.

To put it very simply, the kind of early experience that George and his sister had will have resulted in different brains. George's subsequent improved care at home (since the original email) will have corrected the brain abnormalities to a considerable extent, because his mother acted while his brain was still young and plastic. As a result, he may become an emotionally healthy boy, like his sister may do. However, he will probably differ from her as a result of his early experiences. For example, he will be likely to be the 'brainy' one of the two. It is also possible that in later life, when he has children, he will be a parent prone to easily losing his temper with them. Chapter 6 gives powerful examples of the way in which toxic parental nurture passes traits down the generations.

The broader context of childhood maltreatment

Having presented all this evidence of the impact of maltreatment on sibling differences, it is interesting to reflect that the wider society has a big effect on the meaning of parenting and its consequences. It is an incontestable fact that societies and cultures have huge effects on how mentally ill we are.[85] There are large differences in the amount of mental illness between nations. Evidence from the World Health Organization shows that there is twice as much mental illness in English-speaking nations (23 per cent) compared to mainland Western Europe (11.5 per cent).[86] This is partly to do with how unequal the societies are, partly a result of the amount of me-me-me individualism. There is much less depression in collectivist Asian countries,[87] where there are stronger communities and kinship networks, and less individualism.

All of those 'big picture' factors also affect whether the needs of children get met. Despite being one of the richest societies, America has the highest rate of mental illness (26 per cent of the population in the last 12 months) in every study done.[88] Whilst some like to put that down to a tendency in America towards Woody Allen psychobabbling, one reason is a horrendous failure to meet the needs of too many of their small children. Another is their culture, a third is their inequality. As already noted, an American is over 50 times more likely to be impulsive and aggressive than a Japanese person.[89] In Japan, meeting the needs of infants and toddlers is regarded as essential; in America it is not. But it is also true that Japan has a collectivist culture in which there is a high premium placed on self-restraint and consideration for family at home, and towards colleagues at work. The gap between the highest and lowest paid employees in Japan is much smaller than in America.

Social structure and a society's history have a powerful effect on how we interpret 'maltreatment' in childhood. It is true that World Health Organization evidence shows that, overall, maltreatment causes emotional distress in all societies.[90] But the meaning of maltreatment varies enormously according to culture.

For example, living in a society where all children are openly and commonly hit by their parents can change the meaning of the blows. What is physical abuse in one setting can be 'discipline' in another. In many societies and for most of the history of the world, children have been forced to do the bidding of their parents, often through being slapped and punched. As soon as children are old enough, in the developing world, they are expected to work, whether it be paid labour or domestic. The opening line of a definitive account of the history of childhood[91] reads 'The history of childhood is a nightmare from which we are only just awakening'.

Many years ago, in 1978, I spent three months studying the relationship between mothers and babies in the Ecuadorean jungle. Compared with American mother–baby dyads,[92] there was very little responsiveness. A lot of the time, the babies were left in the care of their older sisters, who frequently ignored them or treated them like toys. The mothers did not relate much because they were busy obtaining food, this being a society in which men played little role as parents, usually having several children by different women in different villages, travelling nomadically up and down the river on which they lived. Also, for mothers to become too attached to small children put them at risk of distress: one in four died before the age of five (usually from infections – without antibiotics, mortality soars for small children).

While the children of the village were generally treated warmly by most adults, expectations of life were not like those in developed nations. Education was minimal, there was no concept of careers or of the individualism we are used to in the developed world. Children expected to become like their parents, living a very simple agrarian life, fishing and growing food.

This had been the life of these people for 400 years. With so little pressure to 'succeed', there was little sign of any mental illness in the adults in the village. Indeed, this is an established fact: mental illness is much less common in agrarian traditional communities, so long as there is enough food and no violent conflicts, like warring tribes or national civil war. For example, in a definitive study of schizophrenia,[93] the frequency in such communities was many times less than in developed nations and the likelihood of full recovery and the speed thereof, much greater. Yet these people had had childhoods which would be predictive of many problems in a developed nation – lack of responsiveness from carers in the early years, being hit if the parents felt so inclined, little education, authoritarian parents, absent fathers in many communities.

The difference in the impact of this care in the case of the Ecuadorean village was the lack of pressure to be an individual. An infancy in which there is an absence of individualised and responsive care is not a problem if you do not have to constantly define who you are and where you are trying to get to, expressed through exam results, curriculum vitae and a charming manner in interviews. In such collectivist societies, your identity is conferred upon you by virtue of your gender, place in the family and your family's relationship to other ones.[94] You just do what everyone has always done, there is no search for self, or a struggle to find an identity separate from that of your parents.

A study of the impact of maltreatment in Nigeria illustrates the power of collectivism to mitigate maltreatment.[95] There is six times less mental illness in Nigeria than in America,[96] yet the study found a similar amount of child maltreatment. This strongly suggests that there is no simple 'early maltreatment always causes mental illness' equation: if Americans and Nigerians experience similar levels of maltreatment, there should be similar amounts of mental illness, rather than six times more in America. The authors pointed to some big differences in the two societies which could explain this.

The amount of divorce and separation is far less in Nigeria. There is powerful evidence that maltreatment has far worse effects when combined with parental disharmony. For example, in one large American study,[97] abused children who also had divorced parents were fully ten times more likely to become mentally ill as adults than children who had suffered neither. But most interestingly of all, abuse alone – without parental separation – only doubled the risk.

Interestingly, in the Nigerian study, even where there was divorce it did not increase the risk of mental illness. This could be explained by the fact that there are extended families, which reduces the disruption to care of the child.[98] Where Nigerian maltreatment does occur, the fact that there are numerous carers provides the maltreated child with much more opportunity to seek solace from alternative sources of nurture if they are feeling neglected, unloved or abused, such as support from older siblings (usually the families are large), aunts and uncles, and grandparents. In the atomised nuclear families of the developed world, the absence of daily contact with the extended family means maltreatment is unavoidable, with no alternative nurture available.

In nations where there is education and more individualistic aspiration, a measure of collectivism can do a great deal to counteract the impact of what would be maltreatment in purely individualistic societies – individualism and collectivism can coexist, as is the case in many Asian societies today. For example, Daphne, a young woman I interviewed in Singapore, was a hard-working, successful medical student who had originally been raised in a Catholic household in an agrarian community in Malaysia. Her father was a mariner who had been absent for ten months of the year for the whole of her life. When present, he was a strict disciplinarian but she expressed no resentment towards him. Her mother was a loving woman but had worked hard during her childhood, meaning that Daphne had a variety of carers when very small. Highly motivated to please her strict father, Daphne did well in her schooling. Although in a strict society where sexual activity was frowned upon, she had a strong sense of agency and had felt able to pursue sexual pleasures during her teens when she felt the urge, avoiding detection. Grateful to have been able to get to medical school and escape the drudgery of her parents' working lives, she was satisfied. She was also very much pursuing success to represent her family and as a poster girl for her wider kin network – cousins, aunts, uncles were proud of her, she raised their status.

Daphne felt a strong loyalty to her parents, although she had no illusions as to their shortcomings – an interesting lack of the falsely positive view of them that *Offspring Stockholm Syndrome* induces. She had the same unconditional love for them that they had always shown to her. Her British equivalent might have psychobabbled about how her father had been trying to oppress her and her mother impose religious doctrines. She did not, although she did have difficulties in allowing others to be emotionally intimate, being shy and keeping herself to herself. In some respects she did not really trust anyone, and was quite isolated. But Daphne got on with secretly enjoying a lively sex life, successfully compartmentalising it from the person her parents wanted to her to be. She was able to feel unconditional love and receive it from them, and although she had some problems establishing stable relationships with men, she flourished. Like George and his successful, obedient self at school, she managed to have different personae in different settings, personae which would have different brain patterns.

Interestingly, though, her brother had been sexually abused by a relative when he was small. He was still in Malyasia. She worried about him because he was altogether incapable of friendships or sexual relationships. He lived in a fantasy world, unable to do more than menial jobs. Living in a rural Malaysian village, he was not labelled mentally ill or given drugs for what psychiatrists would have labelled schizophrenia. His distressed state bears out the broad findings of the World Health Organization[99] finding that childhood maltreatment does account for nearly one third of mental illness in all societies.

This was confirmed by the Nigerian study found: maltreatment did lead to more mental illness, overall. The conclusion seems to be that everywhere, the more childhood adversities a person has suffered, the greater the likelihood of mental illness. However, culture mediates how big that impact is. In our affluenza-stricken society,[100] for example, people who place too high a value on money, possessions, appearances and fame are at greater risk of the most common emotional problems, like depression and anxiety. While nearly all of us have the affluenza virus, the extent to which our parents made love conditional on performance and to which they imbued us with consumerist values affects whether the virus makes us ill: childhood maltreatment makes us more vulnerable to cultural toxins.

That Daphne and her brother had different experiences also suggests that differential care does have different impacts in families everywhere. Daphne was the firstborn and had been the conduit for her parents' ambitions. Similarly, a simple and critical difference between George and his sister is that he was the firstborn. The next chapter explores how our role in the family drama causes differences between us and our siblings.

SO WHAT? 3 TAKEAWAYS

ONE: Avoid stress during pregnancy, especially the last three months
Easy to say, I know, the last three months often being the hardest to get right if you have a challenging job. Nonetheless, given the existing evidence

that pregnancy stress can create problems, and especially remembering that it could turn out that some of what has been attributed to genes is down to the pregnancy, it is well worth taking a lot of trouble to try and chill out, especially towards the end. To get in the relaxed zone, a crucial issue is how you feel about motherhood.

In my book *How Not To F*** Them Up*,[101] I set out the psychology of different mothers in the run up to the birth and during the early years. The evidence suggests mothers fall into three main groups. Stress-reduction in pregnancy for each of these kinds varies according to the group:

THE ORGANISER (about a quarter of mothers)

She tends to see it as necessary for the baby to adapt to her and the needs of the family. She loves her baby as much as any other kind of mother but her attitude is that 'mother knows best'. The baby is a creature without a proper understanding of the adult world, a bundle of hungry needs that require regulation to make them predictable. Insufficiently controlled, the baby can quickly become indulged, selfish and naughty. The Organiser sees it as her job to help it take control of its unruly passions and bodily processes. That is an important part of how she shows maternal love. Hence, she tends to see it as vital for the baby to acquire a feeding and sleeping routine, as soon as possible. She is happy for others to take care of the baby and regards a routine as very helpful for this. As quickly as she can after the birth, she wants to get back her 'normal', pre-pregnant life. She is the one most likely to have a full-time paid job.

As regards pregnancy stress-reduction, she may well be most relaxed if she works up until as close to the birth as possible. Kicking her heels at home may not be her style, she could get very stressed because she is less likely than the other kinds to feel she has a relationship with the foetus, regarding it mainly as a drag on her energies. Rather, she likes to keep busy, enjoys the challenge and identity conferred by work and is content to leave it to the last moment to deal with the birth.

THE HUGGER (about a quarter of mothers)

The opposite of the Organiser, she places the needs of the baby ahead of everything. She is the sort of mum who may have the baby sleeping with her in the bed at night, who tends to feed on demand (when the baby indicates it is hungry rather than imposing a routine) and who regards herself as uniquely able to meet the baby's needs. She luxuriates in motherhood, happy to put her life on hold for at least three years. Overall, she adores being with her under-threes. She is least likely of the three kinds to have a paid job, although some do, but rarely full-time.

She is most likely to have strong feelings about the foetus, aware that it sometimes kicks if she gets upset, believing it will hear her singing soothing songs, and so on. She may want to use her maternity leave to get the maximum time at home before the birth and to give up work altogether when the child is born. Her way of not getting stressed is to spend the pregnancy filled with anticipation of the birth, looking forward to a big change in her life.

THE FLEXIMUM (one half of mothers)

The Fleximum combines both attributes of the Hugger and Organiser mums, cutting and pasting the pattern of care according to what each situation requires. She is aware of the needs of the baby and is led by them but, unlike the Hugger, she never loses sight of her own needs as well. She may have the baby in the bed if it is ill, yet also seeks to establish a sleep routine. She may try imposing a feeding regime, only to drop it if it's not working. Above all, she is concerned to create a 'win-win' situation, where both she and the baby get their needs met. Many have a part-time job, though some are at home or at work full-time, according to financial need.

She tunes in and out of the foetus, sometimes very aware of it, at others on a different plain. She may like the idea of taking as much time as possible off before the birth so she can get organised and because she could do with a rest. If family finances cannot afford that, she can be equally cheerful working close to the birth. Ever the pragmatist, she takes the line of least resistance, doing what works best.

TWO: Tune in to babies, enjoy the la-la land of small children – or if you can't, perhaps your partner can?

As the evidence of this chapter shows, babies need responsive love, and toddlers need adults who provide scaffolding for their play. Under-threes really do not need other children as 'friends', they just play in parallel, taking each other's toys 8 times an hour at the age of 18 months,[102] (and still doing so 4 times an hour at 2 ½). They need the care of a responsive adult who knows them well. Regrettably, throughout the developed world (including Scandinavia), it still falls to women to provide the care in infancy. Yet many men would be wonderful with babies and love hanging out with toddlers, if only they knew it. What is more, people of either sex often enjoy some ages more than others. I love the fantasy play stuff that starts around two years old, I know other men who prefer small babies. It's the same with women. If only we had a system that was flexible enough to ensure that parents could be with their children at the ages that suit them.

Alas, we do not, so, given that it is going to mainly be the woman who cares for the baby, they need maximum support, particularly during the first six months. Isolation is the great peril. In many cases, nowadays, grandparents either live too far away or want to enjoy Saga Tours.

For women who are just not connecting with the baby, they need the support of parent–infant psychotherapists, experts in helping the parent to tune in. That is all too often not available. It is other mothers and friends who have to provide the support and insights.

THREE: Love Bombing

If things have gone a bit wrong early on, or even if they have not, I developed Love Bombing[103] as a technique to reset the emotional thermostats of children aged three to puberty. It entails a period of time alone with your child, offering him or her unlimited love and control. It works for a wide variety of common problems, severe or mild, from defiant, even violent aggression, to shyness, trouble sleeping or underperformance at school. In fact, it's something that all children will benefit from. High on my (now ten-year-old) son's Christmas list this year is 'Doddy' time, a full day in which I am going to have to do everything he wants.

It is not the same as 'quality time', just hanging out with your child. When you Love Bomb, you create a special emotional zone wholly different from your normal life, with new rules.

First, you explain to your child that sometime soon, the two of you are going to spend time together and are going to have a lot of fun. Your child is going to decide what they want to do, and when they want it, within reason. You give the message that this is going to be a Big Event: It's Coming Soon – How Exciting! Your child then draws up a list. It doesn't matter if that includes lots of watching *Spongebob Squarepants*: the key is that it is your child who has chosen it.

Throughout the experience, you are trying, as much as possible, to give them the feeling of 'whatever I want, I get' – a very unusual one of being in control and of being gratified, as well as bombed with love.

You may be thinking, 'Are you mad? My child is already a tyrant – rewarding him like that is just going to make it even worse!' This is an understandable worry. Love Bombing seems to fly in the face of conventional wisdom, which often recommends more control, not less, when a child is not complying, and stricter, firmer reactions to undesirable behaviour.

But the point is the Love Bomb zone is separate from ordinary life. Out of that zone, you continue trying to set boundaries, consistently and firmly. In fact, the Love Bombing experience will feed back in a very benign way, greatly reducing the amount of time you spend imposing limits, nagging and nattering – the 'Don't do that', 'I've told you before, put that down', 'Leave your brother alone', which all parents get sucked into now and then. And it's worth doing with almost any child, even happy ones will benefit.

A key practical decision you need to make at the outset is the length of time you will spend in the zone and the frequency. At one extreme, you can take your child away from the family home for a couple of nights at a hotel or bed & breakfast (or rent a cheap gypsy caravan, as one mother did).

Alternatively, as many parents have done, the rest of your family can spend the weekend with relatives or friends, leaving you at home with your child. There is absolutely no necessity to spend any extra money to do Love Bombing. Many parents have done a day away from home, or just bursts of a few hours.

In the case of Miranda and her depressed son Tim, as a dual-income family, they could afford two nights away at a cheap hotel. They settled in there on the Friday night and set off into town on the Saturday. They did a certain amount of shopping and went on a visit to an aquarium but much of the time was spent just wandering around.

Miranda recalled that just this day 'made Tim feel very special, it definitely worked. I realise not everyone can afford a hotel and shopping. And anyway, when it came to spending money, Tim was reasonable about absolutely everything, much to my surprise.' Children who feel loved are less consumption-obsessed.

After a peaceful Saturday night back in the hotel with a KFC and *The X Factor*, on Sunday they pottered around again, did some more shopping and visited a zoo on the way home.

As well as Tim feeling in control during this time, there was much affection expressed. Miranda recalls that 'Tim spent a great deal of time cuddling up to me and telling me how much he loved me (always reciprocated). It was interesting for me not to be in charge. I do tend to lead. Here, it really was mostly Tim's decision what we did next, what we ate and what we watched on TV.'

In the guidelines I offer for Love Bombing, I suggest getting the child to give the experience a name before doing it, like 'Special Time' or 'Mummy Time' (or 'Doddy' time). Often it helps for them to have got a material object to remind them of the experience, like a stone from a beach or a teddy. Using this and the name to help as prompts, on returning, parents are asked to try and carve out half an hour an evening when they can briefly re-enter the Love Bomb zone together, even if it's only to watch some TV.

Miranda has two other children and for various reasons that half hour each evening proved difficult. Instead, she says, 'I give Tim random bits of time and have recently taken to holding and cuddling him like a baby and even saying to him "you're my baby boy and I love you".' You have to tailor the method to suit your circumstances and the problems you and your child are handling.

The impact of the Love Bombing weekend was immediate and dramatic. Five weeks afterwards, Miranda wrote to me that 'overall he is happier. He still has tantrums, but since the weekend away I haven't heard him say that he hates himself at all – not once, come to think of it.' And 18 months later, she reported that 'It is getting better largely due to the Love Bombing and subsequent changes in our relationship.'

I have had very similar reports of sustained success – followed up one to two years after the Love Bombing – from parents helping children with violent aggression, myriad anxiety problems, ADHD, sleeplessness, perfectionism and even autism.

In many cases, I suspect that the experience stabilises cortisol levels. If too high, the child can be manic or aggressive, or anxious. If too low, blunted, the child may be listless or surly. Even a brief experience of love and control seems to correct that.

The Love Bombing zone need not be a whole weekend. For instance, in the case of three-year-old Sam, he seemed a lot more sensitive than his younger brother, easily overwhelmed by simple situations. Sometimes he would melt down in toddler-like rages. He got very jumpy when separated from his mother, Emma. She said that 'in the house, he wants to know where I am all the time'. If she was upstairs and he was downstairs he would scream asking her whereabouts.

For practical reasons, she planned two consecutive Love Bombing Saturdays away from home with him, rather than a night. The first was named Pirate Day by him because they went to a funfair. He adored feeling in control and his mother's expressions of love.

She told him that she loved him repeatedly. Initially, she made a point of looking at her watch every 15 minutes or so and then telling him. Once into the habit, she just continued.

Since that day they find it easier to frequently express love. She believes they now have 'much, much better communication'. She also says, 'It was good fun, a great day that reminded us of the good times that we can have together, setting us back on that track. It was a truly lovely day.' Often it is not just the child's thermostat that is corrected, it is also the parent's in relation to the child. After Love Bombing many parents report feeling it has been the first time for months or years when they remembered how much they love them.

The second day was based at home and included a complete meltdown by him. It is extremely common during Love Bombing for the child to test out if the parent is for real – really loves them or will still love them if they are horrible. Emma rode it out and they emerged much closer.

Afterwards, she reported that 'He has not had any unreachable tantrums since that one on the last Love Bombing day, four weeks ago.' What's more, his fear of not knowing where she is in the house has disappeared.

Whatever the child's actual age, it can help to think of them as an 18-month-old when in the Love Bombing zone. Parents have reported that their child has brief periods during the Love Bombing when they actually revert to being like a toddler, cuddling and even using baby talk. This is exactly what you are aiming for. You are trying to give them the chance to go back to earlier periods, but this time it is really, really good: they feel totally safe, loved and in control.

Many parents have shown great ingenuity in adapting the method to their circumstances or problems. For example, four-year-old Jeff was having terrible temper tantrums, sometimes directed against his two-year-old sister. His mother Carole introduced twice or thrice weekly Time In Charge sessions, as Jeff named them. These entailed Carole being led in play by Jeff.

A basic game was running races which Mummy had to join in with, holding the baby, charging round the room. However, by far the majority of the time was taken up with fantasy play.

Some were open-ended scenarios, in which imaginary babies would transform into fishes and back again. More commonly, there would be specific narratives that progressed according to his script, sometimes dream-like. He particularly enjoyed disasters, like sinking ships, with his mother and sister employed in a variety of supporting roles.

The impact of this version of Love Bombing was dramatic. Carole reported that 'Immediately after we started the play sessions the temper tantrums stopped. There were just no incidents any more of a significant nature. That has been true for three months now.'

However you do Love Bombing, there is nothing to lose. What's not to like about spending some time having fun with your child? If it transforms them and your relationship, so much the better, but the worst that can happen is you return from the zone having had a good time.

Chapter 5

Your Role in the Family Drama (Why Siblings are so Different, Pt 2)

There is a finite amount of love, time and money for parents to devote to children.[1] When the Spice Girls achieved fame, it was a brilliant marketing ploy to dub each girl with a different persona – Sporty, Baby, Posh and so on. This typology made instant sense to children engaged in the battle for parental resources, niches they partly create for themselves and partly have thrust upon them.

How children politic and what issues they particularly seek to manipulate depend a great deal on the role that has been scripted for them by their family drama. In families, we are very much like actors in a play.[2] As R.D. Laing put it,[3] when it comes to families 'We are acting parts in a play that we have never read and never seen, whose plot we don't know, whose existence we can glimpse, but whose beginnings and end are beyond our present imagination and conception'. Which child ends up in which role depends on a number of factors.

Parents are at variable stages in their lives when their different children are born. The state of their marriage or partnership alters. The first-born has a radical effect, especially upon the mother,[4] usually entailing a transition from worker to full- or part-time mum. Meanwhile, the father may feel excluded by the new arrival or he may be delighted, he may feel under tremendous pressure to be a breadwinner or that his destiny has been fulfilled.

When baby number two comes along, the family has already been altered by baby number one. Perhaps Mum and Dad are not getting along so well in the face of the new pressures, maybe it has brought them closer together. Perhaps they are on the up financially, or money may have become a huge bone of contention. Perhaps they have moved to a new area, upsetting one or both of them. In any of dozens of ways, the emotional contentment and preoccupations of each parent often change considerably from those present at the birth of the first.

As the family grows, the parental resources decrease.[5] Lastborn children get less attention[6] than firstborns. In their early years, triplets get less sensitive responses[7] from their mothers than twins, who get less than individual children, resulting in lower scores on tests of mental development.[8] Parents only have limited amounts of energy and time.

On top of all this, each parent dumps on to each child a furniture van full of historical baggage from their own childhood. If firstborn themself, perhaps the arrival of a second or third triggers memories of being displaced when they were small, making them extra sympathetic to their own firstborn. If lastborn, perhaps they are concerned to ensure that the new child does not get the same 'raw deal' they felt they had. If it is a boy and the father had a bullying brother, if it is a girl and the mother had a sister who was always prettier than her... the variations of birth order and relations between siblings are numerous and the effect on how the parent construes the newborn, profound.

The child's gender also combines with its place in the family in creating dramatis personae for the child as parents rehash their own childhood. Perhaps she was hoping for a boy and got a girl, perhaps he was. The mother may have had an intrusive mother and consequently, be determined to give her daughter space. Perhaps the father feels that his parents were not strict enough and is determined not to make the same mistake. Perhaps a parent was treated cruelly or neglectfully, re-enacting that maltreatment with a particular child by inflicting the same cruelty.

The changes in the emotional state of each parent and of the marriage from one child to the next, combined with the biographical bric-a-brac that each loads separately on to each child, creates a unique psychological environment every time. While some family-wide traits will be demanded by both parents from all their children, like a concern for punctuality, good table manners or good exam results, the remarkable fact is that most of each individual child's nurture[9] is particular to it. They develop their own family niche as a result of receiving radically different care.

Beyond the differential maltreatment and love discussed in the last chapter, sibling differences come from family roles: how our parents react to our birth order and gender, as well as sibling rivalry, favouritism and stigmatisation. All of these interact with each other, rarely is a single one critical.[10] In considering them separately in the coming sections, there will inevitably be some overlap.

Birth order

There have been over 2,000 studies[11] testing the effect of our place in the family on how we turn out. In accord with the fact that offspring compete for parental investment by developing niches, the studies show that firstborns[12] take the line of least resistance: tend to align themselves with what their parents think and feel, and try to fulfil parental expectations, amenable to their wishes and values. That often converts into adults who are more conscientious, responsible, ambitious and organised, compared with laterborns. Firstborns are disproportionally common among leaders, such as prime ministers and presidents. They are likely to be more conservative, traditional and endorsing of conventional morality. For example, if they take a year off before going to university, they are less likely to go on adventurous travels, more likely to do something worthy, like working with underprivileged children or a career-building internship. They achieve more in their careers having done better at school,[13] with parents pitching dinner-table conversation at their level rather than that of younger siblings. The firstborn in a four-children family is, on average, approximately ten percentage points[14] more likely to have their homework monitored on a daily basis than the lastborn. Firstborns are more anxious about their status, more emotionally intense, less quick to recover from upsets. They are more vengeful and prone to anger, often tormented by the loss of attention that results from the arrival of younger siblings. They tend not to enjoy risk-taking in general, and dangerous sports in particular, preferring swimming, tennis, golf and other noncontact sports.

By contrast, laterborns tend to identify less with their parents. There will still be some niches that have not been nabbed, especially if they are of a different gender from the first. For example, our firstborn was a girl. She quickly spotted that I enjoyed watching Chelsea FC and I took her to a couple of games. My son arrived three years after her. Football became less of an interest to my increasingly 'feminine' daughter and he managed to nab this niche off her, by playing a lot of football and supporting Chelsea. She was happy enough to let it go, as she already had plenty of other interests, like painting and reading, neither of which my son challenged her for. Had my son been a girl, it may well have panned out differently and my daughter might still be showing an interest in Chelsea. She might have hung on to that niche, whether also developing 'feminine' ones, or becoming a tomboy.

Laterborns are more open to experience, although they are liable to have been forced to submit to older siblings[15] through physical fighting and greater mental ability. As a result, the later born may empathise with the downtrodden and favour egalitarianism. The later born they are, with more siblings above them, the more they are likely to resist authority and conformity, to be the rebels in the family. They are less self-confident, more altruistic and emotionally empathic. They are less conscientious and less prone to anger and revenge, more sociable and easy to be with – they have to learn to be 'cute' and to rub along with more powerful siblings. They embrace risk-taking and contact sports, are more likely than firstborns to prefer such pursuits as rugby, football, boxing and parachute jumping. For their year off, they may head for the wilds of the jungle, mountains or desert, leaving parents alarmed as months go by without any emails or Skype contact.

Birth order strongly interacts with the baggage parents bring from their own childhood. An email correspondent, with whom I subsequently had several conversations, was the second of two sons. Neither of his parents had been university educated, so the eldest was encouraged academically and became the first child in either family's history to obtain a degree. The younger son, my correspondent, was kept close to his insecure, anxious mother. She made intense demands on him, constantly requiring his attention, just as her mother had done with her. As a teenager, she accompanied him to the drama groups he joined and they became co-dependent. Only in his thirties did he break free from her to develop sexual relationships with women.

Lacking a university degree, he worked in similar professions to his parents, low paid and low status. He was every bit as intelligent as his brother, on to whom the aspirations had been loaded. Purely because of his secondborn position, he did not achieve as much educationally or professionally. He was also the one used as a vehicle for his mother's insecurities. Swapped at birth, I suspect the sons would have turned out like each other, purely because of birth order.

One major reason firstborns are different[16] is that they get the undivided attention of the mother for at least nine months, usually more. While there are big variations, it often means they get more responsive, loving care early on. That can work in their favour but it depends on what happens next.

One firstborn who emailed me an account of his childhood had three years of being the apple of his mother's and grandparents' eye. Along came a sister and he felt a big loss of attention. But that was just the beginning. Another sibling arrived for each of the succeeding four years. By the time he turned eight, he had five siblings. He wrote that 'Although I had a great start, having all these siblings come along turned me into a control freak and someone with a terrible temper – I had big temper tantrums because my ma was no longer paying me much attention. As soon as I was able, I started earning money from doing odd jobs and I used it to manipulate my siblings. For instance, all of us had tasks, like hoovering or washing up. I paid my siblings to do mine.' In later life, the man became a senior civil servant, managing thousands of people, something he attributes to his experience of having to learn at a young age to control his siblings.

Another reason firstborns differ is that parents are generally stricter with them,[17] sometimes to establish a 'reputation' with the younger children. By making an example of the firstborn, the parents hope to indicate to the younger ones what will happen if they misbehave. Parents are also finding their feet with the firstborn and may be alarmed by the challenge of controlling the feeding, sleeping and other routines of the infant and toddler. To cope, they may use strictness, like rigidly imposed routines for feeding, exact times for sleeping and waking. Subsequently, they monitor the child more closely. For example, on average, parents in two-child families[18] spend half an hour more a day providing 'quality time' to their firstborn. It is no wonder that firstborns have higher scores[19] on intelligence tests and get better exam results; their mental development is given much more attention.

As the number of children increases, parents have less and less time and energy to devote to them. This may result in neglect or just in greater freedom for the child. Parents are often much less anxious and less determined to impose themselves, realising that no harm will result if they let the child play unsupervised in sand on the beach or out in the garden. Above all, they have less unfulfilled aspirations for the laterborns;[20] firstborns are the vehicles for that. This is well illustrated by the story of Sir Vince Cable,[21] the firstborn Liberal-Democrat politician. His story also shows how family dynamics can shape political views.

Cable became famous during a two-month period in 2007, as acting leader of his party. This happened to coincide with the collapse of the

Northern Rock bank, the first implosion in what was to become the 2008 Credit Crunch. In making passionate pleas for the nationalisation of that bank, he achieved widespread popularity. His jibe at Gordon Brown, the then prime minister, for having gone from being 'Stalin to Mr Bean', hit the jackpot. Subsequently, as a minister in the coalition government until 2015, from time to time Cable would present himself as the champion of left wing economic ideas, returning to his attack 'on too big to fail' banks.

Yet the fascinating thing about Cable is that he was never remotely a man of the traditional left (i.e., in favour of European levels of public expenditure, against letting a Free Market have its wicked way with the electorate, against large gaps between the average wage and that of senior managers), as he makes abundantly clear in his 2008 autobiography. Misleadingly entitled *Free Radical*, he admits[22] in it that he only adopted left wing positions in order to curry favour with voters. One of the few consistent political beliefs that emerge from his autobiography is a strong commitment to the free market, the cornerstones of modern conservatism and Blairite New Labour. The other main consistency is that he does not feel comfortable in either the New Labour or the Conservative parties, he wants to position himself as the reasonable man in between the two (although there is only a paper thin gap between them). The roots of these political beliefs are clearly to be found in his role within his family as the firstborn.

By being Tory, he is reproducing his father; by being liberal, his mother. It may be that a coalition with the free market Conservatives was psychologically a comfortable position, because of his support for their economic policies.

Cable was born in York in 1943, the eldest of two sons, his brother ten years younger. Not unusually for their generation, Len and Edith Cable, his parents, were consumed by social status insecurities. This translated into ensuring their sons did well at school. Len had worked on the shop floor in the Rowntree's sweet factory in York but through assiduous attendance at evening classes, he eventually obtained academic qualifications and became a lecturer in a technical college.

Len was an extreme authoritarian in every way, to such an extent that at the college his nickname was Hitler. Cable describes him as a 'neo-Nazi', a domineering bully who crushed anyone who could not stand up to him. Politically, in Cable's account, he was a racist colonialist who ranted against socialism.

Len's frustrated ambitions were poured into his firstborn son. In terms of *Offspring Stockholm Syndrome*, given that the terrorist who was holding him hostage was a 'neo-Nazi', Cable had little alternative but to work hard and please him. Success at school was carefully nurtured and ultimately, this investment paid off, with Cable obtaining the Cambridge degree that his father craved for himself. People-pleasing became a critical feature of Cable's personality. However, his relationship with his mother and the position he occupied in relation to their marriage, created a more complicated outcome than Cable only becoming like his father.

Following the birth of his brother, his mother suffered severe postnatal depression. She was admitted to mental hospital for a year and his brother had to be fostered out. When she returned, she was not the same person, a 'damaged' and 'diminished' figure. Len found this intolerable and became extremely aggressive to her. While Cable cannot recall having witnessed physical abuse, his brother can.

Despite Cable's lack of memory of his early life, he does recall one significant incident regarding his political leanings. In 1959, aged 16, his mother broke down in tears and confessed to him that she had that day voted Liberal in the General Election. From then on, the two of them formed a covert Liberal cell in the Cable household.

Although Cable sometimes displays passion in his public appearances, he believes that something in his childhood 'cauterised' his emotions. The obvious scalpel would seem to have been the witnessing of the many rows between his parents, which he knows took place but which he cannot recall. He believes he shut them out and created strong psychological defences against knowing what was happening.

His position as eldest certainly meant that he witnessed his mother's breakdown and the subsequent collapse of the marriage into extreme disharmony. But given the extent of his father's tyranny, Cable must also have developed a hatred of him well before his mother became depressed. He does not report any specific times when his mother was loving before her breakdown and it is highly probable that she was already depressed to some degree long before it.

For he had a largely joyless childhood, a deep cynicism pervading his account of it. He participated in sport, sometimes successfully, but only because it was a means of popularity and to fit in, not for pleasure. On Sundays he attended the Baptist church of which his parents were fastidious congregants, neither of them drinkers or smokers. There he would summon up quotes to impress the congregants with his religiosity. At his grandmother's on Sundays, the climax of his 'weekly cycle of boredom', he would have to be seen and not heard, dressed in his Sunday Best clothes, the slightest sign of bad behaviour slapped down.

Trapped in this life, effectively an only child, for his pleasures he escaped into a fantasy world. He developed the idea of himself as a Big Game Hunter, shooting at cats and dogs with an air rifle. Turning himself into a World War Two hero chasing spies; on one occasion, he even got into trouble with the police for shooting at a neighbour's window. This is an interesting further example of how most of us have many selves. The good boy Vince will have had a different set of brainwaves and chemistry from the one out being a fantasy hero, just as George (from the last chapter) was one person at his school, and another at home, or hard-working medical student Daphne's brain would have had different contents from the secretly sexually active Daphne. But enacted delinquency on Cable's part was extremely rare. The vast majority of his childhood was devoted to pleasing his father and his teachers.

His selves were divided, with the emotionally 'cauterised' people-pleaser nearly always in the driving seat, the father-hating rebel hidden away, along with the fantasy Big Game Hunter who could kill such threatening (neo-Nazi) beasts.

Cable's divided political soul consisted of:

Conservative = Len = Hitler = Being hijacked by a feared tyrant.

Liberal = Edith = Insurgency against the 'Conservative' and

all it stands for = A double agent, betraying his paternal homeland.

This makes sense of his otherwise confusing political positions. Out of fear for his father, he remained true to some Conservative tenets, most notably, free market economics. As a spy in league with his mother and borne of loathing of his father, he supported some Liberal causes. So it was that his role in his family's politics played out in his professional political career.

His brother made a successful business career for himself. I believe it is not fanciful to suggest that, had the two boys been swapped at conception, Cable would now be the businessman and his brother the well-known politician. That is how crucial position in the family is in determining individual differences. While his brother was also hot-housed, the extent to which he was the object of Len's unfulfilled ambitions was far less.

It can be seen from all this that birth order hugely affects what role you occupy in the family drama. But it is equally apparent that it interacts with other factors, like gender.

Gender

Do you think your parents would have treated you differently had you been the opposite of your gender? Of course they would have.

From birth onwards, parents respond differently to boys and girls.[23] A simple experiment is to dress a baby boy in pink, an infant girl in blue, and measure strangers' responses to them. Sure enough, if it's pink there will be a flood of feminising adjectives like 'sweet', 'cute' and so forth; if blue, more masculinising ones, suggesting the baby is 'bold' and 'naughty'. Fathers play more roughly with baby sons, bouncing them up and down, and are more gentle with daughters. As soon as a parent hears the gender of its child, a mass of projections are triggered, beyond the normal stereotypes.

As described in Chapter 1, being the only son with three sisters caused my father to treat me very differently from them. Despite an encyclopaedia of evidence to the contrary, my father continued to tell me, and none of my sisters, that I was 'very clever' and that I could achieve academically what none of my teachers (or my mother) believed was possible. Eventually, his wish was my command.

The projections of the mother on to a daughter can be equally biased. One of my female clients had three sons before her daughter arrived. None of the boys distinguished themselves at school, my client was quite relaxed about their educational performance. It was a different story with her daughter. My client had been the only daughter in her family and her sexist father had been open about his view that the purpose of women was to make good wives and mothers. She had been to university but done little professionally before marrying and giving up work.

A passionate feminist, she was determined that her daughter should have a different experience to her. From nursery onwards, she closely monitored her daughter's academic progress, reading to her, encouraging educational games, hothousing her. Sure enough, the girl excelled, and at grammar school was a star pupil. However, there was a price to pay. At 15, the daughter developed an extreme perfectionism, accompanied by bulimia (overeating then making herself sick) and self-harming (cutting herself). In doing so she was not unusual, the most mentally ill group[24] in our society are 15-year-old girls from the top social classes, the ones who achieve the highest grades. At the last count (2006), 44 per cent of such girls were depressed or anxious. Just between 2009 and 2014, the proportion of 13-year-old girls feeling distressed rose from 13 per cent to 20 per cent.

Neither my client nor her daughter could understand where the intense concern with high performance came from. I have often encountered this mystification, with the girls themselves saying they have not been under any pressure from their parents. Yet when we got into the detail, it soon became obvious to the mother that she had not given her daughter any space to play, to be a child. Indeed, we could trace the problem all the way back to infancy, because it so happened that the father had filmed a few clips of the mother and daughter together when she was a baby. Analysing them, we could see how the mother was unresponsive to the baby's attempts to initiate interactions with a smile or through eye contact, and instead would either ignore her or smother her with intrusive words, or change her position, or make demands that she feed, when these were all too visibly not what the baby wanted.

Once the client had overcome her distress at realising all this, she was quickly able to link it to her own childhood yearnings to be taken seriously by her father and her hunger for success. She altered the way she related to her daughter, who soon recovered from her bulimia and stopped cutting. While the perfectionism endured to some extent, it waned over the three years of my work with the mother. Today it has ceased to be a problem.

Despite the advances that have resulted from feminism, there are still plenty of hangovers of sexist differential treatment of daughters. Among wealthy families, for example, it is still common for sons to be given the lion's share of inheritance in order to keep intact country estates. There are strong traditions in some Asian communities which prohibit daughters from inheriting power. In one family business, the very capable, university-educated daughter was told by her father that she would never be allowed to become his successor as its proprietor because women are 'too emotional'. Her brother was groomed to succeed the father, as he had been by his father. The same is true in some wealthy Caucasian British families.

At a very simple level, despite decades of feminism, throughout our society there are a strong set of expectations which parents are liable to bring to bear when they hear the gender of their child. While the parental rhetoric may be of equality, the reality of parental behaviour is often still different. We have a considerable way to go before we achieve the kind of genuine psychological egalitarianism to be found in Scandinavian nations.

Favouritism

Two-thirds of children claim their parents[25] have shown some form of preferential treatment to one of their siblings. The reasons for it can be as simple as the child's appearance. Beauty or handsomeness[26] affects the reaction of parents, as well as other people, throughout life. But more commonly, favouritism is triggered by the parents' history,[27] causing them to respond preferentially depending on where the child comes in the family and its gender.

Again, my own example comes to mind, and like many favoured children, I remember my father with special fondness. But there are often prices to be paid for special treatment. In adulthood some come to resent it. For example, Pamela, an American woman aged 35, contacted me by email and subsequently she became my client on Skype, with five meetings in person when she came to England. Hers was a mixed experience of favouritism.

She was the youngest of four daughters, born to an affluent family in California. All the girls were mainly cared for by African–American nannies during their early years. Nonetheless, they were tyrannised to varying degrees by Georgina, their mother, a fragile, difficult and depressed woman.

Pamela also suffered from mild depression, a problem we were able to overcome, but her three sisters were far more disturbed, each with major problems, ranging from sex addiction to major mental illness. Pamela was spared these extreme disturbances because she was very much her father's favourite.

From the age of five, he encouraged her to play with her dolls in his study while he was doing his paperwork. When he went out riding on his pony trap, she was taken along to accompany him. He cuddled her, gave her presents, encouraged her schoolwork and called her his 'little princess'. While there was never anything sexually inappropriate in his behaviour towards her, he very much used her as an emotional prop and treated her as an extension of himself. As she got older, he found it hard to accept that she needed independence. None of her boyfriends were acceptable, she was not supposed to do anything that interfered with providing him with her exclusive attention.

The favouritism activated considerable jealousy in her mother. When she was eight, Pamela overheard her mother berating him about their relationship, eventually shouting 'Why don't you marry the darn girl?' Pamela felt powerless: it was not her fault that he favoured her. Equally, when she reached late childhood, his father would sometimes sit on the pony trap and give her more information than she needed about his difficulties with her mother. Again, she felt trapped because there was nothing she could do to change their unsatisfying sex life and marriage. She was distressed to learn that her father had taken lovers, yet she was powerless to prevent him speaking of them, or against her mother.

Her mild depression turned out to be largely due to her sense of impotence in the face of her father's predicament and her mother's tormented existence, something for which she felt considerable sympathy. We worked out that her mother had all the symptoms of post traumatic stress disorder. She had been severely maltreated as a girl, and probably sexually abused. As a result, she was constantly in the grip of fear, and re-experiencing her past traumas. Often she seemed like she was not in the room with her family, staring into the distance. She could lose her temper at any moment for no apparent reason, becoming terrifying, although she never hit her daughters. This intimate terrorism kept the whole family in a permanent state of anxiety.

At mealtimes she insisted on strict protocol and any girl who dared to speak out of turn or who did not eat their food with the right cutlery, in the right way, was liable to a malevolent tirade. Pamela became expert at manipulating the gleaming cutlery so that she could use a knife or spoon as a mirror with which to see the expression on her mother's face in order to take the emotional temperature. It was dangerous to look at her mother directly because if she caught her eye, it might be misinterpreted as a rebellious or critical look ('what are you looking at?'). On one occasion, taken to the cinema, her mother exploded when her daughter failed to pronounce the name of one of the actors in the film correctly, a detonation that Pamela likened to high explosives. Any tiny matter could be the occasion for such eruptions.

The girls were largely kept away from their mother, consigned to the nursery and cared for by nannies. But even when small, Pamela sensed that there was something badly wrong with her mother. She felt sorry for her, as well as resenting her, and was much relieved during the therapy to understand how the PTSD explained her mother's difficultness. What Pamela found hard to forgive was her mother's cruel attitude to her nanny. Georgina would snarl at her, treating her 'as a dog, giving her commands and expecting instant obedience'.

As the favourite, Pamela felt specially entitled and that she should be able to protect her nanny. Yet she also knew there was nothing she could do, she was powerless again.

This mixture of being a chosen one and of helplessness translated into a love of painting. Her father doted on her creations, Pamela went to art college and developed those skills. Becoming a set designer, part of her was satisfied by the backdrops she painted for New York theatres, but another felt that the ultimate control of whether the plays were good was in the hands of the actors and director.

A crucial legacy of the favouritism was that her father, now in old age, still treated her as a crutch. During our work, she attempted to set boundaries on these demands and she also decided to marry her current boyfriend. This decision was treated with horror by her father, who raised strong and irrational objections to the marriage. Her fiancé was a theatre director and her father maintained that he only wanted her for her wealth. Eventually, she came to realise that she had to end all contact with her father.

Ironically, she had the strength to do this because she had been his favourite. It had given her enough confidence to break free of him. Having survived a tyrannical mother, she was able to set sail on her own, unburdened by a parasitical father. No longer plagued by the sense that she was powerless, her mild depression lifted and she was able to leave her parents behind, their difficulties no longer hers to sort out.

In fact, as we worked together, it emerged that she had never been intimate with her father. A self-focused man, he had simply used her when she was convenient. She could not think of a single occasion on which he had sympathised with or consoled her. If she was vulnerable or needy, he had no interest in her. It was her nanny who she turned to at such times, both as a child and as an adult.

This story illustrates that favouritism is not always without its costs. One is that it frequently stimulates sibling rivalry.

Favouritism and sibling rivalry

Lucian Freud, the celebrated painter[28] and grandson of Sigmund, was a favoured middle son. Famously, he had a deep enmity toward both his brothers, his younger one being Clement (the media personality, chef and ex-MP), the older being Stephen. In his autobiography, Clement wrote that when their mother came into the nursery 'she nodded to Stephen and me, and sat down with Lucian and whispered. They had secrets'. Although she showed a much greater interest in Lucian than his brothers, this does not seem to have pleased him. He told his biographer, Geordie Greig, that he found her attentions oppressive and as soon as he was old enough, distanced himself from her.

As children, Stephen and Lucian sometimes ganged up on Clement, sometimes cruelly. Raised in Berlin before the Second World War, they persuaded the young boy to go up to a Nazi soldier and ask him if he had seen a monkey. When Clement returned to report that the soldier had not, they gave him a mirror to look at. These kinds of cruel 'jokes' seem to have been a regular part of the boys' subculture.

It so happens that my mother, Lydia (née Jacobs), was a contemporary at Dartington Hall School, where all three boys were sent almost as soon as they arrived as escapees from Nazi Germany in 1932. She was scathing about Lucian. He was obsessed by horses (as was she, at that age), sometimes sleeping in the stables with them. My mother summed up how anti-social and unpleasant she found him with the claim that he tried to kill her horse by feeding it raw barley.

In later life, Stephen and Clement remained on civil terms. Lucian, however, had long periods of disenchantment with Stephen, resulting from a row over a debt. He was consistently scathing about Clement, saying he always despised him. He called him a liar and commented 'He's dead now. Always was, actually'. They did not speak for the last forty years of their lives.

The greatest single reason for problems between Lucian and his brothers is that they claimed he was the result of a marital affair, and was not the biological son of their father, Ernst. Even at the age of 87, Lucian still raged about this slur on him and his mother. Given her special interest in him, it is understandable the brothers might have believed it or that it could even have been true, although in appearance, he looked like a Freud. It may, of course, have simply been one of the brothers' 'jokes'.

The three boys turned into very different men. Stephen seems to have been unambitious, content to run an eccentric shop mostly selling door-knobs. Lucian was possibly the greatest portrait painter of the twentieth century. Clement became a celebrated chef, comedian and politician (Lucian is said to have refused a knighthood on the grounds that Clement accepted one). Apart from the fact that two of them became famous and that all three were keen gamblers, it is hard to find any other similarities. The favouritism shown to Lucian created a lifelong sibling rivalry of remarkable enmity.

Another interesting example of favouritism mixed with sibling rivalry comes from the childhood of Janet Street-Porter.[29] She is a journalist who worked for many years as a television presenter, then as a producer and executive. I got to know her quite well in the 1980s, both professionally and personally. She has always been highly competitive and, at times, downright aggressive. As well as being highly entertaining and having considerable charm, as an employer she could be tyrannical, demanding instant obedience. She was constantly office politicking, often with considerable success.

The opening pages of her autobiography are a lament to the fact that she is becoming like her mother. 'Why am I turning into her?' she asks. By the end, neither Janet nor the reader is any the wiser. In fact, it appears that she turned much more into her father than her mother, because of a mixture of favouritism, her gender, birth order and intense sibling rivalry with her younger sister.

Her father, Stan, was a bully, the centre of attention in their family. Her mother, Cherrie, lived in fear of him, including of physical abuse. She became subservient and passive, adjectives that no one who knows her would apply to Janet. Stan never failed to make everyone feel inferior, it seems, and could be a 'mini-dictator'. He insisted that the home be run according to his rules, and demanded absolute control. When people were of no use to him, he discarded them.

In many respects, Janet was also like this when I knew her. One reason for the similarity was the accident of being the firstborn.

Her only sibling, Pat, was two years younger. A war developed between her parents, which seems to have been played out between the two daughters. Above all, Janet was favoured by her father and she took his side in the marital battles.

Her father was a distant man who had no close friends and he took Janet with him to see his beloved Fulham Football Club and to watch motorcycle racing. He had wanted sons and treated Janet as one, so she developed classically boyish interests. Given a doll for Christmas, she ripped off its arms and legs. When her mother had the doll repaired, Janet repeated the mutilation. After that, she got the Meccano sets she wanted.

Whilst her dominant personality came from her father, her hyper-competitiveness and penchant for manipulative game-playing resulted from intense sibling rivalry. Always flat-chested, Janet abhorred the fact that Pat was not. Janet wrote that 'I bloody loathed her'. Pat had a friendly, cheery disposition, was popular, whereas at 13, Janet describes herself as having been an unpopular 'moody cow'. They grew up barely tolerating each other.

Although Pat was also intelligent, their father treated Janet as if she was the 'brainy one'. She wrote that she was 'obsessed with winning everything, from cards to spelling to maths to rounders'. Janet reports having won a prize for writing a 'heartrending' story at school about a downtrodden seaside donkey. She shows no sign of realising that she might have felt like that persecuted creature. Perhaps she dealt with those feelings by some extreme bullying of her sister, mirroring the control-freakery exercised by her father over her mother.

Sharing a room with Pat, Janet drew a line down the middle and warned that crossing it would lead to her being 'dead meat'. So frightened was Pat of crossing the line, she would tie her leg to the bedstead in case she sleep-walked across it in the night. Janet used piercing gazes to terrify Pat, writing that 'I definitely intended to show that bitch a lesson for growing breasts before me'. She was so envious of her sister that she made two attempts to kill her.

Waiting until Pat was about to walk down the stairs, Janet pushed with all her might. Fortunately, Pat only received a cut to the head. Despite being hit for this action by her father, Janet repeated the attack two weeks later. She suspects Pat had anticipated such an eventuality and this time rolled smoothly down the stairs, turning only to give Janet a V sign before escaping at the bottom. Following that incident, Janet writes 'I was in total despair. I had to escape from the prison that was my life with my family, how I didn't yet know'.

What is striking about the stories of Lucian Freud and Janet Street-Porter is that favouritism and sibling rivalry contributed to their considerable differences from siblings. Although extreme cases, the stories illustrate the norm. As parents, all of us inevitably prefer some features of our children to others. To some degree that goes down gender lines, so mothers may have more in common with daughters, fathers with sons. Parents will say they go to great lengths to treat all their children equally and they may succeed in practical and material matters, like bedtimes at certain ages, amounts of pocket money and so forth. But at the emotional level, it's often beyond a parent's control. A mother who loathes a lot of her daughter's lifestyle preferences cannot help feeling warmly to the other daughter who shares her own. Part of having a personality is preferring some things over another, parents cannot avoid that. Part of having had a childhood is that we emerge with strong tastes and distastes. Part of life is that we can be eight months pregnant and not want to have the baby. Which brings us to stigmatisation as a family role.

Stigmatisation

A significant number of children are born unwanted, often with damaging effects. In one study, the negativity of mothers towards their babies[30] during the first month was measured. Tested 40 years later, children of mothers who felt negatively were 18 times more likely to be insecurely attached adults (which means they would be nearly twice as likely to be mentally ill[31]) than babies whose mothers felt positive to them all those years ago.

A rather clever Czechoslovakian study[32] identified 220 children whose mothers had given birth to a child they had twice been refused a request to abort. Compared with wanted children, the mothers of the unwanted were less likely to breastfeed and at age nine, the children were doing markedly worse at school, were less diligent than their schoolmates, more prone to explosive irritability and defensiveness. Aged 15, the unwanted children were still academically worse, reported by their teachers to be less conscientious and obedient. When asked about their mothers' attitude to them, the children claimed she showed less positive interest. Either they felt neglected by her or she was interfering and over-controlling. In accord with this, subsequent large studies[33] have found that an adult is three times more likely to have the severe mental illness of schizophrenia if the mother had not wanted the baby during pregnancy.

A study of five- and seven-year-old siblings[34] in 172 families reveals some of the underlying causes of adverse differential treatment. Whereas most of the children claimed they were treated differently by both parents, only a small proportion of fathers or mothers thought they did: surprise, surprise, parents do not want to admit they have favourites. If a child claimed difference, the parent very rarely also reported it. That strongly suggests parents (understandably) like to think they are fair, but it is likely the children know better.

There were big differences between mothers and fathers. Maternal levels of emotional 'malaise' (measured as prolonged feelings of sadness, despair, loss of appetite, enjoyment, lethargy and thoughts about suicide) predicted differential treatment. The same was true of anger. Neither of these predicted it in fathers, illustrating the crucial role played by mothers. This is as one might expect. In most families, mothers continue to be more involved in childrearing (time spent present with children, as well as actively engaging with them) than fathers. Mothers shoulder more of the responsibility for childcare tasks (taking children to and from school, for example, scheduling dental appointments). Sheer quantity of involvement alone would make it likely that any tendency to treat their children more differently would show up more. Combine that with malaise or anger and it's easy to see how the impact of maternal differential treatment would be greater.

In the study, there was also more stigmatising in chaotic households (noisy ones with lack of routine and untidiness). Under stress, any differential tendencies may be harder to control and exacerbated. Overall, single mothers were more likely to differentiate than ones in couples, exacerbated if they had high levels of anger. The stresses on single mothers are usually very considerable, not least lack of time and money.

When all the measured factors were taken into account, they explained 17 per cent of the differential nurture. But the study did not examine the role of parents' personal histories. It is likely to be critical, as we shall see in the next chapter from the potent evidence that there is intergenerational transmission of traits through nurture, not nature. Families are like dramas and the parents' own childhoods are the main scriptwriters, which in turn are heavily influenced by their own parents', and so on.

Consciously not wanting a child is an extreme. Commoner is for parents to simply develop a milder dislike or disdain for aspects of a particular child owing to its gender, birth order or perhaps because it triggers resentment the parents are carrying from their own childhood. A good example of a stigmatised child is Penny Leach, the author of influential parenting books.

The middle child of three sisters, I interviewed Leach for a newspaper article in 2003. She told me that her father favoured her older sister over her: 'We never clicked. He was devoted to my older sister until the day he died. To him, she was everything a girl and woman could possibly be – and she is a gorgeous lady who I adore myself. Perhaps if I'd been a boy, maybe that would have been more interesting to him, but really, he couldn't be bothered with a second daughter, although years later he did better with a third.'

Leach's parents divorced when she was 12 and there were a couple of years when she had to traipse between her parents, caring for her sister, who was seven years younger. This sister 'was very much my first baby. We would be sent down on the train to stay with my father, which neither of us wanted. He'd never been a very hands-on father and there was no mother-figure there. Five-year-olds aren't good at coping with that. If you can't have your own mum, being somebody else's is a good alternative. I'm still angry on her behalf – which is probably really my anger, a straight projection.' In other words, she felt unloved by her father and dealt with that by caring for her sister when on these trips (what might be characterised as *I'm Not Okay, You Are*).

Being unfavoured by her father may have increased Leach's intense concern to help parents to see things from the child's standpoint. He was an authoritarian, where the adult view is imposed, while her mother was much more child-centred. 'Don't let her argue with you,' her father would roar regarding Penny. 'How can she learn if she can't argue?' her mother would reply.

She recalls that 'Mummy was the light of my life, very, very much the special person for me. She was not permissive, exactly, just very devoted, interested, intelligent, warm.' In writing her books, it could be that Leach is taking her mother's child-focused side in her parents' dispute.

The fires of indignation still burn brightly. Asked to consider Gina Ford's advice to mothers of tiny babies to wake them every two to three hours for a feed during the day to maximise their own chances of a good night's sleep, she responds 'If they kept waking somebody in an Iraqi jail we'd call it torture. Good infant care is being responsive. If you don't give babies the chance to realise they're hungry, ask for food and discover the satisfaction of feeding and getting full, you're not doing that.'

Leach's disfavour from her father, because of her position in the family and her gender, influenced her subsequent theories of child rearing and the passion with which she holds them. The same was true when I spoke with Gina Ford, author of the influential *Contented Little Baby Book*, in the same series of newspaper interviews.

Whether you see Ford as The Great Satan or as The Saviour of Modern Mothers, hardly any parents are neutral about her. Contrary to what some of her critics claim, Gina emphasises her approach is absolutely not about starving babies or leaving them to cry and adds all her routines are about putting baby's needs first. Her writings are passionately prescriptive attempts to introduce routine into the lives of both parents and children. I explored the origin of her ideas with her over the phone for several hours, spread over two days.

She was the only child of a single mother, born 54 years ago on a farm in south-east Scotland. She is an example of the impact that being an only child can have, a situation which can result in a form of victimisation. While parents of an oldest child pour their parents' strongest beliefs, virtues and pathologies into them, the arrival of siblings means that this is subsequently watered down. Being the only child increases the intensity of parental influence. This is an extreme impact of birth order.

Ford's father left the family soon after her birth; there was very little money. So impoverished were they that even working-class people seemed 'posh'. Fortunately, the farm was a mini-community, so she was not solely dependent on her mother for nurture, there were other relatives nearby. Ford recalls plenty of love in this set up and does not believe there were tremendous pressures. Nonetheless, all was not well for her mother. Hospitalised with depression from two or three months after the birth, there was a prolonged period in her first year in which her mother was absent. Ford recalls with sadness that the depression endured for the rest of her life and that she took tranquillisers throughout.

Perhaps astonishingly from the author of books which implore parents to train their children to sleep alone, Ford slept in her mother's bed until the age of 11. It was then that her mother remarried and Ford recalls feeling upset at having to sleep alone.

She directly relates the fact that she is an insomniac – always a nifty trait for a maternity nurse – to having slept in her mother's bed: she never learnt to get a proper night's sleep on her own.

You don't have to be Sigmund Freud to leap from this experience to her becoming the author who wants to disentangle us from our children to help them sleep regularly and to establish clear 'boundaries'. In getting us to do so, she may be trying to ensure that our children get the sleep she never did and that they do not become the sleep-disordered adult that she is.

There is no doubting the passionate identification Ford has with 'her' infants. She likes babies, is intrigued by them. She finds it hard to comprehend how anyone can find them dull. But the greater identification is with their mothers, perhaps traceable back to her mother's troubles.

Many studies show that children of depressed mothers[35] often become super-empathetic to the needs of others. Worried by their mother's long faces and dark moods, they are constantly seeking to understand what is wrong and trying to make the mother better. If Ford felt like this about her mother when small, it could also explain her tremendous concern for the mental health of mothers and desire to write books that protect them – she might have become a social worker or therapist; it so happens the books were her way of expressing the empathy she felt.

That she may be more preoccupied by the plight of the parents than the baby is suggested by her retort to accusations that her books encourage mothers to leave their infants to cry themselves to sleep. She maintains that a few evenings of brief periods of crying do no permanent damage. She believes the high divorce rate is evidence of what happens if parents are driven to distraction by crying babies and exhaustion, and if they have no time together.

When I put it to her that her books might be an unconscious attempt to provide her mother with the tools that might have prevented her depression (and her father's departure soon after her birth) she agreed. However, she also believes her concern for mothers might reflect a need for love and support for her 'reclusive', Howard Hughes-like self. She wished that she could have a Gina Ford to look after her, providing the support that she gives to mothers when working as a maternity nurse. But most of all, she is giving mothers the experience her mother did not have. She mothers the mothers and wishes someone could have mothered hers when she was small.

Her intense identification with the agonies that her 'over-permissive' mother suffered may be what fuels her almost strident tone in trying to persuade modern mothers to take the advice that she believes will protect them from breakdown. She feels it is good for us to be in control of our lives and that her methods enable mothers to take control of theirs.

This goes to the heart of her difference from more child-centred baby-care experts, like Leach. They object that she is placing the mother's need for control and order too far ahead of the needs of the infant, at the expense of its mental health. Ford disputes the latter, while admitting that the prescriptive nature of her routines is as a deliberate antidote to the chaos of motherhood. Mothers, she feels, just want to be told what to do.

Above all, it is interesting to note that, had Ford not been an only child and had she been the secondborn, it is extremely unlikely she would have written the books that she did. Because of her position in her family, she suffered considerably.

Whatever the rights and wrongs of the child- versus parent-centred debate, the stories of Leach and Ford sharply illustrate the cause of sibling differences. Both women were maltreated, to some degree, the precise details of which led to very specifically different views about motherhood. It is differences in maltreatment that set the scene for what happens when the infant becomes a child old enough to participate in the family drama. Differential maltreatment is a key cause of sibling differences, both by affecting the child's role, but most potently of all, by directly causing emotional distress.

What is especially interesting about the stories of the successful people described in this chapter is that their ambition is clearly to be found in their family histories. The idea that some children are born talented is a fiction. Both ambition and its successful fulfilment are the result of nurture, as we shall see in Chapter 7.

One of the most startling implications of what you have read in this book so far is that it also explains why traits run in families. In treating children in very particular ways, causing different learning, modelling and identification, and by maltreating or loving them in specific ways, parents pass on patterns that have, in some cases, been in the family for generations. This leads to a remarkable conclusion, one that flatly contradicts modern accounts of human psychological evolution. It is not genes that pass traits between generations. It is patterns of nurture.

SO WHAT? 3 TAKEAWAYS

ONE: Tease out your role in the family drama

Try writing down the roles you feel you occupy – clever or stupid at maths, best or worst at sport, favoured or disfavoured and so on. An interesting additional plan is to quiz your siblings and if possible, parents, about their view of your role. You do not need to make a big deal of it. Just say 'I have been pondering what kind of child I was and how I was regarded in the family. What do you think was my role – the clever one, the stupid one, the late/early, lazy/conscientious one?'

It is also valuable to identify the roles played by your siblings. Question your siblings as to what roles they think they occupied.

Once you have identified the roles you believe you and they played, you can have a bit of fun with them. The next time your family are all gathered together, make a big effort to behave in the opposite way to the roles you believe you have. If it's Christmas time, for example, and you are all staying at your parents' house, if you were the one who was characterised as always talkative and argumentative, try being quiet and uncontentious. If you are supposed to be lazy when it comes to doing the washing up, be the first to do it.

What can be fascinating about this is the extent to which families will continue to attribute your role to you, regardless of whether you have changed. Indeed, returning to our family, we often do get put back into that box. Dominant and aggressive chief executives can become silent and compliant in the face of their parents and siblings. If you have been deliberately enacting the opposite of your expected family role, do not be surprised if there are attempts to reimpose it.

As an exercise, it may be therapeutic to force yourself to act against type. As a shy or extrovert person, for example, you can have a new experience of feeling what it is like to be otherwise. That could be the germ of a new you in that respect, the beginning of exploring what it is like to be someone other than the person your family tried to make you.

TWO: How did your birth order, gender and so on, affect the script of your role?

Having identified your role, the next step is to analyse how it came about.

Perhaps you have always been the relatively unambitious, laid-back one. Perhaps you were the youngest, with some fearsomely pushy older siblings. If you dared to present a challenge to the clever, sporty or attractive siblings in their area of success, they quickly knocked you down. Your way of coping was to develop a relaxed, uncompetitive persona.

It can be as simple as that, but usually there are also projections of roles on to you by parents, often based on their own histories. Perhaps one of your parents also occupied that role in their family and has settled on you as like that. As the youngest, it was hard to get attention so you cosied up to them by playing that role.

Equally, as the youngest, maybe you were neglected on a practical level: your parents were so busy driving your older siblings to their extra-maths tuition, ballet lessons and football coaching that you had to just tag along for the first five years, always in the slipstream, ignored emotionally.

Also, you could have been neglected because your parents had run out of parts of themselves to attribute to you. Perhaps they both longed for an academic achiever and the eldest has nabbed that niche. In a large family, where you are number four or five, there are no unfulfilled ambitions left for them to pin on you.

Analysing how birth order, gender, sibling rivalry, favouritism and stigmatisation panned out in your particular case can be very rewarding. Whereas self-help can be hard for the problems created by your early life described in the last chapter because they are so difficult to remember, this is stuff you can recall and which you can get information about from relatives. By piecing together your story, you can be freed from enduring stereotypes.

It's worth remembering that a good deal of what is going on may be the result of events several generations back, as we shall see in the next chapter. It can be an amazing insight if you understand that your negative trait (laziness, ill-temper, workaholia) is a role that has been passed down with the same implacability as succession to a royal throne.

THREE: Positives of parents' unfulfilled ambitions

Although most of this book has focused on adverse consequences of parental projections on their children, it needs saying that it is hugely important for us that parents do confer identity.

I have never forgotten the first client I was assigned during my training as a child clinical psychologist. She was a 12-year-old girl who had been raised in an institution since early childhood.

Her face was blank, emotionless. At no point during our sessions did she express any enthusiasm for anything at all. Doubtless this was partly due to my callowness, perhaps she just thought I was the latest in a long line of unhelpful, meddling professionals whom she had no intention of engaging with. But it was also clear from what she told me that she had suffered a lifetime of neglect in which no adults had ever consistently expressed pleasure at her existence or joy at her achievements, big and small.

This had occurred since birth. Donald Winnicott's dictum that 'there is no such thing as a baby' is true. He meant that unless someone provides positive and responsive mirroring to babies, they do not develop a strong sense of self. Only through that sensitivity can babies feel 'this is my mouth receiving this milk, this is my stomach going from empty to full'. My client had not had such experiences.

My first client also illustrates John Bowlby's assertion that love is as important to the health of a baby as vitamins. Without love, babies can die. In the existential sense, my client had died.

As we move out of infancy into early and middle childhood, we need our parents to express pleasure at our choices and consequent actions but more than this, we need them to have aspirations for us. However much we reject or adapt or adopt them, without parental hopes for who we should be, we flounder.

Chapter 6

Why Traits Run
in Families

I vividly recall meeting a research neuro-psychiatrist at a friend's house over dinner - a doctor who has trained in the workings of the brain with a view to providing physical treatments for 'mental illnesses' just like any other diseases. He had a senior position at Britain's leading hospital for treatment of brain disorders. 'Because schizophrenia runs in families it must be a genetic trait,' he intoned with absolute medical authority. Alas, I am afraid there are still too many psychiatrists who would have a similar view today.

He was puzzled when I retorted that the transmission could be through the way parents care for children, repeated down the generations, rather than genes. Indeed, it took several minutes before he actually grasped what I meant. When the penny finally dropped, he admitted the idea had not occurred to him and that he had never had it explained to him as a possibility by his teachers. During their training, doctors are inducted into the biogenetic explanation of mental illness and studies show that this leads to a remarkable ignorance of the extensive evidence of environmental causes.[1] This is not surprising when you grasp the stranglehold the medical profession and drug companies have on research. In the case of schizophrenia, 45 times more studies are devoted to biological causes or drug therapy than to environmental causes or treatments,[2] even though it is now beyond doubt that maltreatment is the main cause. What is more, the drug companies overlap closely with the medical profession and use their financial clout to promote their biochemical message. The public are systematically misled,[3] with 40 per cent of mental health websites having drug company funding. These sites present mental illness as an illness like any other, but one that cannot be cured, only managed (with drugs and by temporarily changing the way you think), because it is a lifelong destiny.

What was undisputed between the neuro-psychiatrist and I was that most traits, like shyness, high intelligence and mental illnesses, do tend to run in families. Whilst they do not do so nearly as much as is often thought, as explained at the start of Chapter 4, it's true that family members are more like each other than non-family. A first-degree relative of someone who is depressed is three times more likely to suffer than a person with none.[4] For anxiety, depending on the kind, it is four to six times more likely.[5] Intelligence broadly runs in families,[6] personality traits less so.[7] But the fact that a trait is familial tells us nothing about cause: it could be passed down through nurture every bit as much as nature.

Schizophrenia may run in families,[8] but so does one of its main causes, sexual abuse.[9] Having a schizophrenic mother makes you about nine times more likely to suffer than someone with no affected relative[10] (interestingly, though, having a schizophrenic father rather than mother is half as likely to mean you develop it[11] – mothers spend that much more time engaged in nurture). A review of 59 studies[12] found that 47 per cent of women diagnosed as psychotic suffered sexual abuse. This review shows that symptoms are more likely if there has been incest, rather than abuse by someone outside the nuclear family. Repeated penetrative incestuous rape is most harmful. If there is now no doubt at all that sexual abuse is a significant cause of schizophrenia, there is also no doubt that such abusive behaviour runs in families: the brother of a man convicted of a sexual crime is five times more likely to also commit that crime than the brother of someone with no convictions.[13]

But it's not only sexual maltreatment that causes schizophrenia. Reviews of the evidence show that all kinds are two to three times commoner in the childhoods of schizophrenics.[14] Interestingly, it is emotional, not sexual abuse that is the strongest predictor: over-controlling parents, intrusiveness, hostility, victimisation.

The fact that the impact of maltreatment is dose-dependent has been shown to strongly suggest that it is causal[15] – the more and worse the maltreatment, the greater the risk. People who have endured three different kinds of abuse are 18 times more likely to be diagnosed as schizophrenic than people who have suffered none.[16] This rises to as much as 193 times more likely if they have endured five or more kinds. The more severe the particular maltreatment, the greater the risk: severely abused children are 48 times as likely to be psychotic adults compared with twice as likely if the abuse is mild.[17]

There is similar evidence for the causal role of childhood maltreatment in other severe mental illnesses, like bipolar disorder (extreme mood swings)[18] and personality disorder (febrile emotions, me-me-me narcissism).[19] It is also much more common in the depressed and anxious,[20] compared with people who do not have these problems.

Nor do genes explain why intelligence runs in families. Despite huge publicity[21] being given to the results of twin studies which purport to show that genes are critical, no genes have been found to have a significant effect.[22] It is simply not true that genes explain exam results at age 16, as was claimed in extensive media coverage in Britain in 2013. The evidence for that claim was based on increasingly discredited studies of twins (see Appendix 2), not of genes.

For over a century, eugenicists[23] have maintained that people with low incomes are less intelligent because inherited genes caused their ancestors to slip to the bottom of society. Since we now know that there are no genes for ability,[24] the consistent finding that being raised in a low-income home lowers IQ scores is causal, not correlational: low-income homes have fewer books,[25] are less stimulating of the cognitive skills required to do well in IQ tests and exams; when children from low-income homes are given extra help to boost their skills, it works.[26] It's not genes that cause the low IQs which lead to low incomes, it's nurture.

Little attention is paid to the evidence that when children are adopted young,[27] often into middle-class homes from low-income ones, on average their IQ score is fully eighteen points higher than that of their biological parents. It is hard to correct early emotional damage but is very possible to stimulate intellectual development despite it. Indeed, one study showed that children of heroin-addicted mothers[28] who are adopted at or near birth, usually into more settled, middle-class homes, have significantly greater mental abilities, typical of their class of adoption, compared with children who stay with their heroin-addicted mothers. Part of the reason why the ones who stay with their heroin-addicted mothers have lower abilities compared with heroin-free ones is that they cannot concentrate. Half of them are likely to have attention deficit hyperactivity disorder (ADHD) caused by what might be called maternal deficits in attention and chemicals passed to them in the womb. When on heroin, it's hard for a mother to attend to her infant and toddler's needs.

As for personality, again, it does run in families to some degree but if the findings of the Human Genome Project are to be believed, the reason is not genes. Enormous publicity has been given to the twins reared apart study in Minnesota, which falsely claimed large heritability of personality (see Appendix 3). But almost none has been given to a much more convincing study done in Colorado.[29]

A sample of 469 adoptees was identified who had, on average, been adopted 29 days after birth: unlike with so many of the subjects in the Minnesota study, in this one the biological parents had very little opportunity to have any effect on them. The biological parents' personalities were carefully measured around the time of the birth of the Colorado children. When the children's personalities were measured at ages 9 to16, there was no significant correlation between the biological parents and their offspring. Personality was not heritable.

If mental illness, intelligence and personality do run in families and if the reason is not genes, the mechanisms of transmission described in Chapters 1, 4 and 5 become critical. Whilst there are very likely to be physical mechanisms too which have so far not been discovered, as with my son's dribbling, the way traits are passed down the generations is clearly to a large degree through learning (teaching, modelling and identification), and maltreatment and love.

How traits run in families

Near the start of the twentieth century, a mother perceives her newborn daughter as ugly. To conceal this ugliness from the gaze of visitors – and of herself – she often places a veil over the infant's face. The mother comes from a modest home. Married to an upper-middle-class man, she fears social humiliation. She tells her 'ugly' daughter in later life that she will never find a husband, complaining to her diary 'what did I do wrong to have such a socially unsuccessful and unprepossessing daughter?' Decades later, in old age, that daughter writes of herself, 'the sad truth is that I confess I lived and have lived in a world of the imagination, I cannot bear much reality at all'. A muslin veil had been drawn over it.

The supposed ugliness of the infant (she is just premature and underweight) is a projection of the mother's own sense of inadequacy and social unattractiveness. It's a case of an *I'm Okay, You're Not* attribution of unwanted feelings from a parent to a baby, transposing her own social ugliness on to her baby's physical appearance.

The baby herself becomes a mother in the 1940s. She writes that one of her daughters 'was impossible. She yelled and shouted until she got what she wanted. She did that noisily and uncontrollably and went on doing it continuously from birth until teenage.' She writes of this girl as if tormented and tyrannised by her. She believes the problem is 'in' the girl.

In the 1970s, the 'impossible' daughter gives birth to one of her own. She complains that her daughter is insatiable, constantly screaming as a baby and 'very difficult' all the way through childhood and teenage. Like

145

her maternal ancestors, she experiences her daughter's difficultness as being 'in' the girl, a problem that is not created by the way she has related to her.

In 2013, the girl has become a mother and sends me an email about her daughter who is aged seven. This child is volatile in the extreme, prone to anger attacks on a daily basis. She becomes incensed by attempts to control the clothing she wears, the food she eats, or when and whether she goes to school. The anger attacks are reminiscent of those of a toddler, puce-faced rages, scratching and slapping of her mother. The girl tyrannises the mother, telling her where to stand, attacking her from the back seat of the car, having refused to walk to school.

Four successive mothers have been persecuted by their daughters, tyrannically so in three cases. This pattern runs down the maternal line of the family. What is the mechanism by which it has been transmitted?

Until the findings of the Human Genome Project, it would have been plausible to suppose that each daughter had been born with a genetic code that predisposed them to be difficult. The DNA sequence would have caused certain difficultness-causing chemicals to be released and, regardless of how the girls were cared for, they would have been difficult. Just as people born with certain DNA sequences suffer from rare and proven genetic illnesses, like Huntingdon's chorea or Down's syndrome, so with the difficultness. That was what the vast majority of geneticists predicted but the model has been wholly discredited and there are hardly any who would now advocate it. Virtually no scientists still believe that there are specific 'genes for' intelligence, personality or, in this case, behavioural problems in children.

However, there are still some who believe in the 'bit of both' model, the combination of nature with nurture. The daughters could have inherited genes that made them vulnerable to difficult behaviour, but only when combined with adverse parenting. Equally, such genetically vulnerable children would particularly benefit from especially sensitive and nurturing care. In this model, neither the genes nor the adverse parenting on their own cause difficult behaviour, it requires the presence of both.

There is a gene associated with the hormone serotonin (which plays a role in both aggression and depression). Some reviews of the evidence suggest that certain variants[30] in it seem to increase the damage done by parental maltreatment or increase benign outcomes if care is good.[31] However, this has been contradicted by many other reviews of the evidence[32] reporting many studies which did not repeat the finding. Even where an effect of the gene is found, it is not nearly as big as that of maltreatment on its own. The same is true of other 'candidate genes'[33] supposed to create a vulnerability to aggression when combined with maltreatment: none have consistently been shown to have this effect when studies are replicated.

Whereas there are now big doubts about any role for genetic variants in causing difficult behaviour, there are no doubts that parenting is crucial. There have been numerous studies[34] following children from young ages into adulthood showing that childhood nurture is the major cause of behaviour problems, like disobedience and aggression. In the first instance, these prove that unresponsive early care makes children more insecure and less able to regulate their emotions, making them overreactive. They are more fearful and liable to respond with anger as a way of coping with threats. Lack of parental warmth at all ages makes the child more liable to be aggressive, so does parental hostility and aggression. The studies prove that difficult children are likely to have had parents who try to control them through 'coercive' parenting. Instead of staying calm and using gentle persuasion, the parents try to force their children to obey them.

Their repeated 'nattering',[35] a drip-drip-drip of 'don't do that', 'I said Don't Do That', 'I SAID DON'T DO THAT', crescendos into screaming and shouting. It is liable to climax in physical violence, which has been proven to directly cause aggression in childhood and subsequently, violence in adulthood, regardless of genes.[36] The parenting is also more likely to be accompanied by inconsistency in discipline, so what was punished last time may now be rewarded.

In a nutshell, there is incontrovertible evidence that children who are aggressive and disruptive have been inadvertently trained to be so by their parents. Its kernel is the tendency for the parent to completely lose control, becoming as red-faced and emotionally incontinent as the toddler or child they are trying to discipline. While most, if not all of us, have sometimes done that (and in my case, bought the T-shirt), for some parents it becomes a regular event, increasingly repeated. The nattering starts to pollute almost every exchange with a child, who becomes so accustomed to it that it takes hardly anything to set the child or parent off. They are primed to expect it, so just a word or a look from either is enough to activate the cascade of warring behaviour. The problem is that the parent is increasingly incapable of remaining adult: calm and rational, capable of a measure of detachment.

The reason such parents are like this is, surprise, surprise, that they themselves had parents who were incapable of 'authoritative', adult parenting.[37] Faced with the normal exuberance and self-expression of a toddler or small child, because they were subject to temper tantrums and anger attacks from their own parents (for whom it was the same and so on back, for generations), this is how they react. This is partly simple modelling, partly identification and partly a trauma resulting from the maltreatment of being screamed at by parents who have repeatedly lost control.

That 'anger attacks' cascade down the generations is illustrated by the mothers described above, all of whom subsequently wrote about their experiences. All perceived the difficultness of their daughter as being a defect 'in' the girl, with no awareness of how this difficulty has come about. In the cases of the last three mothers, they felt tyrannised by their daughter. Having been maltreated as children, they felt that their daughter was maltreating them. Indeed, their daughters were all truly very difficult. But the mothers were unable to see that they provoked them to be so, by nattering, anger attacks and then physical abuse. Having created a daughter who was just like how they were when small, they then proceeded to maltreat that girl, just as they were.

For example, in the case of the last mother, who became my client and whom I shall call Amy, when I first asked her what sort of childhood she had had, she replied 'awful', and burst into tears. Her mother had been unable to tune into her as a baby, as was the case across the generations. Amy was a difficult baby who cried a lot and seemed to her mother insatiable. That created an insecure template for what was to follow.

Her mother was an 'angry', 'judgemental' woman who hit Amy from a young age. During violin practice, the mother struck Amy with the bow just for disagreeing with her opinion. Out shopping, her mother hit her when they disagreed about purchasing a dress versus some trousers, shaming Amy in front of the onlookers.

Even worse than the violence was the fact that being in her mother's presence was like 'walking on eggshells'. She was 'explosive'. On one occasion, her mother had a temper tantrum, rolling around on the floor like a toddler because Amy had not packed a suitcase. Tidiness, food choices, there were a host of issues over which her micromanaging mother would pick fights. Amy's choice of music was a particular bugbear, as her mother insisted that only the classical kind was acceptable, Amy's preference for Abba was ridiculed and prohibited.

On a Saturday morning, her mother would walk into the middle of the bedroom, hurl clothes and objects into a pile and demand it be cleared up. Having created the mess, she would then lambast her children for untidiness. Her own internal mess was frequently converted into a problem in Amy.

Her mother's behaviour was a form of what is known as intimate terrorism.[38] Found in spousal abusers as well as parents of this kind, it consists of using any or every domestic or social arrangement as the means for instilling fear in the victim through rages and the final threat of physical violence. This intimate terrorism passed down the generations, having originated in the first mother, or perhaps her antecedents.

Amy's mother would be cruel, mocking her in front of others. Having upset her, she would sneer 'Look, Amy's turning on the tap', implying that Amy was only crying to seek pity and to manipulate, belittling her genuine distress as acting.

A perfectionist, her mother had excelled as an athlete in her youth. She held Amy to her impossible standards. This was one of many ways in which Amy was not granted any autonomy: her mother did not respect her separate, independent existence as someone with a right to a different point of view.

Amy could think of only one occasion in her whole life when her mother took responsibility for her domineering or excessively aggressive behaviour, and then only implicitly, by offering a gift, with no words of regret. She was someone who never admitted that she was wrong, seeing the world in black and white, no shades of grey.

Amy was portrayed as a defective child, one who had something wrong with her. She would sit on the stairs listening to her mother debating what was the matter, terrified that she would be declared mentally ill and carted off to a mental hospital, her father patiently listening (he was also terrorised, coerced into collusion with his wife's totalitarian regime). When older, it particularly annoyed Amy that, on reading Lionel Shriver's book *We Need To Talk About Kevin*, her mother implied that Amy was also a crazy, menacing child like the boy portrayed in the book. This entailed a massive confusion of the mother with Amy. In reality, she was the scary person, not Amy.

Even today when they are both supposedly adult, if Amy were to say this to her, it would evince a furious, childish response. This places Amy in an impossible position: on the one hand, she will be falsifying herself if she agrees with her, accepting her mother's view that she was a disturbed, troubled person, although it is all too apparent the troubled one was Amy's mother; on the other hand, if she disagrees with her view, she risks a torrent of hostile words. Impossible positions were the currency of Amy's childhood.

The diaries of all the mothers reveal similar stories, a catalogue of abusive *I'm Okay, You're Not* passing down the generations, often with the exact same details of the maltreatment. However, through our work together, my client was able to dam the cascade of emotional abuse. The great struggle was to *Believe the Unbelievable*: that her mother really had maltreated her in those ways, that it was truly not her fault, that she did not have some inbuilt defect which had justified them. Gradually Amy became able to have sustained periods of not believing her mother's account of her. From time to time she would become worried that I thought of her as mad or bad, that I might call in the men in white coats. I recommended that she watch *The Sopranos* television series, in which it takes a great deal for the son, Tony, to accept that his mother was willing to do almost anything to serve her own purposes, at his expense.

Amy was unusual in that she had started our work knowing that she had had an unhappy childhood. *Offspring Stockholm Syndrome* usually makes us loyal to maltreating parents. But it was still hard for her to believe the truth of her maltreatment. Over time, she came to feel a sense of security, what she called 'a warm glow', through having a different experience with me from the one she had had with her mother.

Importantly, as a result of our work, she largely ceased to have anger attacks towards her daughter. She did Love Bombing (see TAKEAWAY 3 in Chapter 4) with her and it ended the daily occurrence of her daughter's tantrums.

Over the next year, the number and intensity of her daughter's anger attacks decreased. While there were periods when they recurred and it seemed as if nothing had changed, these always receded. Her daughter became fundamentally different in key respects, for example, being able for the first time to enjoy the company of peers and to flourish at school. There is a real chance that when this girl herself becomes a mother and, if she has a daughter, that she will pass a much more positive set of traits down to the next generation through more benign nurturing. The evidence that both positive and negative parenting patterns pass down the generations is overwhelming. Contrary to the beliefs of the neuro-psychiatrist with which this chapter began, it's not genes but patterns of nurture which transmit traits intergenerationally.

The intergenerational transmission of traits through parenting

There are at least ten studies[39] proving that difficult behaviour in children, like anger attacks, is passed down the generations through nurture. As in Amy's family, the transmission mechanism is harsh and cruel parenting, not genes. These studies examine the care a sample of children receive and then explore whether it results in parenting that induces difficult behaviour in the next generation. For example, one study showed that children whose mothers had been angry and aggressive to them[40] became like that as parents. If this pattern of parenting was not present, it was liable not to be present in the next generation.

Intergenerational transmission through parenting has been shown for other traits in studies proving it could have nothing whatever to do with genes. For example, whether or not a person suffered persecution at the hands of the Nazis during the Second World War could not be due to genes. Trauma is still evident in the descendants of Holocaust survivors two generations later, the method of transmission being the way the trauma has been played out in patterns of parenting. Half a century after the holocaust, offspring of survivors and their children were still being made emotionally insecure by their ancestors' trauma.[41] A high proportion of holocaust survivors suffered post traumatic stress disorder (PTSD) and that inevitably affects parenting, with more emotional abuse and neglect.[42] This, in turn, affects how the child parents when they grow up.

The same is true of combat veterans and their children.[43] Specifically, PTSD and related problems in the parents result in high levels of distress in the children. Absence of parental PTSD means distress is significantly less likely in offspring.

The child of one female survivor of the holocaust contacted me to explain how she had been affected. Her mother had a large collection of books and videos about the holocaust which she exposed her five children to from inappropriately young ages. The mother suffered from PTSD, making her prone to terrifying rages. She sleepwalked and would wake her children in the night, talking to them as if she was still in the concentration camp, sometimes imagining she was one of the guards, menacing them. While one of the children was favoured by her father and emerged calm and emotionally healthy, her siblings all suffered nervous breakdowns in later life.

Distress can also be passed down generations if parents are emotionally insecure (fear of rejection or abandonment in relationships, confusion and disconnection from feelings). For example, some parents have what is known as an 'unresolved' pattern of attachment: asked about their childhoods, they have only fragments of memories, traumas and losses which they cannot properly feel or think about but yet, which they know are there. Eighty per cent of children with parents like this have what is called a 'disorganised' pattern of attachment, in which they have confusing ways of coping with relationships.[44] Sometimes they feel rejected, sometimes abandoned, often they seem lost and their minds appear to be elsewhere. Disorganised attachment in childhood often results in an unresolved adult pattern which, in turn, leads to 80 per cent of their offspring having disorganised attachment.[45]

That parents repeat or react to how they were cared for as children has been also proven by studies of animals. For example, the kind of early care a monkey receives precisely predicts the kind of adult it will become, including its brain chemistry.[46]

Compared with mother-reared ones, Rhesus monkeys separated from their mothers at birth and reared only with their peers until the age of six months, are more easily scared of strangers and unfamiliar experiences. They slide to the bottom of monkey status hierarchies, whereas the more secure, socially assured, mother-reared monkeys are at the top.

Less extreme variations in early care also have big effects. If a group of monkey infants are only briefly and occasionally separated from their mothers during the first fourteen weeks of life, they are fully as insecure as young monkeys reared solely away from their mothers. Tested at four years old they still have depleted brain chemicals.

Above all, patterns of mothering are passed down from mother to daughter. When peer-reared female monkeys become mothers themselves, they are significantly more neglectful or abusive of their offspring than those that were mother-reared, repeating the cycle of maltreatment.

The specific amount of care received in early life predicts how the monkey will subsequently mother. Amount of contact with mother precisely predicts the amount that she bestows on her own daughter. The same is found in rats: the more a mother is licked as a pup, the more she does the same with her offspring.

The similarity in mothering across generations could be simply a genetic inheritance but this has been disproved. The amount of contact with the particular monkey daughter has been compared with *the mother's average care for all her daughters*. A daughter's subsequent mothering reflects her particular experience rather than the average for all her sisters. The unique care received determines subsequent patterns of mothering, rather than a genetic tendency inherited from the mother.

Another theory is that a genetically difficult baby could make the mother uncaring. This was contradicted by a study of what are called highly reactive infant monkeys – ones that are very difficult to care for because they over-react to the slightest sound or movement, probably because of difficulties during the pregnancy or birth.

They were fostered out to either average mothers or exceptionally nurturant ones. The exceptionally nurtured young monkeys who had been born over-reactive actually grew up even more socially well adjusted than normal infants fostered by average mothers. In other words, good nurture was so influential that it could turn a difficult infant into a superior adult. Furthermore, when the generation of offspring in the study grew up and themselves had infants, their parenting style, whether exceptionally nurturant or average, precisely mirrored the kind of care they had received as infants. This was regardless of whether their original infant personality had been highly reactive or not. Much, although not all, of what goes for monkeys seems to go for humans.

It's a simple but important point: babies and toddlers need consistent loving care if they are to grow up secure and mentally healthy, and to become nurturing parents themselves. This was explained in more detail in Chapter 4, but to take just one of hundreds of examples, a study of over 1,700 maltreated children showed the crucial role of nurture.[47] Measured as infants, 85 per cent of the sample were neurologically impaired and at high risk of behaviour problems and language deficits – the sample were specifically chosen because they were likely to be difficult to nurture. Followed up at 18 months and three years, it turned out that the more their maternal or other nurture improved, the greater the likelihood of the babies having overcome their initial impairment.

For at least two decades, the myth has been doing the rounds that babies' temperaments determine the care they receive, not vice versa. This study was able to show quite clearly that it was how the environment reacted to the babies that was crucial in deciding outcomes. A calm mother can nearly always calm a tempestuous baby. This is hardly surprising, considering how powerless babies are, yet the myth of the genetically unchangeable baby is still propagated widely today.

The classic debunking of that myth was done by a Dutch researcher, Dymphna Van den Boom.[48] She embarked on her research because, while working as a teacher of troubled children, she had become convinced that innate difficultness of babies was a major cause of later problems.

To test the idea, she selected 100 infants whose postnatal personalities should have placed them at very high risk of being emotionally insecure. They had been measured as highly irritable immediately after birth, easily upset and annoyed, harder to cope with than smiley, placid babies. If the irritability was a genetic trait it should translate into insecurity a year later, regardless of the kind of care received.

When the babies were aged six to nine months, 50 of the mothers received counselling sessions to increase their responsiveness and sensitivity to their difficult charges. Prior to the help, these mothers tended to have become discouraged by their baby's lack of good cheer, ignoring them. Customising her help to the particular problem, Van den Boom taught techniques for soothing the baby, encouraged play and helped the mother to connect.

Meanwhile, the other 50 mothers and their irritable babies had received no extra help. When the level of emotional security of the two groups was tested at one year old, the contrast in the outcomes was remarkable. In the group who had had no help, 72 per cent of the children were insecure whereas in the assisted group, only 32 per cent were. The only difference was the counselling sessions, so the implication was that even the most difficult babies can be turned around by their mothers.

More recent studies have demonstrated the same basic point. Overall, children born with low birth weights[49] are at greater risk of inattention and hyperactivity at school age. Identical twins rarely weigh the same when born. For every pound less that an identical twin has when born,[50] the likelihood of ADHD in later life increases significantly – a strong proof the low birth weight, not genes, is an important cause of ADHD. But if the mother is warm and supportive in early life the likelihood of ADHD is much less. Another study showed that children whose mothers drank a lot of alcohol[51] during pregnancy are generally at greater risk of a low IQ, but not if the mother is emotionally sensitive and mentally stimulating.

Above all, the evidence shows that there is a strong tendency for mothers to care for their infants in similar ways to how they were nurtured.[52] For example, in one study of 180 mothers,[53] 70 per cent of those that had been maltreated as children either maltreated their own children or provided unresponsive care. As a consequence, at age 19, 90 per cent of the maltreated children qualified for diagnosis with at least one psychiatric illness. By contrast, only one of the children who had had good care from their mothers qualified for a diagnosis. Thirty per cent of the mothers who had been maltreated did not go on to maltreat. What allows some to break the pattern?

Humans have complex language which enables us to use concepts, creating self-consciousness. Because of this faculty, we can deliberately control ourselves and our environment to a far greater degree than monkeys. As parents, we can make the choice to care differently from the way we were. While overall, humans tend to follow the pattern which was imposed on them, a proportion decide to do the opposite or in some cases create a different pattern from the one they experienced, which is neither a repetition nor a reaction against.

It is difficult for all of us to break parenting patterns. A famous example is Mia Farrow, the actress and ex-wife of Woody Allen. Born the fifth out of eight children, aged 19, she expressed regret about her family's size, saying that 'A child needs more love and affection than you can get in a large family.' Aged 25, she gave birth to her own first children (twins), and soon afterwards a son followed. Now she could give them that life in a moderately sized family that she had never had herself. Yet within a year she had adopted two Vietnamese infants. Over the next 12 years she produced one other child and adopted a further six. In all, 12 children called her Mother. At this point she said 'The benefits of large families are enormous. I want to re-create my childhood environment.' Either she had changed her mind or somewhere along the line she had lost track of what it felt like to be lost in a large family and, instead, imposed that experience on a dozen children.

Of course, intergenerational transmission of traits is not only of maltreatment and negative outcomes. Love, wise instruction and sympathetic support are passed down the generations every bit as much. There is strong evidence that parents who had responsive care when they were children become responsive parents themselves. Several studies have observed the care children received when small and then followed them up when they became parents,[54] showing that a parent hands on responsiveness to their child, just as much as misery. A particularly telling study[55] observed 200 children from age three into adulthood and then filmed them interacting with their own children when small. Warm, sensitive and stimulating parenting, whether received in early or middle childhood, or during their teenage years, strongly predicted the same type of parenting when they became parents. Similar studies have demonstrated that positive parenting from fathers results in the same when the sons become fathers.

Since no one has a perfect childhood, there are always negative ghosts as well as positive angels from the nursery, haunting us when we become parents. As we parent, the two wrestle with each other, depending on their relative strength. The evidence clearly shows[56] that the angels win out more where the parent is unconsciously drawing on a large fund of positive experience. However, some parents who have suffered considerable maltreatment can be particularly loving as compensation for the suffering they endured. In giving the baby or toddler the love they never had, they identify with it and heal some of their own wounds.

Evidence from samples of mothers[57] who were at high-risk of finding it hard to be sensitive and warm show that the 30 per cent who managed not to maltreat their own young children were disproportionately likely, relative to women who did maltreat, to have had an emotionally supportive and non-abusive adult available during early childhood. They were also more likely to have undergone extensive therapy during their lives. A loving relationship with a partner also helped. These factors – a supportive alternative carer when small, therapy or a loving partner[58] – have also been shown to reduce the likelihood of parental maltreatment in samples of parents who had loving childhoods themselves. Loving partners are particularly shown to help.[59] A caring partner enhances the parent's ability to keep their emotions under control when children are being difficult, by offering a positive alternative model. They also enable the parent to tune into the child's perspective, creating patience and understanding instead of incomprehension, sadness and rage.

It should be clear from this chapter that there are compelling reasons to suppose that parenting is the main reason that there is transmission of traits down the generations. The next explores how parental projections – not genes – are the foundation of achievement. It also shows that the way in which parents convey them determines whether the high achiever is miserable or emotionally healthy.

SO WHAT? 3 TAKEAWAYS

ONE: Identify intergenerational patterns in your family

When I worked in television I suggested an idea for a series. Instead of the BBC programme *Who Do You Think You Are?*, in which genealogists trace the long distant forebears of celebrities, I suggested 'WHY do you think you are?' The trivia of whether your great-great-grandfather suffered agonies as a soldier in the Boer War or nearly perished in the Irish Potato Famine – cue celeb tears – is as nothing beside the psychological traits that pass down.

One way to access your family's patterns is to write accounts of what it was like to be your mother and your father, aged 10. How were they cared for? What were their predicaments? That forces you to try and imagine what their parents were like and how they were cared for. It also helps to replace blame with empathy for them.

In researching your accounts of them, you will want to consult every possible source. Surviving relatives who knew them when small are a rich seam. Any letters they wrote to their parents or other written material, like memoirs making sense of their past, are likely to be invaluable. Likewise, pictures of them in their family can be revealing – the scowl at the camera, or equally, a Say Cheese fake smile through gritted teeth.

Of course, the most revealing potential witness could be your parents themselves, if they are still alive. But that is rarely a simple matter. For all sorts of reasons, parents spin their childhoods when speaking to their children about them. Some are extremely reticent, some overshare with distorted stories, some gloss it because of an enduring *Offspring Stockholm Syndrome* fear of the truth. Often they are more honest and accurate when speaking to their friends about it than to their children. So your parents' closest friends could be a treasure trove.

This work of personal archaeology should be fascinating but its purpose is to help you identify the negative patterns that need exorcising so that you can break them. A particularly moving example of someone who achieved this is Alexander Waugh, son of the writer Auberon and grandson of the famous novelist, Evelyn. In a book on the subject,[60] Alexander showed how the cruelty of father to son down several generations had played out. In a moving documentary[61] he implicitly demonstrated that he had broken the cycle by the warmth and humour he displayed towards his son. He began the programme with the words 'To understand how a man behaves as a father it is useful to know how he was treated as a son'. In examining his paternal ancestors, he explains to his own son how he came to be who he is.

Perhaps you can do something similar if you can uncover the intergenerationally transmitted maltreatment in your family history.

TWO: Embrace the angels in the nursery

Positive psychology encourages salesmanship of the positive to oneself – regardless of the negative truth, it calls black white. It is therapeutic Elastoplast. More profound is to identify the roots of the good that has been passed down to you.

In my case, for example, on my mother's side, there was her Tasmanian nanny. Until my mother married in her early thirties, her nanny lived with her. I remember the visits to her in an old people's home, and my mother's intense mourning when she died, in sharp contrast to how she was when she lost her parents. Her father committed suicide when she was 14. I asked her how upset she was about that and she replied 'I didn't really know my father. I was at a boarding school and they came and told me it had happened. I don't remember being very upset.' It was her nanny who gave my mother the (despite everything, not inconsiderable) capacity to care for us in a benign fashion. On my father's side, his father was truly scholarly and passed that on.

Of course, not all the good there is in us comes from distant ancestors, some comes from the particular love, wisdom and playfulness our parents directly expressed, sometimes despite the past, rather than because of it. My parents prized playfulness and in doing so, broke with their pasts. But there is an important extent to which we are also direct vessels for the good that was in our ancestors.

THREE: P-A-C, a top tip for changing the intergenerational record
Transactional Analysis,[62] created by Eric Berne, proposes that at any one time we can be in one of three fundamental states:

Parent: In which you mimic your parents.
Adult: In which you are able to be relatively detached from emotion, seeking an objective view of the situation you are in.
Child: In which you are in the grip of how it was for you when small, reliving that even though you are now grown up.

More than any other single model, I find that clients can instantly relate to P-A-C and apply it. Being in Parent or Child mode is not 'wrong' at all times, indeed, when it is the angels in the nursery that are pulling the strings, they are benign. But most of us can grasp that when things are going wrong, the Adult mode is very helpful.

It is especially so when trying to work out how to relate to your children in a different way from your forebears. For example, a repeated situation all parents face is our children refusing to do something we feel they need to do for their own good, and perhaps displaying defiance or stubborn disengagement. We are liable to become frustrated and then angry, or find ourselves fighting back the rage or, alternatively, become passive and paralysed. Either we revert to Child mode, perhaps becoming red-faced and tantrumming, or we go into Parent mode, be that coercive or permissive. From the Adult position we can appraise the child's emotional state, remain calm and perhaps see if there is a way to help the child plug into the self-interest in pursuing the goal we want them to seek. If the child can find a way of their own to decide to do their homework or use the potty or sleep in their own bed, that is the most desirable outcome.

You can ask yourself at any moment in the day which mode you are in. For example, right now, which is it? You may be finding this exposition dull as ditchwater, perhaps your Adult just does not buy into what I am writing. Or perhaps it makes sense. Or you may be having a strong emotional reaction to it, perhaps driven by your Child or Parent modes.

In the case of Amy, the woman whose family was described in this chapter, during and after the Love Bombing, when she was working at changing the way she related to her daughter to avoid repeating the *I'm Okay, You're Not* pattern, invoking Adult Amy proved very helpful. She would catch herself about to lose her temper or embark on a nagging session and choose not to by deciding to move into Adult mode.

The battle to wrest fate from destiny is lifelong. The quintuplet of Melrose novels[63] by Edward St Aubyn explore this with particular precision. Melrose was sexually abused by his father and severely neglected by his mother. The novels evoke this childhood and explore its consequences for him, including heroin addiction, cruelty on his part to others (especially women), and a dreadful despair and confusion. But they also itemise how it is possible to grasp small portions of volition from the chaos. Gradually the central character of the novel stabilises. By the end, he finds himself able to make real choices, using his Adult mode.

Part of how he achieves this is by a profound understanding of the intergenerational nature of the trauma. He identifies the horrors inflicted on his parents and uses that to empower him not to repeat the past, especially as a parent himself. While by no means self-help books, the Melrose series offers a fine model of how we can make a present of our pasts. It is in our hands, not our genes, to pass something different and better to our offspring.

As I pointed out in the Preface, politicians play on our desire to improve our material circumstances in order to provide a more affluent life for our children. If only we could see that, once a basic level of material security has been achieved, it is far more important to pass love down the generations, not property or stocks and shares.

Chapter 7

The Real Causes of Ability

Most parents are delighted if their child excels in some way but mistakenly suppose that excellence is innate. No one is born that way, not anyone. Ability, or the lack thereof, is the result of the combination of the early care we receive and our role in the family drama, themselves strongly affected by intergenerational transmission of traits. There is no inborn talent or stupidity, no hard-wired quick-wittedness, exceptional capacity for abstraction, inborn drive to succeed. The DNA of exceptional achievers has never been shown to differ from that of the average person in any significant respect.

Locating the issue in the genes and brain of the child displaces the focus away from the family that created it and the society which created that family. The fact that about one quarter of British children[1] leave school without five grade A–Cs at GCSE has nothing to do with genes, and everything to do with the high proportion raised in low-income families. It is now clear that IQ scores are a proxy for privilege, not for inborn mental ability:[2] on its fifth birthday, the average child from the top social class has received five and half times more positive (relative to negative) feedback from parents than a working-class child.[3] Children in low-income families are read to less, taught less maths, and have much less pressure for academic success from their parents. This is before they go to the state schools, which have much lower expectations than the private ones where 7 per cent of children are educated. The vastly better educational performance[4] of Scandinavian countries compared with Britain can be largely explained by their much lower numbers of low-income families – only 6 per cent in Denmark, for instance.[5] The proportion of children in low income families[6] when Margaret Thatcher was elected in 1979 was 19 per cent; it was 31 per cent from 1981 onwards during her reign. Alas, it has stayed thereabouts ever since.

There are no 'gifted' children. Just as there is an industry based around the premise that many children are born with genetically inherited mental disabilities, so it is with the gifted. The professionals mistakenly suppose there are cognitive capacities that are wholly detached from the personality and deeper motivation of the child. In fact, ability derives from more or less unconscious motives arising from our unique nurture.

Indeed, having an exceptional IQ is not a strong predictor of subsequent excellence. Many decades ago, the American psychologist Lewis Terman[7] identified 1,500 'exceptionally superior' IQ performers with a score of 150 or more (the general average is 100, so this is a huge score) and they have been followed up to the age of 80. There were no artistic geniuses or Nobel prize winners. While they achieved more than the average American, they did no more than the average for their social class. Most startlingly, the 5 per cent of Terman's group who had IQs of over 180 barely achieved anything more in their careers than those with 150.

In this chapter, I will focus on exceptional achievers because their stories bring into sharp relief the forces that determine ability levels in all of us. The principles apply to underachievement as much as to its opposite. As in all traits discussed in this book, the study of ability illustrates the extent to which the main reasons we are similar to or different from parents and siblings spring from nurture, not nature.

Healthy and unhealthy hothousing of skills

Large amounts of the right kind of practice has been proven in numerous different studies to correlate with competence. That applies as much to poor as to good performance, to my low-grade golfing as much as to Tiger Woods. It takes 10,000 hours of practice[8] to achieve exceptional skill in a wide variety of fields, including chess, golf and playing the violin. The classic illustration is that top professional violinists (soloists) have done 10,000 hours whereas good ones (orchestral players) have done 8,000 and music teachers 4,000. In the study that showed this, there was not a single good player or music teacher who had done 10,000 hours; all the exceptional players – the soloists – had.

All prodigies, without exception, seem to be the product of hours practiced, not some inbuilt capacity.[9] What is more, prodigy is overrated. Most do not continue to be prodigious and most exceptional achievers were not prodigious. While it is startling and headline-grabbing, prodigy is not what it is cracked up to be by the media, a freak inborn phenomenon. The notion of talent as a thing, a capacity fixed in the brain at birth, has been completely discredited.

If practice makes perfect, not just any practice is required. Crucial is that the person is constantly seeking to improve performance (known as Deliberate Practice[10]). It entails identifying deficits and correcting them, constantly striving to do better. This has been shown to affect both the size of different parts of the brain and its morphology. Famously, a study of London taxi drivers found that there is enlargement in the part of the brain concerned with mapping because of the many hours of learning different street names.[11] Other studies have shown that there is more myelin in the neurones of exceptional violinists, increasing the speed of passage of nerve signals.[12] This is caused by practice, not genes.

Some of the most effective practice is solitary, done for hours on end: David Beckham still perfecting his dipping free kick at age 10 long after the other players have gone home, the Williams sisters bashing the ball back and forth all the way through their childhood holidays (from 8 a.m.

to 3 p.m., every day) when their peers had headed off to watch TV or go swimming. Whereas I am delighted by a well-hit golf shot and am not too much distressed by my many botched ones, an exceptional achiever is aiming for perfection every time. Anecdotally, you notice this in major competitions in golf or tennis. Even when at the top of their game, the very best players are castigating themselves for first serves that go out or difficult putts that do not drop.

That the practice starts young in many cases is noted by popular authors writing about exceptional achievement but none seem to understand its true significance. They simply regale us with the early beginnings as evidence of hours and kind of practice. Three crucial questions are ignored or sidestepped:

> ⟩ What is the reason why some people do 10,000 hours of practice, but not others?
> ⟩ Of those that do complete the 10,000 hours, what causes the difference in success of the winners and the also-rans?
> ⟩ Of those that do 10,000 hours and become exceptional, what causes some to be desperately unhappy, others to be emotionally healthy?

The last of these is possibly of greatest interest to the reader, whether as a parent or in your own life. The answer to all of them lies in the precise details of early nurture described in Chapter 2 – learning (teaching, modelling, identification), and maltreatment and love. All but teaching are largely ignored by scholars of this subject. Insofar as they address my questions, they put the differences down to the extent to which achievers believe themselves to have fixed rather than flexible capacities. As noted in TAKEAWAY 2 in Chapter 1 and Appendix 4, there is no doubt that believing your ability is a genetic destiny can limit it. Teaching children, students, teachers or parents that it is not fixed can improve performance considerably.[13] But that does not answer my questions.

Take Wolfgang Amadeus Mozart's assiduousness,[14] an oft-told parable of the popular books on achievement. It is wheeled out to illustrate how sheer quantity of practice leads to skill but is much more revealing than that. His composing began at five years old, his performances for the aristocracy at the age of six. His father was a domineering, famous composer and performer, who trained Wolfgang from the age of three. The fact that the father was using Wolfgang as a vehicle for unfulfilled ambitions rather than his sister is not discussed, nor the nature of his father's coercion, his domineering insistence. Nor is the prodigiousness of his sister.

Called Nanneri, she had also been hothoused, becoming exceptional for her age as both a pianist and violinist. But family roles and social mores (equality of opportunity for females did not exist) were crucial. Nanneri was the oldest child and used as a guinea pig, her skills not nurtured to anything like the same extent as those of Wolfgang. He had already put in 3,500 hours of practice by age six. It was purely by virtue of his gender that Wolfgang became the historic genius, not his sister. His father, fuelled by a pious and ferocious religiosity, needed a boy to identify with in order to create a genius. But rather than explore that issue, it is simply pointed out by authors discussing this case that the Suzuki method now reliably creates prodigies every bit as proficient as the Mozart children, that hours and kind of practice create proficiency. The family politics that favoured the boy over the girl are ignored.

An equally telling and oft-told tale is that of the Polgar family.[15] This is interesting partly because it is so cut-and-dried an example of the role of nurture over nature in causing exceptional achievement. But always ignored by authors considering its importance, it also provides a glimpse of the crucial difference between the origins of distressed versus emotionally healthy outcomes among exceptional achievers, the issue raised in my third question, above.

In the 1960s, Laszlo Polgar was a Hungarian educational psychologist who had written several scientific papers on the effectiveness of practice in creating excellence. As was common behind the Iron Curtain, he used pen pal letters to make friends in other countries and through one of them, met a Ukrainian woman, Klara. He explained his passionate conviction that excellence can be nurtured and she fell for him as well as his arguments. They agreed to have children and to turn them into chess grandmasters, choosing that game because it has an incontestable, objective metric by which achievement can be measured.

Polgar was a mathematician by specialism and doubtless that helped in implementing his plan. But he was not exceptional, so it cannot be suggested that he passed genes for exceptional pattern recognition to his children (not that such genes exist). He played the game as a hobby, his wife did not play at all. Having read up on the best means for teaching it, he prepared to conduct his unusual experiment.

As luck would have it, Klara gave birth to three daughters. There had been no female grandmasters and it was widely assumed that females were born with brains less capable of the mental operations entailed for exceptional chess playing. If he could create a female grandmaster it would be all the more telling, since the administrators of world chess forbade women from top tournaments.

But the most interesting thing about the Polgar story is the way in which the nurturing of the skill was done. Starting with his eldest daughter Susan, Polgar was careful to treat it as a playful activity, turning it into a fantasy of dramatic wins and losses. By the time she turned five she was excited by playing and spent hundreds of hours practising. Entered in a local competition for children of all ages, she treated it as fun and won 10–0, causing a sensation. Meanwhile, her younger sisters were intrigued by this activity and Laszlo allowed them to feel the pieces, seeing them as toys, without giving any formal tuition until they were aged five.

Interviewed recently, all three girls[16] described playing the game as something that they loved doing, it was not a chore. Instead of messing about playing Monopoly, netball or going to the local swimming pool, chess was just what they enjoyed in the Polgar family.

Sure enough, in 1991 the eldest daughter became the first female grandmaster. Although the second daughter did not achieve that status, in one tournament she had ten straight wins against male grandmasters, a performance rated the fifth best in the history of chess. Her younger sister did become a grandmaster at the prodigious age of 15, the youngest ever (of either gender). She became the greatest-ever female chess player.

It is a matter of public record that Polgar declared his intention of creating grandmasters before his children were born. Neither he nor his wife were exceptional in the relevant skills needed to play chess. It is very hard to dispute this story as proof of the overpowering importance of nurture rather than nature in causing exceptional chess achievement. But more than that, it is interesting in terms of how to create emotionally healthy high achievers, as opposed to the many highly distressed ones.

That Polgar understood the benign effect of not coercing his daughters into playing is clear: he grasped that small children need to enjoy fantasy play through which they develop self-determination and imagination. Consequently, his daughters all seem to have grown into satiable, well-balanced people rather than hungry success addicts. There is no need for Tiger Mothering to produce exceptional achievers.

The term Tiger Mothering[17] achieved international attention in 2011 as a result of a book by Amy Chua. She suggested that the strict approach to learning used by the Chinese was superior to the more gentle American one. She was remarkably frank about how humiliating and aggressive she had been with her daughters. For example, she called one of them 'garbage', something her father had called her (a transgenerational trait). On another occasion, Chua described how she got her unwilling younger daughter to learn a very difficult piano piece. Chua stated that 'I hauled Lulu's dollhouse to the car and told her I'd donate it to the Salvation Army piece by piece if she didn't have "The Little White Donkey" perfect by the next day. When Lulu said, "I thought you were going to the Salvation Army, why are you still here?" I threatened her with no lunch, no dinner, no Christmas or Hanukkah presents, no birthday parties for two, three, four years. When she still kept playing it wrong, I told her she was purposely working herself into a frenzy because she was secretly afraid she couldn't do it. I told her to stop being lazy, cowardly, self-indulgent and pathetic.' They continued practising through dinner without letting her daughter get up, not for water, not even to go to the lavatory. At the end, the daughter mastered the piece and was said to be 'beaming', wishing she could play it repeatedly.

While this kind of coercion can produce a prodigy, it is also potentially emotionally toxic. In marked contrast, the dynamics of the Polgar family emerge from a fascinating footnote to their story.

When the eldest daughter had been crowned as the first female grand-master, forcing the sport's organisers to change their rules, a Dutch billionaire offered to pay Polgar to adopt three boys from a developing nation to show that the experiment could be replicated. Polgar was keen on the idea but his wife turned it down. A relaxed, warm woman unmotivated by money or fame, she felt they had already made their point and that to do it again would take more energy than she had.

She had given her daughters a very solid early infancy and secure life as toddlers, standing them in good stead for the pressures of top chess competition. She was not someone who would coerce them. Just as her husband had conducted the experiment in nurture with full awareness of the need for small children to enjoy the delights of la-la land for much of the time, so she had provided the loving, responsive base, which is the foundation of emotional health.

The Polgars are a refreshing exception to the rule which most popular books on exceptional achievement either ignore or show a baleful unawareness of: the great majority of exceptional achievers are borne of adversity. The single strongest proof of this is the fact that in all fields where the matter has been studied, one in three exceptional achievers lost a parent before the age of 14.[18] This applies to American presidents, British prime ministers and entrepreneurs. It applies across a wide variety of fields of endeavour. One third of the 600 people with the most space devoted to them in the British and American Encyclopaedias suffered parental loss young. When combined with certain kinds of nurture before and after the loss, the experience impels some children to seek to wrest fate from destiny, to take control of their lives. In some cases it results in dictators (like Napoleon, Hitler or Ho Chi Minh) who will trust no one and kill all possible rivals, in others it leads to great scientists (like Charles Darwin) or artists (like Paul McCartney).

The evidence that high achievers of all kinds are more likely to suffer mental illness is considerable.[19] Chief executives in America are four times more likely to be psychopathic than the general public.[20] British ones are significantly more likely[21] to have certain personality disorders (such as narcissism) than mental hospital patients. In the performing arts,[22] one study compared creative with non-creative people. Comics scored significantly higher on four negative traits, especially introvertive anhedonia (a form of depression – inability to feel pleasure, including an avoidance of intimacy). The researchers pointed to similarities in what it takes to be funny and the mindsets of people with schizophrenia or bipolar disorder. Both require thinking outside the box and with manic speed, making up original connections. Actors also scored significantly higher on three out of the four traits but not on introvertive anhedonia. Both comics and actors were far more likely to be high on the traits than people from other professions.

The cliché of the tears of a clown in comics appears to be true. Interviewing young comedians for two television series in the late 1980s (some of these interviews can be seen on my website http://www.selfishcapitalist.com/index.php/tv/ go to room 113), many of whom subsequently became world famous, what startled me was how very distressing their childhoods had been. Robbie Coltrane had been thumped about by his dad until the day he was big enough to thump him back. Stephen Fry's intellect and personality had been cruelly, severely belittled by his father. Ruby Wax had a mother who was so badly affected by hysteria and obsessive-compulsive disorder that it nearly drove Wax mad. Aged five, Julie Walters came upon her father sitting dead in his armchair. There were others, and only Ben Elton had nothing extreme to report.

What is important about the study of performing artists is that it demonstrates links between a specific pathology and a specific profession: depression and comedy. What is completely lacking from the analysis of the results is their wider meaning: that the precise way we *are* precisely reflects how we have been cared for in childhood.

We know that children's fantasy narratives[23] reflect the specific care they receive. The physically abused make up different stories[24] from the sexually abused, who are different from the neglected, reflecting the actual care they receive. This translates into adult symptoms: there are now a host of studies[25] linking specific childhood adversities to specific adult psychiatric symptoms. Specific kinds of childhood maltreatment are related to specific adult psychotic symptoms. For example, sexual abuse correlates with auditory hallucinations[26] whereas erratic and emotionally neglectful care is associated with paranoia.

In short, it is clear that childhood maltreatment is not only the principal cause of mental illness but also, of much exceptional achievement. While there are refreshing exceptions, like the Polgars, it seems clear that it is usually a way of expressing childhood maltreatment. This is well illustrated by the sad story of Tiger Woods, to which I will devote much of the rest of this chapter, since it is so telling.

As well as showing how Tiger Mothering maltreatment becomes achievement, the Woods story is a particularly telling illustration of the intergenerational nature of family traits, in this case, the will to exceptional achievement. I will use detailed exposition of it to explore why so many exceptional achievers are desperately unhappy. Along the way, I shall explain how self-control works in normal and exceptional people.

The rise and fall of Tiger Woods[27]
In 2009, Tiger Woods was revealed to have engaged in multiple affairs and sexual encounters with dozens of women. It came as a considerable shock

to anyone familiar with his squeaky clean public image. He was forced into various *mea culpa* public announcements and it became apparent that he had been a deeply troubled person for many years. His difficulties stemmed from his upbringing.

Tiger's parents

Tiger's father Earl was born in 1932 in the midst of the Great Depression, the youngest of six children. Miles, his father, was already 60 when Earl was born, having fathered five children with a previous wife. A harsh, unyielding and punitive patriarch, he eked out a living as a stonemason.

Earl's mother, Maude, was twenty years younger than Miles. She took the view that education was crucial for the advancement of her children. Miles was forced to commit to a strong emphasis on schooling for their children as a condition of their marriage. She encouraged her children to see themselves as being as good as anyone, but impressed upon them that they would need to work extra hard to overcome the prejudice against their skin colour. Along with strong pressure to excel in their schoolwork, the children had to earn their keep. Earl's role was to clean and feed the chickens, and when the time came, to slaughter them.

From a young age, Earl expressed an interest in baseball. Seeing potential in his son, Miles arranged for him to act as batboy for the Kansas City Monarchs, the local Negro League team. Earl was left in no doubt as to the purpose of this arrangement. Miles told him that 'you need to play for the Monarchs when you grow up'.

Aged 11, Earl's father dropped dead and his mother dubbed him the new man of the house but only two years later, she also died suddenly. Potently self-sufficient, Earl gritted his teeth and fortunately, his aunt was able to move into the house and support him. The twin bereavements only served to increase Earl's determination to succeed. Had he been born in an era when it was more possible for blacks to reach the top, it is conceivable that Earl would have joined the ranks of early bereaved exceptional achievers. As it was, although he achieved a good deal himself, his son was to be the intergenerational conduit for that success.

In later life, Earl played fast and loose with the truth when speaking of his own and of his son's histories, a blagger. Nonetheless, he had substance. As the first and only African–American player in the 'Big Seven' conference baseball league, he played successfully in the face of savage racial taunts from the crowds. In due course, aged 19, he was offered a contract with the black professional side, the Kansas City Monarchs. Following his mother's dictat that he must complete his education, he turned it down. This created the unfulfilled aspiration of an outstanding sporting career; Tiger was to be the vehicle.

On leaving university, Earl married and joined the army. Over the next decade he served all over the world, including several tours in Vietnam. He fathered three children, although he largely missed out on their early years, absent through his military career. His relationship with his first wife came to an end.

Earl pushed on with his career and at the age of 35, qualified as a Green Beret, a legendarily gruelling experience akin to the British Special Air Service (SAS) training. In 1968 he was stationed in Thailand, having achieved an unusual degree of power for an African–American in that era, responsible for the leisure activities of 100,000 soldiers. It was through this role that he first cast eyes on his second wife, Tiger's mother, Kultida.

She was 24 when Earl Woods walked into the office where she worked, startlingly attractive, diminutive but self-assured. From an affluent, established Thai family, her father was an architect who also owned a tin mine. Her self-assurance sometimes tipped from assertive into aggressive: she was opinionated and independent-minded. She would normally have married into the Thai ruling elite but was sufficiently of her own mind to take the step of tying the knot with a foreigner, and a black one, at that.

Her parents had divorced when she was aged five, and sent her to boarding school until she was ten. By the time she left school, both her parents had new families and the stepparents in both cases rejected her. She was peddled between the households, a lonely and unhappy childhood that forced reliance on her own resources. She found solace in Buddhism.

Having been spurned by her family, she had no compelling reason to remain in Thailand once she she fell in love with Earl. By now a confident, swaggering charmer, he was bowled over by her, and they set off for America and married within a few months of meeting, in 1969.

The hothousing of a golfing genius

Earl was a reluctant second-time father, but Kultida insisted on it. After the birth of Tiger, in 1975, she was told that she could have no more children. A lorry-load of expectation was to be placed on their only child's shoulders.

Earl had had to boost himself in his own eyes in order to overcome his considerable childhood adversities. There was a ruthless, angry, pragmatic materialism about him, alongside an overblown, sales pitch of a personality, wrought of insecurities. He would never have been satisfied by anything less than a top winner in his son. He felt he had failed the children from his first marriage. Now, aged 43, he was determined to make a big paternal investment.

For Kultida, this was to be her only offspring. Tough, as pragmatic as Earl and damaged by her unhappy childhood, she was equally single-minded in making it clear to Tiger that he must succeed. Her aspirations for Tiger were remarkably similar to those of Earl's mother, Maude: he must obtain a good education before pursuing his sporting career. Neither of the mothers seems to have made a point of caring for their sons as loveable or playful children, success appears to have mattered most.

Both of Tiger's parents were physically undemonstrative, there were no hugs, and love was conditional on performance. An altruistic concern that the child develop his own self-determined identity would have been lacking, the kind of parental love which contains the potential for later emotional health.

Earl regarded his position in relation to Tiger as the trustee of a special talent, long before Tiger had had a chance to display any. He spoke of him as the Chosen One. In some of his pronouncements, it sometimes sounded as if he felt like Joseph, Kultida was Mary, Tiger the baby Jesus. Except that it often seemed as if Earl regarded himself more like God than Joseph. Earl said that he had a sense from the birth onwards that something was different about this baby and that he would eventually become 'the greatest man to walk the earth'. This speaks of Earl's enormous narcissism and delusions of omnipotence. He was dealing with his own sense of hurt and of humiliation by projecting on to the baby a set of exceptional attributes that could repair those feelings. No infant could behave in ways which indicated they were going to be 'the greatest man to walk the earth'.

Once the Chosen One returned with his mother from the hospital, the parents sat down and had a hard-nosed conversation about how to raise him. They agreed to sacrifice their lives, he would be the priority. There would be no nannies, no babysitters, at all times one of them would be present. Earl had hopes of his son becoming his best friend. Being a narcissist, he was lonely. For her part, Kultida wanted an ambitious child with the manners and skills to succeed. Her hunger for this and her critical role in Tiger's golfing killer instinct has sometimes been lost amid the deafening noise of Earl's increasingly pompous pronouncements. But in later life Tiger was to put his golfing killer instinct down to his mother, not to Earl.

The story goes that, aged nine months, Tiger would sit in his highchair watching Earl practise chipping golf balls into a cup. Earl maintained that his son watched what he was doing with intense fascination. When Earl put a mini club in his hand just before his first birthday, he swung the club precisely mimicking his father. His astonishing two-and-a-half-year-old golf swing can be viewed on YouTube today[28] because he appeared driving a ball on American TV's *Mike Douglas Show*. Capitalising on his year spent as an army publicity officer, Earl had pulled off the first of many media coups.

He began Tiger's training in dealing with the press when he was still tiny. He taught him never to supply more than the question demanded.

He would ask Tiger how old he was and if he replied 'Three, I'll be four in December', Earl would say 'That's not what I asked you.' In later life, Tiger would be notorious for his parsimony in dealing with the media, becoming a master of the Delphic soundbite, repeated monotonously.

At the age of three, Tiger played round the first nine holes of a local course in 48 shots (for non-golfing readers, that is the most basic level expected of a fully grown adult – over 18 holes, it would be a handicap of 24, the starter level). I repeat that this was *at the age of three*. Anyone who has both played golf and who has experience of what a three-year-old is like, physically and psychologically, will realise that is scarcely credible. So fluid and perfectly aligned was his swing, it looked like that of a professional. Aged four he was the subject of a short piece in a golfing magazine, aged five he appeared on the network ABC show *That's Incredible!* [29] For once, the superlative was apt. He spent most of his waking hours chipping and putting golf balls around his house, not just the garage. He was well on the way to completing his 10,000 hours.

It might be supposed by some that his commitment was the natural consequence of a boy wanting to practise a genetically inherited superhuman skill. We can be certain that this is not true. Rather, Tiger was responding to his father's determination to create the world's greatest golfer. It was much like Laszlo Polgar and his daughters, but with money and fame as the drivers, not scientific curiosity, and with ruthless, cold bullying as the means, not playfulness and love. That Tiger's skill was the product of relentless and carefully calculated grooming, not genes, is suggested by the fact that neither of his parents were exceptional golfers.

Aged seven, lining up a putt on their local course, Tiger was distracted when Earl jingled the change in his pocket. He asked his father to keep quiet. When he was all set to do the putt again, Earl let out a loud cough. These distractions continued every time the putt was attempted, Earl pointing out that Tiger had to learn to block out everything when playing his shots. Earl later explained that 'I wanted to teach him mental toughness. I knew it was annoying ... plus it was always fun to give him the business.' This latter utterance was accompanied by a grin: there was a sadistic component to Earl's training regime, one completely absent in the Polgar household.

Both father and son always maintained the training was done out of love, that it was fun and that it bonded them. While there were elements of truth in that, Earl's primary motive was to create a world-beating golfer who would become rich and famous, making Earl rich and famous as well – the primary concern of the narcissist.

The extent to which Tiger had no choice in the matter is revealed by a six-month period of 'special training' that Earl introduced when Tiger was 11. Earl admitted that 'it was brutal, prisoner-of-war interrogation techniques, psychological intimidation – it went on and on'. Drawing on his experience of being brutalised during his Green Beret training and also on his own tough, strict upbringing as well as his many experiences of racism, he would get into Tiger's face, taunting him, with cruel, vicious barbs. While there was also encouragement, it was close to brainwashing and torture, with a great deal of bullying. Even Tiger would later say that the experience left him feeling 'frustrated' and 'insignificant'. These feelings must have been the tip of the emotional iceberg because, due to *Offspring Stockholm Syndrome*, Tiger was always highly protective of his father and very reluctant to reveal any details about his emotions.

Earl later claimed that Tiger had requested the 'boot camp' treatment and revelled in the discipline. Tiger also stuck to that story but he did admit that he shed tears of frustration over it. Earl maintained that he never made Tiger feel that love was contingent on winning, but that was precisely the truth. Ever the public relations spin doctor, Earl was canny enough to realise that exact criticism would be made and knocked it on the head by naming it. Golf was all Tiger wanted to do and Earl offered that as evidence for the idea that the impulse to play came from his son. The real reason was to get his father's approbation and affection.

In later life when Tiger got angry with himself at missing a putt, Earl would maintain that his role was to help his son see it was not the end of the world. But that account left out the extreme fury or nasty psychological mindgames that Earl had earlier inflicted on his son when he had made any mistakes. Right from the start, Earl could be very unpleasant if Tiger did not deliver.

It is common for parents of perfectionist and often very high-achieving children to stress that the child puts the pressure on themselves. That can be true of children as young as five: the child may indeed be frantically trying to work late, do better and so on. But that statement ignores the more or less subtle ways in which the child has been coerced into regarding perfection, often from birth, as the only way in which to extract a genuine smile or loving cuddle from their parent. When the child is older and craving perfection, the parent can say to themselves and to others, 'I wish they did not put so much pressure on themselves, it comes from within'. They may never have realised their role in creating it.

Contrary to misleading newspaper reports that perfectionism is caused by genes, it is well proven to be caused by helicopter parenting.[30] Over-control by parents, usually expressing their own perfectionism, puts intolerable stress on the child to meet impossible standards. Such parenting leads to eating disorders[31] and many other problems, including anxiety and depression,[32] loneliness,[33] compulsiveness,[34] feelings of being an imposter[35], suicidal tendencies[36] and cortisol dysregulation.[37] Love and warmth can mitigate the effect of over-control, depending on familial and national culture. In one study, samples of British and Italian families were compared.[38] While the Italian mothers were significantly more over-controlling, they were also warmer. This compensated for the over-control, making their children no more at risk of suffering anxiety than children without over-controlling parents. A lack of warmth from Kultida could have been critical in creating later problems for Tiger.

There is also an important distinction to be drawn between adaptive and maladaptive perfectionism.[39] In the adaptive variety, your best is good enough. That was the case for the Polgar girls but may not have been for Tiger. In the maladaptive variety, there is a toxic lack of self-forgiveness for imperfection (a phenomenon that has been specifically tested in athletes[40]). This was something Tiger felt and displayed only too audibly and visibly on the golf course, whereas the Polgars did not.

As a child Tiger was subjected to perfectionist pressure. Whether it was homework, housework or respect for his elders, coercion was the punishment for falling short of the expected high standards. Tiger was spanked repeatedly, what might now be termed physical abuse. Just as Earl's mother had believed, Kultida felt that sparing the rod spoiled the child. Tiger feared her. He had to be a good boy, polite, well mannered and neatly turned out, or he would face physical wrath, or a cold brush-off, a withdrawal of approval.

As part of her regime, they did a nightly Buddhist meditation. This may have helped him to calm down after what must have been stressful days but it was yet another imposition – he had no choice in the matter. That is suggested by the fact that he dropped the practice once he became an independent adult. Kultida believed that she could reach ultimate enlightenment through her Buddhism, something Tiger always doubted about himself: her insistence on perfectionism was no less than her husband's. As already noted, it is to his mother rather than to Earl that Tiger attributes his exceptional competitive drive.

When Earl followed Tiger on to the golf course during the years of tournament play in his teens, he sometimes consoled Tiger if he slipped up. Kultida was less forgiving. Having been an aggressive, argumentative young woman, she was implacably hyper-competitive. On the occasions she accompanied her son, her face would be a picture of concentration, creased with tension, never satisfied unless Tiger was making no mistakes. She hardly ever smiled on the course, whereas Earl often did, partly because he enjoyed the attention and played to the gallery.

Tiger's rise

Earl groomed journalists to report on his golfing prodigy as he repeatedly broke records. Tiger first beat his father at the age of 11 with a score of 71 (for non-golfers, this is 'par', the number of shots a really good player would be expected to take in completing all 18 holes on the course). Starting at the age of 13, he won the Junior World Championship, doing this six times, winning consecutively for four years. At the age of 15 in 1991 he won the American Junior Amateur Championship, the youngest ever to do so (the age limit was 18) and voted Junior Player of that year. Coached by Earl, he chanted the vacuous, brand-associating soundbite: 'I want to be the Michael Jordan of golf'.

Aged 18, he became the youngest ever American Amateur Champion (the best amateur adult American). The flamboyance with which he did it was a sign of things to come. Six shots behind the leader at the start of the last round, he won by two.

In moving to Stanford University to study business, Tiger took his first step to becoming his own brand manager. He studied economics because 'I want to be able to manage the people who manage my money'. By this time, there was no question that he would be making millions as a professional.

Just before he took that step he signed endorsement deals worth $60 million. Earl summed up the scale of expectation that preceded Tiger's professional career with these words: 'There is no comprehension by anyone on the impact this kid is going to have not only on the game of golf, but on the world itself. The Lord sent him here on a mission and it will transcend the game.' The messianic imagery verged on the delusional. But the idea that Woods was going to be a poster boy for race relations was ludicrous and partly a publicity scam. It would take a great deal more than Tiger's success to shift entrenched American racial prejudice. Nor was Woods motivated by this, he just wanted to please his parents.

His first major victory in 1997 – the Masters at Augusta – shot him to global fame. Prior to his appearance there, only four black players had even been invited to this preppy, establishment tournament. He won so emphatically it really did seem as if the Son of God had taken up golf. At the end he was *twelve strokes* ahead of the runner-up and the confidence, style and virtuosity of his golf was unprecedented, he was also the young-est ever winner. 'We did it, Pop,' he whispered into his father's ear as they embraced. The 'We' expressed the extent to which it had not been him, it had been his father in him. It would almost have been more accurate to say 'You did it, Pop', although that would have been to forget Kultida's contri-bution. It was probably what Earl felt, unconsciously.

The Woods name became a global brand immediately, as recognisa-ble as Pele, Princess Diana and Bowie. This was the culmination of the creation in Tiger of what is known as The Marketing Character.[41] Such people regard themselves as commodities whose value depends on their success, saleability and approval by others. They distinguish themselves and others by what they own and have achieved in the eyes of others, not who they are. They are focused on Having rather than Being. *Homo consumens* is a thing to be bought and sold, like a car, a home or a corpo-ration. Woods' brand was traded by corporations.

Studies of such characters[42] show them to be conventional in their ideas, comparing themselves obsessively and enviously with others, always wanting more, and prone to being angry, anxious and depressed. They aim to keep emotion at bay. Objects in a 'personality market', they work hard at selling themselves as a nice 'package', coming across as cheerful, sound, reliable and industrious. Those for whom love has been conditional on success, like Tiger, are much more vulnerable to becoming Marketing Characters; so are many successful people.

The creator of this concept, Erich Fromm, portrayed America as a Marketing Society.[43] Consumers must be permanently dissatisfied with themselves and their possessions for consumption to be constantly growing. Work must have a central place in their lives to pay for their insatiable desire to consume and to bring the status that comes from wealth. With no deep feelings or convictions, the standardised tastes conveyed through advertis-ing replace any profound understanding. Tiger and Earl were steeped in this way of thinking and Tiger became one of the icons by which advertis-ing controls our values.

'Tiger' the brand had been conceived (literally, as well as figuratively) as a product by his father and marketed as such, starting with his appearance on the *Mike Douglas Show*. The concept of a child prodigy black golfer had been carefully orchestrated, including the prodigiousness itself. That was not a scam: Tiger really was a golfing genius. His parents having created a Blue Chip human product, Blue Chip corporations queued up to associate themselves with it. Golfing equipment and clothing companies wanted to use Tiger's brand on their products so that consumers would feel that in buying them, they would be connected to a golfing phenomenon. In the woo-woo fuzzy magic by which advertising works, some of his skill would rub off on the consumers if they used 'his' clubs and wore 'his' clothes.

A separate group of corporations with no golfing products wanted to use his brand to strengthen theirs. His image as a young, handsome, self-made and phenomenally successful man would rub off on them. That he was a squeaky-clean African–American gained them credibility, suggesting they were without prejudice. By subtle implication, they would seem in favour of equal opportunities for other disadvantaged groups, like women, if they were identified with a person of colour. Hence, Accenture, a global corporation in the business of consultancy and people management (the exploitation of 'Human Resources'), could use the Tiger brand to give the impression that they backed excellence without reference to race, gender or religion.

The investment paid off handsomely for both them and him. Over the next 12 years, Tiger won 13 more majors. He acquired a personal fortune of one billion dollars. He purchased two homes in Florida, two in California, one in Dubai and an estate for his wife in Sweden. One of the homes cost $38 million, another $23 million, his yacht $22 million. His Marketing Character had created huge professional and material success. But behind the façade and the brand, a human being still existed, one that had been set on this trajectory by specific childhood experiences and family dynamics that contained the seeds of emotional collapse and career destruction.

Tiger's fall

When Tiger won his first major in 1997, Earl was 65 and had already had a triple-bypass heart operation. He kept a close eye on Tiger's career and remained a crucial motivator. Having smoked two packets of cigarettes a day throughout his adult life – a habit Tiger abhorred – and having had a relentless diet of junk food, in 2006, cancer and a weak heart claimed him. The death left Tiger more than bereft, he was unable to accept it. The press release and his automatic pilot utterances seemed to acknowledge the death. He spoke of having lost his 'best friend and greatest role model'. But internally, Tiger could not cope with the absence. His father had hijacked him so young and so completely that there was no Tiger if there was no Earl.

Pathological mourning takes two forms.[44] One is to repress the death altogether, simply denying that it has happened, so that there are no tears and the bereaved person carries on as if nothing has happened. Quite often, the person will have a severe reaction, amounting to a breakdown, usually on an anniversary, like that of the death. The other form, which was Tiger's, is to experience the person as still alive. When playing tournaments, at times of stress, he could be seen speaking under his breath to his father. While intellectually he knew his father had died, at another level he still felt he was there. Earl had always maintained that he and Tiger could communicate telepathically and Tiger now reported that he could still hear his father's voice. So completely had Earl dominated his son, through the mind games and bullying, it looked almost like a case of spirit possession. It was as if Earl still lived on through him, God still on earth through his son. Just as Earl had suffered an early bereavement, probably without healthy mourning, so Tiger was unable to metabolise the death of his father.

Those close to Tiger reported that he was still severely distressed two years after the bereavement, quite unable to come to terms with his father's death. Tiger had become irritable and compulsive. He had spoken of his father as his strongest role model. There was one particular respect in which this now came to the fore: rampant sexual promiscuity.

Tiger's sexual life had been initially difficult. In his early teens he was a golf nerd, uncool and forgettable, not a popular boy, largely ignored. However, by the age of 16 he was a rising star in the golfing firmament – although most of his peers did not know this – and as a Marketing Character, he decided on a makeover. A handsome six-footer, he replaced his Coke-bottle glasses with contact lenses, cut his hair and bought some hip clothing. Shy, quiet and reserved, his polite, soft-spoken style appealed to some girls. To begin with, he managed only to be their best friend.

He worked out that he needed a high-status girlfriend as a way to signal his attractiveness, so that other girls would want him if he had such a commodity by his side. To this end, he dated a cheerleader called Dina, the first of a long line of leggy blondes. The concept of having such a trophy seemed more important to him than any intimate connection. He stayed with her until he enrolled at Stanford University at the age of 18, ending the relationship when he went there, on Earl's advice.

At Stanford, Tiger rapidly became nationally famous, increasing his allure. At this stage, he was much like any other high-profile male undergraduate, moving between parties and one-night stands, living it up. The shyness was replaced with his father's swagger and confidence. A handsome and always quite gentle man, he had no difficulties in attracting women. Once he became a global figure at the age of 21, he embarked on the promiscuous sexual career so common among young men who become famous.

A crucial factor, however, was that his 'greatest role model' had been the same. Earl had been a philanderer throughout his life. When he was younger it upset Tiger, so that his first girlfriend claimed that he once rang her up in tears speaking of an affair his father had had. But as he got older, father and son had an unspoken pact in which sexual infidelity and promiscuity were an accepted practice. In fact, Earl was proud of his son's sexual prowess and as Tiger became famous, he was a beneficiary, more women wanting to sleep with the father because of the son.

Tiger's sexual exploits were kept out of the press by his publicity team. However, the Marketing Character would need a wife and children if the brand was to be strengthened. Tiger was also feeling lonely and unsatisfied by his roaming. Having consumed dozens of leggy blonde products, he needed something more to fulfil his emotional needs. By 2001, aged 26, he was in the market for a wife and Elin Nordegren was suitable for the merger, although in some respects it was not an obvious fit.

Nordegren was the Swedish daughter of a prominent journalist father and politician mother. On a whim, she had dropped out of her psychology degree to act as the nanny to the family of Jasper Parnevik, the golfer. Although she had done a bit of modelling, she was a very different person from Tiger. Like most Scandinavians, as the studies show,[45] she was much less interested in bigging herself up than Americans. She had no desire to be thrust into the public spotlight. At the time she met Tiger, she had a boyfriend back in Sweden, a forklift driver. She was not interested in displays of wealth or bravado. When Tiger first asked her out, she turned him down, feeling he was not her type.

He persevered, egged on by her reluctance. There were few American women who would not sleep with him, and he saw her as a challenge. At his fifth request, she finally agreed to a date, hoping that this would bring an end to his phone calls. By now she had split up with her boyfriend and on their first date she was surprised by Tiger's amiable companionability. The dinner and a movie were pleasantly normal, she had expected him to try and impress her with more expensive options. Ever the marketeer, Tiger had taken advice on what this consumer would prefer. However, she did not dive into the relationship because she had heard of his philandering ways and was aware that he was one of the first golfers to have a genuine groupie following. First she needed to reassure herself he wasn't cheating on her. If he did, she would leave.

After more dates, their differences gradually stopped mattering. She liked a night in at home, was well mannered, genuine and engaging, unconcerned with externally valued achievement. He was shy beneath the marketing façade, frequently rude, aggressive (his audible and visible 'fucks' when missing putts in tournaments had become accepted by broadcasters and the public alike as a sign that he was human after all) and determined to rule the golfing world. But she also enjoyed a caustic humour with him, and had a competitive, loud side to her, which they shared by playing video games and ping-pong.

Perhaps the crucial factor was that her parents had divorced when she was aged six, and she had been shuttled between them, just as Tiger's mother had. This insecurity meant that she fell for Tiger's romantic gestures, not just expensive presents but also apparently genuine little notes and other intimate signs of love. In many respects, she was like his mother, a woman with values and integrity, but the child of a destabilising divorce, who was willing to leave her home land and make a new life with a successful, impressive American. In fact, there is a large body of evidence that we are attracted[46] by characteristics of our opposite-sexed parent in choosing mates, so Tiger was not unusual in being attracted by aspects of his mother and her history.

The first study proving this was done in Hawaii in 1980,[47] where there are many mixed-race marriages. One thousand men and women who came from mixed parentage were identified. In two-thirds of cases, their first marriage had been to a partner who was of the same ethnic origin as their opposite-sexed parent – for example, if your dad was a person of colour and you were a girl, in two-thirds of cases you would marry a man of your dad's skin colour, likewise sons with their mothers and wives.

The cleverness of this study was that the sample had all divorced and remarried. Sure enough, in two-thirds of cases their second partners were also of the same ethnicity as the opposite-, rather than same-, sexed parent. This is powerful evidence that how our mum or dad looks affects who we shack up with (and perhaps also shows that we do not learn from our mistakes).

Subsequent studies show we are more likely to pick partners with the hair and eye colour[48] of our opposite-sexed parent, likewise their smell. It applies to traits as obvious as what our opposite-sexed parent's face looked like and as obscure as whether they smoked.[49] But it also extends to whether or not we were emotionally close to them. A study of 49 women[50] mapped precise dimensions of their fathers' faces (distance between eyes, size of nose and so on). The women were then shown pictures of 15 men's faces. If they had a positive relationship with their dad, they were significantly more likely to pick out the picture that resembled his dimensions. A particularly telling study[51] used a sample of adopted girls. Only if they had been close to their adoptive dad did they end up marrying a man who looked like him. This proved it was all about nurture and could have nothing to do with nature.

It is not clear how soon after their opulent wedding Tiger continued to have affairs and one-night stands, but at a certain point he continued exactly as before. Those who knew him found it odd that he would maintain how much he loved Elin, despite flirting with girls before their eyes. He appeared to feel there was no connection between the man who had recently sworn to be faithful to Elin till death did them part and the man who was constantly on the prowl for other women. A year after the marriage he said of it that 'I love the idea of growing old. I want to have a relationship where we can change for the better and continue to get closer'. He probably had no sense of self-contradiction when he said those words. Tiger had been used to living a double life since he was a baby. The façade he had to present to his parents, his good boy false self, had been running on parallel lines with his inner world. He had witnessed his father lie about his affairs to his mother with casual ease. On a more practical level, he had no fear now of being exposed. He had lawyers behind the public relations team who manicured his image, and anyway, it was in everyone's financial interest – corporations, the media – to keep it clean.

Before he became a father he said 'I would rather have no children than one child'. This is a rare implicit public admission that his childhood had been less than perfect and seems to address the fact that he had had to carry all his parents' expectations. The arrival of the first of his two children in 2006 did nothing to change his philandering but the death of his father did. His sexual hunger became a frenzy. He began picking up women in bars just ten minutes' walk from his home and now he sometimes slept with them in his marital bed. His behaviour became riskier and riskier. Not long after the birth of his second child he said 'I have been blessed...I love being a husband and father. It's who I am'. Yet he was flaunting his sexual profligacy, a desperado in search of the next fix, a car crash waiting to happen. On the evening of 27 November, 2009, his car literally crashed and his downfall began.

Tiger ran out of his home barefooted and climbed into his black Cadillac. Accelerating away, he lost control and crashed into a tree. Subsequent investigations showed no signs of a head injury, yet he seems to have been in a semi-conscious fugue state afterwards. He did not respond to questions, his eyes rolling up in his eyeballs.

A week before, the *National Enquirer* magazine had run a story with explicit details of an affair he had had. His public relations people had not been concerned because *Enquirer* reports are generally treated as works of fiction by the rest of the media. However, the crash received worldwide coverage. Within a short time, a voicemail from Tiger to a cocktail waitress in Los Angeles was widely reported on the Internet and migrated into the mainstream media. The waitress had 600 texts to support her claim of an affair and the floodgates opened. Dozens of women came forward reporting their liaisons with him. Within an astonishingly short period of time, the Tiger brand became toxic. He had become the world's most famous sex addict.

The philanderings of famous men are so well known and commonplace as to be unsurprising. Whether it be Michael Douglas or Russell Brand, we have heard it all before. One view of celebrity promiscuity is that it is a simple matter of opportunity. Even male gargoyles seem to attract many more women once they become famous. Indeed, there is evidence that women[52] who sleep with high status (rich) men have more orgasms. There is no doubt that men are more prone to casual encounters than women. In a famous study,[53] an attractive young man and a similar woman walked around a campus asking opposite-sexed students if they would consider sleeping with them, then and there. None of the women who were propositioned by the man agreed to the plan, whereas a high proportion of the men were only too happy to oblige the woman.

Fame increases attractiveness but the sort of people who become famous are a group with personalities making them prone to promiscuity. There is good evidence that a high proportion[54] were already narcissists before they became famous. Narcissists are more prone to promiscuity.[55] Since narcissists are also more likely to have many psychopathic traits (like lack of empathy and selfishness), and since the psychopathic are also more promiscuous, this increases the likelihood of promiscuity. The same is true of the Machiavellian: the Dark Triad of narcissism, psychopathy and Machiavellianism is a personality constellation prone to both exceptional achievement and promiscuity.[56] Tiger has many of these traits.

Another common concept is that of the addictive personality. Impulsivity is one of the traits in the Dark Triad and it makes promiscuity more likely. The idea that they have an addictive personality has proved useful as a way of thinking about themselves for people with many forms of compulsion, particularly alcoholics and drug abusers. The Twelve Steps Programme helpfully promotes total abstinence, enabling many people to take the initial move away from their addiction,[57] although there can be problems in sustaining this for some people.[58] The programme implicitly endorses the concept that addictions are interchangeable and that it is a genetic propensity. In fact, there is no evidence whatsoever that addicts of any kind have differences in their DNA which make them significantly more at risk than non-addicts, this is wholly without scientific foundation. Rather, there is considerable evidence that childhood maltreatment puts them more at risk.[59] Less well known is a particular factor in the case of high achievers known as the problem of 'ego depletion'.

Good and bad self-restraint

Exceptional self-control is essential for high achievement. It is required by top sports performers and especially golfers. They must practise their skills for hours every day, they have to manipulate their emotions to deal with disappointment after playing shots that do not turn out as intended. For all of us, self-control entails altering our responses in line with internal standards, such as ideals, values or morals. Every day, people use it to resist 'bad' impulses. These impulses might include the wish to eat fattening foods, to be hurtful to partners, to play instead of work, to engage in inappropriate sexual or violent acts, and so on. If we carried out these acts we might feel immediate pleasure but they carry long-term costs, such as incurring punishment or unpopularity for violating rules of behaviour.

Sigmund Freud's point in his famous book *Civilization and its Discontents* was that the cost of repressing our true desires is that they express themselves in other ways which may seem irrational or inexplicable. At a simple level, my decision ten minutes ago not to eat a fattening cake could result in a stroppy response to a request from my child to download a new app for their phone. Having recently suppressed my impulse, I am doubly annoyed by the idea of fulfilling someone else's, even those of my beloved son or daughter. The ferocity of my reaction might be so intense that it seems inappropriate to the stimulus. The displacement of my repressed desire could also lead to a redoubling of its strength. It might be that, after several days of cake-denial, on attending the birthday party of one of my children's friends, I suddenly engage in an orgy of cake consumption when offered some.

Over one hundred experiments (mostly conducted in the last decade[60]) show that after having to engage in self-control, we are more easily tempted to behave in impulsive, out-of-control ways: if we are good, it makes us more at risk of being bad. This could help to explain how some highly controlled high achievers are prone to act in promiscuous ways. It goes some way to explaining those otherwise puzzling incidents we read about entailing indecent acts by judges or politicians in public places.

Forcing yourself to do what you do not want to, using self-discipline, means that subsequently other parts of yourself seem to be more able to grab the controls and steer you in 'bad' directions. Our capacity to suppress ourselves and persist in dutiful tasks is depleted, and we are at greater risk of succumbing to short-term pleasure-seeking.

For instance, in one of four seminal experiments,[61] students were placed in a situation where there was the tempting smell and sight of chocolate cookies but they were encouraged instead to eat radishes. Afterwards, the cookie-deprived persisted for less time on an insoluble jigsaw than the ones allowed to eat cookies: suppressing the urge to eat them reduced staying power on the task. Since those studies,[62] controlling one's thoughts, managing one's emotions or overcoming unwanted impulses (like drinking alcohol, smoking cigarettes, eating fattening foods) have been tested. Exercising such self-control has been shown variously to lead to eating among dieters, overspending, aggression after being provoked, lack of kindness in response to a partner's bad behaviour, the telling of more lies and exaggerated racism in people already prone to it. When people choose water instead of alcohol[63] in experimental settings, they subsequently find it harder not to binge on booze. The more the person was already prone to a lot of alcohol, the greater the subsequent loss of control. When people put a positive gloss on their lives it subsequently reduces their self-control.[64] It has also been shown to have that effect on enactment of sexual impulses. All of which evidence is consistent with the idea that, having had to be so self-controlled as a result of his childhood maltreatment, Tiger may have been more prone to sexual incontinence.

This makes sense, and yet it is also common sense that self-control is essential for success in most spheres of life. Indeed, the evidence shows that people with good self-control are more likely to do better academically and in their careers, and to have better mental health.[65] Low self-control is associated with the opposite: relative failure at school and work, greater mental illness. It seems like a conundrum. How can people who are self-controlled be made more impulsive, because ego-depleted, yet also be more successful and mentally healthier?

The main theory to explain ego depletion is that self-control is a finite resource and that when it gets used up, we become uncontrolled. Some studies have found that people have diminished glucose levels following self-control.[66] In those studies, if glucose is added to the bloodstream, ego depletion ends. However, other studies have not found such a simple chemical relationship, suggesting that the process may be more complicated than a purely physical one.[67] Rather than regarding the energy model of willpower as literal, many authors have proposed it is figurative.

Richard Ryan and his colleagues have built up a large body of evidence that a sense of autonomy – self-determination – is crucial for human thriving. They have shown that this derives from a childhood and subsequent environment in which 'intrinsic' motives and goals are allowed to evolve, rather than doing things in order to please authorities like parents, teachers and bosses, what they call 'extrinsic' motivation and goals. It was with this model that Ryan approached the contradictions thrown up by the ego-depletion evidence.[68]

The self-determination model was applied to the issue of choice.[69] The authors pointed out that in previous ego depletion experiments, subjects had not been offered real choices; rather, they had been pressured into one course of action rather than another. Sure enough, when given real choice, allowed to be truly autonomous, there was no ego depletion. For example, this was true of students given the option of writing an essay for or against the teaching of psychology in secondary school. Those who truly opposed it could do so; those who did not, could put that view. By contrast, another group of students were instructed which case they had to make and indeed, ego depletion succeeded such loss of autonomy. It did not do so if the students made a free choice of the position they took.

Activities that are externally driven, like the pursuit of money or to obey authority figures, require more self-control and result in more ego depletion than ones more freely chosen. In the first of three experiments,[70] students were paid not to laugh at a funny film or alternatively, simply paid to participate. Those paid not to laugh were more depleted. In the second experiment, participants were paid to describe their perfect day and to use as few 'filler' words, like 'ummm', as possible (requiring self-control). One group were told they would only be paid if they used less than 15 fillers, the other were told they would be paid however they performed, although they were asked to use as few fillers as possible. Those put under external pressure by the threat of no payment were more depleted afterwards. Their sense of autonomy was lowered. The third experiment was as in the second, except that an additional group were included who were solely asked to describe their perfect day with no mention of the need to avoid fillers, so they had no sense of external pressure whatsoever. Sure enough, they had the least loss of autonomy, which, in turn, predicted their lower degree of ego depletion. The conclusion was that 'Self-control that feels more externally determined is more depleting than self-control that feels more personally chosen ... it appears that even small changes in feelings of autonomy surrounding the activity can affect how depleting the task is.' Two further studies supported those conclusions.[71]

Tiger's fall as ego-depletion

Ryan's theory could explain some of Tiger's compulsive sexual behaviour. Despite appearances – on the golf course he seemed a man with an astonishing capacity to control his fate – he had very little sense of self-determination. His phenomenal golfing discipline from a very young age was driven by fear of an emotionally abusive mother and a bullying, game-playing father. Severely ego-depleted, he used risky sex – and it became ever riskier following the death of his tyrannical father – as a way to restore the balance. That is not to say there were not other factors. He was world famous, handsome and extremely rich, giving him access to a great many willing women. He was also feeling emptied by his Marketing Character, lonely and needy, and used sex to fill the emotional hole. But ego-depletion also probably played an important role.

For Marketing Character Tiger, the damage to the brand that resulted from the public revelation of his sex addiction was almost disastrous. After brief deliberation, the corporations worked out their response. The golfing equipment companies decided it was in their interest to stick by him, while those who had solely sought to add lustre to their reputations dumped him. Accenture, for example, withdrew their sponsorship with a remarkably frank statement of how they wished to position themselves in relation to this person-product. With a large peg plugged on to their corporate nose to reduce the unsavoury smell, they stated that Tiger's 'achievements on the golf course have been a powerful metaphor for business success in Accenture's advertising'. However, they felt that 'he is no longer the right representative' for their advertisements. With pious sanctity, they wished him and his family the best. What they really meant was that they wanted nothing more to do with him and he would have to fend for himself.

In his public statements, Tiger was initially reluctant to admit he had been a wildly sexually promiscuous husband. However, having served his time in a sex addiction residential clinic, he emerged with a new marketing brand, that of the penitent. There was nowhere else to go. He (or his publicist) produced a persuasively remorseful speech: 'I thought I could get away with whatever I wanted to. I felt that I had worked hard my entire life and deserved to enjoy all the temptations around me. I felt I was entitled. Thanks to the money and fame, I didn't have to go far to find them ... It's up to me to start living a life of integrity'. Integrity was a good word. He had been dis-integrated, living multiple sex lives that did not join up. When he crashed his car it would appear he was close to a psychotic episode, a complete lack of coherences. At the risk of stretching the famous metaphor, it might be said that he blew his mind out in a car, he didn't notice that the lights had changed.

The divisions in himself had been extreme since very early in his life, having to keep his true wishes, insofar as he ever knew what they were, private from his parents. Developing so young a false self, what my father termed Premature Ego Development,[72] interfered with him knowing what he wanted. His father hijacked him as a vehicle for his own narcissism. His mother spanked and glared away any resistance, and also demanded perfection. Poor Tiger had to get what pleasures that were truly for himself where he could, and like so many famous men, that was through admiration from and power over compliant young women (drugs are not an option for most professional sportsmen). It had seemed completely natural to live this double life. He truly did not have a sense of self-contradiction when moving between his husband/father self and that of the lothario.

However, Elin Nordegren was unable to forgive his disintegration. While she had been aware from the outset that he would be away from home for nine months of the year on the golf circuit, the reality of his infidelity and the fact that he clearly had significant emotional investment in his innumerable affairs – these were often not just one-night stands – proved too much for her. A child of divorce, she had to accept that it had happened to her. Whereas Earl had managed to keep his other life secret from Kultida, although she may well have suspected it was going on, that was not possible for the famous Chosen One.

Elin received around $100 million in the divorce settlement. The Woods corporation, so to speak, had to accept this 10 per cent loss of its net assets as a write-off for his infidelities. The product was damaged by its loss of brand sponsors but the money kept flowing from golf equipment manufacturers. Following his fall, although Tiger's golfing remained excellent enough for him to win the number one spot several times on the American Tour in the succeeding years, he has yet to win another major.

Before the fall, then aged 33 with 14 majors under his belt, no one doubted that he would exceed the 18 majors of Jack Nicklaus. He has not won one since 2008. Tiger seems a completely different character. The narcissistic flair and sense of omnipotence are no longer evident, except in brief patches. The internal relationship with Earl on which they were based seems to have changed. He can be seen talking to Earl, asking him for guidance, as he goads himself to do something special. But the Son of God is alone now. Without his father, he lacks the extra dimension, the almost divine intervention which enabled the near perfect performances he achieved in some of his early victories, such as the first one at the Masters in 1997.

Emotional health and pathology in exceptional achievers

The dominant model of mental illness is that it is a genetic destiny. It cannot be cured, only managed. The main methods of management offered by the British National Health Service are drugs and Cognitive Behavioural Therapy (CBT). As noted in TAKEAWAY 2 of Chapter 1, CBT explicitly discourages clients from considering the childhood causes of their problems. The medical and psychological establishments largely continue to ignore the persuasive evidence that the main cause of mental illness is childhood maltreatment.

One of the ways in which the received account of mental illness as genetic and needing management through drugs and CBT is promulgated is through public figures. After Tony Blair's departure as prime minister, a number of the leading figures from his close circle publicly announced that they had suffered from depression. His publicist, Alastair Campbell, has been open about his battle with depression and the use of anti-depressants in its management. Labour-supporting comedian Stephen Fry made two BBC TV documentaries in which he embraced a diagnosis of bipolar disorder, including genetic causes. Comedian Rory Bremner, another Labour supporter, made a BBC Radio 4 documentary about how he suffers from adult attention deficit hyperactivity disorder (ADHD).

The media keeps up a steady drip of stories that ultimately serve the interests of the drug companies and the purveyors of a management model of mental illness, like practitioners of CBT. The implication of such yarns is that you should grin and bear it. Take the pills, do your CBT course and keep your chin up.

None of the right lessons get learnt from the famous examples that the media purveys. Two particularly dispiriting examples are the rugby star Jonny Wilkinson, and the England cricketer, Marcus Trescothick.

Trescothick's autobiography[73] makes baleful reading. Having suffered severe depression, he shows few signs of understanding its true causes. Nor does he appear to believe he will ever escape it. Instead, he buys into the medical account, taking antidepressants and undergoing CBT. He quotes from a book by a psychiatrist to explain it: 'Depressive illness is not a psychological or emotional state and is not a mental illness. It is a not a form of madness. It is a physical illness.' When he starts his CBT, the therapist tells him 'You are exhausted. You can see your body is saying that's enough. It needs a rest...Why has it happened?...the exhaustion you are suffering from has led you to be physically depressed.'

Although Trescothick does not realise it, his autobiography provides strong clues as to the real causes. Both his parents were fanatical about cricket. At the time of his birth in 1971, referring to the infant Marcus, a local newspaper article had the headline 'On the Team for 1991?' His father is quoted in the article as saying 'I was secretly hoping for a boy, and he will have every encouragement to become a cricketer when he grows up'. His mother recalls that he had a cricket bat 'thrust' into his hands at 11 months old. At two, his mother was bowling to him at every available moment, at four he was smashing balls around the house, breaking windows without his parents minding. At six he was telling friends he would be a cricketer when he grew up. But at 11, he went away from home for a cricketing tour with his team and suffered severe anxiety, he was 'terrified'. From then on he always felt deeply upset if he had to be away from his parents or family.

When Trescothick regales his CBT therapist with the story of his severe separation anxiety, there is no attempt to explore its meaning and its connection to his subsequent anxiety as a professional cricketer at being away from his wife and family. It is hard to imagine a more blatant clue that Trescothick was suffering from severe attachment disorder, something that would have its roots in his relationship with his parents. Nor is there any sign that the therapist explored the extent to which his parents placed a huge load of expectation upon him.

The book ends with Trescothick quoting extensively from the letters of 'fellow-sufferers'. He reports how he has gained enormous solace from coming out as a depressive, he has enabled others with his illness to feel they are not alone. But he is. At the end, he is left with the conviction that he has a physical illness that he can do nothing to cure. He does not notice that, long after he ceased to be physically exhausted – the cause offered by his therapist – he is still depressed. It is tragic to think that a therapy that explored his early relationship with his parents and their ambitions for him would still be able to cure him.

Jonny Wilkinson's story is equally disheartening.[74] Right at the start, he tells us he is not sure if he was born a perfectionist or if he had unconsciously chosen it. Aged seven, he has to jump out of his father's car to be sick on the way to play a rugby match, so filled with fear and doom is he at the thought of the game not going well. He is fine on training days but on match days, wakes early with his heart racing with fear. He tells his parents he cannot go to the game, pleading with them to tell the coach he cannot play that day. It is like this for every match. But that is not all, it is the same with going to school. Every morning he goes crying to his mother, desperate to avoid failure. just one letter out of place on a spelling test will throw him into a panic.

When we learn about his childhood, surprise, surprise, and in accord with the evidence on perfectionism presented above, it turns out his father is a rugby player and Wilkinson is desperate to please him. This is illustrated in a particularly sad story. While still young, he goes on a local radio station to talk about winning a competition. He forgets to mention how much he owes to his father and he beats himself up about it for months afterwards, showering the radio station with letters asking them to let him mention his father. Like Trescothick, it turns out that he is made insecure by being away from home. He cannot sleep, lying there feeling 'I need my dad'.

While Wilkinson's ailment appears to be compulsiveness and perfectionism (and no small measure of self-absorption), there is equally much obliviousness to the probable causes. No therapists appear to work through with him how his childhood has created these states. In his very first comment, he has the clue: that his perfectionism was neither a genetic destiny nor something he had chosen. He is asking the wrong questions. The missing bit is that he had to be perfect in order to fulfil his role in his family drama, to play his part in the script. Like Trescothick, we leave him at the end of his book trapped. He sees no hope of understanding and altering his perfectionism.

Conclusion

At the outset of this chapter, I asked three questions that are normally ignored:

> 〉 What is the reason why some people do 10,000 hours of practice but not others?
> 〉 Of those that do complete the 10,000 hours, what causes the difference in success of the winners and the also-rans?
> 〉 Of those that do 10,000 hours and become exceptional, what causes some to be desperately unhappy, others to be emotionally healthy?

There are some strong clues to the answers in the Tiger and Polger stories.

The answer to the first one is that in pretty well all the recorded cases of people who practised for 10,000 hours, as a result of their family drama, their parents had a strong investment in the child doing so – this child, rather than the other siblings. Remember Wolfgang Mozart and his sister?

The answer to the second question is that the unique combination of factors in the family drama produced the right blend of mental and physical attributes. In Tiger's case, his father was a cunning, devious man who manipulated his son, his mother a ruthless taskmaster. They managed to make it a matter of life or death for him to be the best of the best. Whether nurtured by coercion or by encouragement of the intrinsic, the winners emerge out of unique family dynamics that enable them to deal with the pressure at the very top.

With regard to the third question, we can see that Wilkinson and Trescothick are examples of exceptional achievers who ended up miserable. While neither of them provide sufficiently precise details as to how their nurture led them to be exceptionally miserable, the scientific evidence presented in previous chapters provides plenty of clues as to what might have happened. For example, Wilkinson's perfectionism was clearly maladaptive – his best was not good enough. The evidence suggests this happens when love is conditional on performance. His extreme anxiety, expressed in compulsive thought patterns, is very likely to have resulted from feeling insecure in his early years. The same is strongly indicated regarding Trescothick. His terror at being separated from his family suggests an insecurity that resulted from his nurture in infancy and as a toddler.

With Woods, we have a startling contrast from the Polgar sisters. They come across as girls and women who played chess for fun, as well as to win, and as offspring who felt unconditional love from their parents. By contrast, Woods was in a totalitarian family regime from the beginning, one that had its roots in Earl Woods' unfulfilled ambitions.

What will it take for our system to change so that the likes of Woods, Wilkinson and Trescothick can get the kind of help they need, not to mention the many millions of less successful people who share their kind of background? The genetic myths of talent and mental illness continue to be promulgated. The miserable talented will continue not to have the childhood causes of their problems properly treated. Books promoting Tiger Mothering will continue to be given mass publicity, and more or less distressed prodigies will continue to be produced.

There is a limit to how long a society can promulgate ideas which are false and harmful. Just as buried childhood trauma always finds a way to express itself in the individual, eventually the truth has a way of forcing itself into the consciousness of societies.

SO WHAT? – 3 TAKEAWAYS

ONE: Distinguish good ambitions from bad, using emotional health as the arbiter

In recent years, there has been a big emphasis placed on happiness as an internal goal but I profoundly disagree with this. Happiness is a temporary state, mostly derived from material pleasures like food or sex. It is a mug's game to chase happiness, a chimera.

More meaningful and realistic is the concept of emotional health (described in my book *How To Develop Emotional Health*). This has six components:

> ⟩ Living in the present
> ⟩ Authenticity
> ⟩ Insightfulness
> ⟩ Fluid, open relationships with others
> ⟩ Playfulness
> ⟩ Vivacity

Emotional health is the sense that what is happening, is happening now. It is first-hand, immediate, rather than only knowing what was experienced when you reflect about it later. You are, as the sports commentators put it, 'in the zone'.

You feel real rather than false. You are comfortable in your skin: you do not wish you could be someone else, nor do you look down on others for not being like you. You know what you are thinking and feeling, even if sometimes it is only that you know that you don't know.

You have your own consistent ethical code which enables you to distinguish right from wrong. You are stoical in the face of adversity, realistic in your ideas and often seem to be wise in your judgements. You have the capacity for insight into your own actions. You can sometimes spot in advance when you are about to make a mistake and avoid it, or can see when you are reacting irrationally to a situation and correct yourself. This gives you that nectar of the soul, the capacity for choice, and therefore, for change. Such self-awareness is what sets us apart from other animals.

In your moment-to-moment dealings with other people, you are a good judge of what they are feeling and thinking. You are able to live in the place where self and others meet without tyranny. You do not get 'jammed on transmit', nor 'jammed on receive'. You live without flooding or dominating others, nor are flooded or dominated.

You are adaptable, but without losing yourself. When in social or professional situations which demand a measure of falsehood, you can 'put on a face to meet the faces that you meet' without losing your sense of authenticity. Your real self is as close as possible to the one you are presenting to others, depending on what is feasible. If a lie is necessary, you lie.

Your vivacity – the liveliness you bring to any situation – is striking, but it is not frenetic and does not smack of 'keeping busy' to distract from bad feelings. You are spontaneous and always searching for the playful way to handle things, retaining a child-like sparkle, a conviction that life is to be enjoyed, not endured. You are not bogged down in needy, childish, greedy, game-playing manipulation.

You may suffer depressions, rages, phobias, all manner of problems from time to time. You make mistakes. But because of your emotional health, you are far better at living in the present and finding the value in your existence, whatever is going on, making you resilient.

When people leave your company, they often feel better able to function, more vivacious and playful. Your emotional wellness rubs off on them. You are no martyr but you are widely regarded as a valuable contributor to your social and professional circles.

Have you ever met anyone like this? No, nor have I. None of us are emotionally healthy at all times, in all these ways. For most, it is only in some respects, some of the time. A very few are, in many respects, much of the time – perhaps 5 or 10 per cent of us. Emotional health is a state that we can approximate to, more or less, and is not absolute, like happiness.

There is, of course, a constant tension between the pursuit of emotional health and of the glittering prizes of social and career success. In the society in which we live, it tends to be assumed that acquisition of wealth or the possession of beauty will bring emotional health. This is far from what I believe to be the case.

Although there are no studies testing the matter, I suspect that the emotionally healthy are more to be found among people with relatively low conventional aspirations. It is hard to imagine how someone who works seven days a week for decades can be emotionally healthy; the pressures to focus on the future, to be game-playing rather than playful and so on, would seem to make that unlikely.

The best way to arbitrate between good and bad ambitions is by asking whether they will nurture emotional health. The challenge in our own lives, and in the motives and goals we nurture in our children, is to balance the pursuit of emotional health against the pursuit of conventional achievement. The best solution to that enigma is self-determination. If you and your children feel you are doing things because they matter to you, rather than to people-please, you are most likely to achieve success and emotional health.

TWO: Avoid ego-depletion through self-determination

Ego-depletion does not occur when you feel self-determined: i.e., when you do things because you want to, not in order to please others. Of course, this is not as simple as it sounds. A good deal of pleasing myself entails pleasing others.

Part of enjoying my weekend or holiday is making sure that my children are enjoying theirs (not least because they will make my life hell if I do not). If driving them to and from their friends makes them happy, while it may be a pain in the neck, it makes me happier. If I want this book to be good, that includes adapting it so it will appeal to you. Tiresome and exhausting though it may seem at the time, I might need to respond to suggestions from my editor or agent in order to achieve this.

How are we to work out where to draw the line between pleasing others and ourselves? The distinction has its roots in how our parents cared for us.

It requires a strong sense of self, originally created by having our needs met in infancy. Subsequently, if our parents respected our autonomy, we know what we think and feel. At the same time, we need our parents to have had aspirations for us. When benevolently nurtured, with our parents not living their dreams through us, they provide identity.

On top of this, we have constant battles between what is 'for me' and what is for a future me. The tension is between our short-term and long-term desires, requiring decisions about whether to delay gratification, now, to achieve a longer-term goal, then. If I do not want to get fat in the future, I had better not eat this ice cream, now. If my child wants to get those exam grades, they had better put off watching that episode of their favourite TV programme and do their homework. This requires identity, knowing who you want to be. It also demands self-control.

As discussed in Chapter 4, all toddlers must learn to find the pause button and that depends on nurture. Whether about to grab another child's toy or in the midst of a temper tantrum, when self-regulation is still in its infancy, this process needs the scaffolding provided by a responsive adult. But the problem of self-discipline does not end at age three. Insofar as we are feeling coerced to go to work, to go out to supper with people we do not really like and so on, self-discipline is demanded, a grinding of a conscientious gearbox with no oil in it. The struggle is to colonise these experiences and make them our own.

Cognitive behavioural therapy (CBT) suggests you can do that by mental tricks, like reframing. Just by telling yourself that your job as a supermarket checkout operative is not all bad, that it has this and that advantages (you get paid, it's not as stressful as your previous job and so forth), you can change how you experience it. This is bilge.

No amount of sophistry can make the unwanted, wanted. What we need is identity and the ambition for emotional health in order to satisfyingly do the unwanted. Very few things are really all bad. Without having to call black white (CBT), if it is from a position of knowing who we are, we can find the enjoyable in almost any situation. Identity and the sense of self can transcend the most boring job or supper when it is accompanied by emotional health.

Just by aspiring to live in the present, have two-way communication, insight, playfulness, vivacity and authenticity, it is possible to enjoy almost anything. The feeling of neediness and hunger for 'something for me' and 'me-time' dissolves.

THREE: Have the right ambitions for your children

The average parent is not hoping for an exceptional achiever, like the ones described in this chapter. Yet their stories apply directly to you. Whether you long for a happy child who would be satisfied working in a supermarket, or whether you are Earl and Kultida Woods, there is no difference in the kind of mechanisms by which ambitions are transferred from parent to child – learning (teaching, modelling and identification), and maltreatment and love.

Your children need you to have hopes for them, otherwise they are liable to lack identity. In middle-class homes, superficially, the hopes can usually be boiled down to a wish for them to be reasonably well mannered yet spontaneous and happy, and for them to get 'reasonably good' exam results.

At a deeper level, we have all kinds of implicit ambitions for them. These have their roots in what your parents' aspirations were for you. The starter for one is the child's gender.

There are still many mothers who feel that they have not yet fulfilled the opportunities provided by feminism, because of the nurture they received. They often have high-achieving daughters. They may maintain that it's most important to be happy and that exam results do not matter for the sons, but subtly convey a very different message to their daughters.

Equally, old-fashioned sexism still exists as regards paternal aspirations: in the end, the daughter is going to get married and have kids; the son will need to be a breadwinner, the father may think, even if he does not say it.

A good deal of what passes down is benign. You may be an upwardly mobile person who has become the lawyer, accountant or doctor that one or both of your parents might have been. In many such cases, a good deal of love went with the nurture of this achievement and you are living a satisfied life.

Sometimes the aspirations are largely modelled. Perhaps your parents were caring people whose wise didacticism and concerned engagement with the community provided a strong model. You feel most comfortable working in a caring profession as a result. The same applies to other fields, be that family businesses or commercial professions.

Then again, you may be working in a job that is a reaction against your parents. Perhaps you are a female professional whose father was 'a failure' and whose mother was 'only' a housewife. You wanted to do something that brought in a decent income and made an impact on the world.

Alternatively, you may be someone who feels deeply frustrated by your lack of achievement. This could be because you reacted against parental pressure – a fair number of high achievers at school do not shine afterwards, 'first in school, last in life'.

Often crucial is the intergenerational transmission described in the last chapter. You may be part of a family tradition which is quite happy to achieve no more than your forebears. More common in an era in which self-advancement is strongly fostered in schools, and by the media and by politicians, is a wish to be exceptional. The commonest ambition among boys is to be a Premiership footballer, among girls to be a pop star or model.

Whatever the details, the point is that it behoves us parents to work hard at analysing where our ambitions for our children came from. Having sorted that out, the crucial distinction is between putting pressure on, and having fun with, them in the pursuit of the goals. Insofar as you are able to model emotional health, they will follow that. The details of the ambitions will be insignificant.

Conclusion

It's the Environment, Stupid!

If it is true that the Human Genome Project has disproved the importance of genes in explaining why children are like parents, why traits run in families and why siblings are different, here are my choices, from the many, for the top five major implications.

ONE: Genes do not explain why the rich are rich, and the poor, poor. If so, changing our society could largely eradicate poverty. Given the right parenting and a supportive society, the children of the poor could perform at school and in their careers just as well as those of the rich.

TWO: Genes do not explain why some of us excel and not others. If so, almost anyone can be talented. We need an education system which makes this assumption and implements it, like that in Finland.[1]

THREE: Genes do not explain mental illness. I have provided a mass of evidence in this book that the combination of early nurture and the kind of society we are in largely explains it. If so, change the way we parent and change our society, and we could largely eradicate mental illness.

FOUR: Genes do not explain our individual psychology. The assumption that there is such a thing as 'bad seed' needs to be eradicated. If so, genetic testing for psychological traits is a waste of money and should be exposed as fraudulent. Adopted children should be discouraged from seeking out their birth parents, insofar as they are hoping to get clues as to why they are like they are because they assume they have inherited traits from them. As with all of us, they need to examine the nurture provided to them by those who raised them. Genes do not explain why traits run in families. Schools and universities should cease teaching students the idea that genes play a central role in transmission of psychological traits. The myth that we are carcasses for reproducing our selfish genes should be replaced with the fact that traits are passed down through patterns of nurture.

FIVE: If genes are so unimportant, we need to revise how we raise our children and how we treat emotional distress in adults. At present, official psychology encourages mothers to leave their infants to cry, then, when the infant becomes a confused and angry toddler, to put them on naughty steps or leave them to stew in their poisoned juice alone in their rooms. In many cases, desperate to pay the mortgage and to escape their difficult child, the mother returns to work. Mostly against their better judgement, they put the child in day care where their problems are exacerbated by lack of constant security from an adult who knows them well and loves them. As soon as you're born, they make you feel small, by giving you no time instead of it all, said John Lennon.

In the middle classes, a crazed obsession with early learning means the miserable three- to six-year-old is assailed with reading and arithmetic when it should be enjoying the wonderful, rich La-La land of children's play. Their hyperactivity and angry behaviour is medicated with Ritalin, rather than understanding and attempts by therapists to help the parents engage with them and reset the emotional thermostat. Increasingly, a place is found on the autistic spectrum disorder for the ones who have shut down and ceased responding. In ADHD and ASD, the parent is told the child has a biogenic disease which is incurable, only manageable by strict routines as well as drugs.

There's room at the top they're telling you still, but first you must learn how to smile as you kill, said John Lennon. Having endured an ego-depleting education system which programmes them to tick exam boxes rather than acquire a love of learning and a capacity to question the status quo, at university they medicate their misery with binge drinking, illegal stimulants, loveless sex, and an obsession with physical appearance, fame and consumption. Emerging into the job market already prone to depression and anxiety, when they visit their GP they are told they have an incurable illness which requires antidepressants or cognitive behaviour therapy, neither of which usually help much.

Instead of all this we need to enable parents to be with their children and provide the love they need, not routines that are there for the benefit of parents. When both parents work we need a national nanny care system, not national day care – the politicians who advocate day care do not use it for their own children, they have nannies. Why is it a case of day care for the poor and middle class, nannies for the ruling elite? (We could easily afford it – how about selling off some off some of the 1 per cent of the British landmass owned by the Ministry of Defence?) When adults are distressed, rather than the Elastoplast of CBT and antidepressants (although they can reduce symptoms, most have considerable side-effects, notably the loss of the sex drive) we need long-term therapies that illuminate the childhood causes and provide a new emotional platform for how relationships can be. We could afford that too.

Alas, I am not optimistic that these implications will be accepted immediately. It can take decades or even centuries for the Establishment in a society to accept it has been completely wrong about one of its primary tenets. Anyone hoping for rapid change in beliefs should recall the fate of Galileo Galilei in the sixteenth century, whose advocacy of the idea that the earth revolved around the sun nearly proved fatal to him. In that case, religion proved the barrier to truth; in the modern age a major obstruction is the media. There is an increasing reluctance or incapacity of the media to properly research the truth of the stories it tells. It will take time for the genetic religion to be discarded, Robert Plomin's faith in heritability even when genes have been disproved.

Consider the case of mental illness and genetics. Particularly in the last 20 years, the scientific and medical establishment, heavily influenced by the drug companies, have succeeded in persuading the media that mental illness (as well as intelligence and achievement) should be understood as a genetically inherited destiny. That is bizarre, given that the Human Genome Project has virtually proved the opposite during this period.

The trusted journals of the establishment, like the *British Journal of Psychiatry*, continue to publish and endorse very questionable, if not plain dishonest, views. The science correspondents in the media, like Tom Feilden of the BBC, continue to give distorted coverage of the findings of studies that, when looked at closely, do not support the exaggerated claims made for them.

I can vouch for how hard it is to change this situation, having made several attempts. For example, on 28 February 2013, on the BBC *Today* programme the presenter Sarah Montague heralded the publication of a new study in *The Lancet* medical journal.[2] She introduced the study as proving that five major psychiatric illnesses 'all appeared to be caused by variations in just four areas of our genome'. Asking for clarification of the meaning of the study from Tom Feilden, he stated that 'I think it is really quite an important moment for the whole field of mental health . . . a handful of the same or similar gene variants or regions on two particular chromosomes are playing a key role in a number of this big five, if you like, mental disorders'.

The idea that this was an important moment for the whole field of mental health turned out to be a grotesque misrepresentation of the significance of this study. In fact, the scientific paper revealed that these variants were able to explain almost nothing; Feilden got it wrong when he claimed they had been proven to be playing a 'key' role. Possessing the variants was unable to explain hardly any of the difference between mentally ill and mentally healthy people. Yes, these variants clustered in the mentally ill, but they explained hardly any of the reason for the illness. It is hard to escape the conclusion that Feilden had simply regurgitated the blurb from the publicists' handouts.

I raised my objections to the coverage on the BBC *Feedback* programme on 6 March. No one from the *Today* programme was willing to appear.

Meanwhile, as has been happening for ten years, scientific paper after paper continues to be published showing that genes explain either very little or none of why some people are mentally ill. In October 2013, a telling example was published,[3] entitled 'No genetic influence for childhood behaviour problems from DNA analysis'. This was truly a remarkable finding, given that the study had taken every imaginable step then possible to identify such DNA differences.

I forwarded it to the *Today* programme, asking them to balance their coverage by reporting this paper to publicise the true situation: all HGP studies of human psychological traits, not just this one, show little or no causal effect of specific gene variants. I got a reply from Dominic Groves, the assistant editor. He wrote that 'I'm afraid we have decided not to pursue the paper you forwarded to us. I would however reiterate that we strongly reject any suggestion of inaccuracy or bias in our coverage on this issue. We shall continue to explore significant new insights and developments in this area as and when they arise'. No further explanation was offered. Why was a paper appearing to prove that genes play no role in autism, ADHD and conduct disorder not a 'significant new insight'? Sure enough, the commitment to the misreporting of genetic findings continued with a *Today* report about an obesity gene on 29 May 2014, and there have been further ones since.

Yet I do not despair. Eventually the medical and scientific community will be forced to publicly acknowledge the true findings of the Human

Genome Project. When that happens, the science correspondents of the BBC and newspapers will fall into line.

In the meantime, if you are still reading these words I have to assume that you have found some value in this book. My earnest message to you can be condensed into three simple suggestions.

Firstly, do whatever it takes to understand how the past is operating in your present. As well as how you were nurtured as a child, do not forget to take a long hard look at how your ancestors were nurtured.

Secondly, using those insights, change the way you relate to your children, if they are still young or even if they are grown up.

Thirdly, allow yourself to believe that we could radically alter our society for the better if we changed the way we cared for children. A system which puts the profits of the few ahead of the mental health of our children is not inevitable.

Of all the points I have made in this book, there is one which I feel is the most important. In most developed nations we are obsessed with passing wealth to our offspring and in the age of supposed meritocracy, with encouraging them, usually through pressure to do well at school, to surpass our levels of material and career success. But once basic levels of affluence are achieved, like a roof over our head and enough to eat, these ambitions dwindle into nothing compared to the alternative which this book offers: passing love and emotional health to our children.

Appendix 1

Not in Your Genes: Time to Accept the Null Hypothesis of the Human Genome Project?

(Reproduced from ATTACHMENT: New Directions in Psychotherapy and Relational Psychoanalysis, Vol. 8, November 2014: pp. 281–96.)

Introduction

The hypothesis of the Human Genome Project (HGP) was that differences in genetic material contribute significantly to explaining why one individual is more likely to possess a trait than another. This would be tested by comparing groups. For example, when 10,000 people suffering from major depressive disorder are compared with 10,000 who do not qualify for this diagnosis, the HGP hypothesises that there will be differences between the two groups in a single gene*, or groups of genes, or in numerous tiny variations in genetic material, that explain a significant (usually regarded as greater than 20 per cent) amount of the reason (known as variance) why one group is depressed and not the other. Replicated in other samples, the HGP expected to establish reliable genetic causes of traits like depression: specific differences in genetic material that were proven to directly contribute to such traits to a significant extent.

The null hypothesis of the HGP is that differences in genetic material play little or no role in explaining why one individual is more likely to possess a trait than another.

It is a little known fact outside the world of those directly concerned with molecular genetics that, so far, the HGP has been unable to identify genes, groups of genes, or small variations in genetic material that explain more than a tiny proportion of why two groups differ in any psychological respect at all. This applies whether it be depression, schizophrenia, anxiety disorders, or any other mental illness. The same is true of mental abilities and of personality. In all cases, genes explain only about 1–5 per cent of the variation (Plomin & Simpson, 2013; Wray et al., 2014). As Robert Plomin, one of the leading figures in the field, put it during an interview with Peter Wilby (the respected ex-editor of the *Independent* newspaper) in the *Guardian* newspaper in 2014, 'I've been looking for these genes for 15 years and I don't have any' (Wilby, 2014).

Although the reader might find it hard to believe, it is completely uncontroversial – an established and oft-repeated fact within the scientific literature – that, so far, genes identified by the HGP explain only 1–5 per cent of the variance between groups for psychological traits of all kinds. This assertion is not an interpretation of the evidence, it is accepted as fact by virtually all scientists working in this field (Wray et al., 2014).

The debate concerns whether the HGP will discover genetic differences explaining more of the variance in the future. So far, to put it bluntly, the HGP has proved that genes play virtually no role in explaining our psychological differences. Precisely at what point the principal scientists in the HGP will accept its null hypothesis is an interesting issue.

The main empirical evidence upon which the HGP hypothesis was based were familial studies of twins and, to a lesser extent, adoptees. For example, twin studies find heritabilities of 50 per cent or more for many major mental illnesses, like schizophrenia and bipolar disorder (Kendler, 2001). They also do so for scores on tests of intelligence (Deary, Johnson, & Houlihan, 2009).

Because there is such a yawning gulf between twin study findings and those of the HGP, rather than simply accepting the null hypothesis, researchers have dubbed the absence of significant findings 'missing heritability'. Ignoring the many strong reasons to doubt the scientific validity of twin studies (James, 2005; Joseph, 2013), the researchers obtained grants to examine larger samples in order to identify this putative absence. When study after study (and there have been hundreds) continued to find virtually no genes explaining significant amounts of variance in traits, hardly any of the researchers even considered the possibility that the heritability was not missing, it simply does not exist – although there have been a handful of exceptions (e.g., Sonuga-Barke, 2010).

As methods for studying differences in genetic material became faster and cheaper, they were able to test for differences at greater and greater numbers of genetic locations. The latest technology can search millions of different locations on each individual's genome in samples of many thousands. On top of that, scientists started to pool their findings to create larger samples.

While they have managed to find some differences in sequencing of DNA* between groups for some illnesses, these differences are unable to explain more than a tiny amount of the variance in illnesses. For example, a recent study examined the genes of 150,000 people, of whom 36,989 had been diagnosed with schizophrenia (Schizophrenia Working Group of the Psychiatric Genomics Consortium, 2014). This is a huge sample. The study identified 108 genetic locations where the DNA sequence in people with schizophrenia tended to be different from those without the disease. Yet, taken together, the total variance that these differences in DNA sequence explained was a paltry 3.4 per cent. An important proviso about this study is that a considerable number of the genetic locations in the study had not been replicated: again and again, studies have purported to find new locations that subsequently turn out not to replicate.

Remarkably, this study was heralded on the BBC *Today* programme as 'a huge breakthrough' (BBC *Today* programme, 2014). Taken at face value, it could be suggested that the study proved that 96.6 per cent of the difference between schizophrenics and non-schizophrenics is non-genetic. If the study was indeed a huge breakthrough, it was because it proved that schizophrenia is almost completely not caused by genes, the exact opposite of the way in which it was portrayed by the BBC.

In this paper, I shall first provide a brief survey of the findings of the HGP regarding mental illness to date. I will then summarise the areas of research that are still held to be promising in establishing a role for genetics in causing mental illness. I will briefly consider the implications of the HGP findings for twin studies and offer an alternative interpretation of their supposed findings of high heritabilities. I will end by considering what will be accepted as evidence for the null hypothesis of the HGP.

The findings of the Human Genome Project for mental illness

Only a few years after the announcement of the mapping of the human genome in 2000, leading figures in the field stated emphatically that they had already established that single 'genes for' psychological traits did not exist. In 2000, with the HGP results about to be published, Robert Plomin predicted that 'within a few years, psychology will be awash with genes associated with behavioral disorders' (Plomin & Crabbe, 2000). For decades Plomin had been predicting genes, or groups thereof, for specific mental illnesses (and for intelligence) in highly influential scientific papers and textbooks for students (Plomin, 1990). His colleague at the Institute of Psychiatry, Peter Mcguffin, had been equally emphatic about genes for schizophrenia (e.g., Plomin, Owen, & Mcguffin, 1994).

By 2003, based on the complete absence of any such genes having emerged from early HGP studies, both had admitted they were wrong in expecting groups of 'genes for' common traits and that the truth was there would be a very large number of tiny variants, each contributing small effects. Only extremely rare disorders would be caused by monogenic, Mendelian genes. For example, in 2005, Plomin and colleagues pronounced that 'Common disorders of the sort seen in child psychology and psychiatry ... are likely to be caused by multiple genes of varying but small effect size' (Harter et al., 2005).

The hunt was on for large numbers of tiny parts of genes, rather than groups of genes, associated with specific mental illnesses. The small effects of each little difference would, together, amount to similar heritabilities to those found in twin studies, it was believed. The method for finding them was called Genome Wide Association (GWA) studies, an atheoretical genetic fishing trip. Instead of starting from the assumption that specific candidate genes would explain differences, researchers started looking for any kind of difference across massive numbers of locations in large samples of people. In 2009, Robert Plomin was bullish about the prospects for GWA studies: 'Conceptual advances ... have led to a revolution in molecular genetic research: genome-wide association ... In just a year's time, GWA studies have come to dominate the gene-hunting literature' (Plomin & Davis, 2009).

There are some three billion base pairs* on the double helix of the DNA of each individual, of which 99 per cent are the same from person to person. The 1 per cent difference is the focus of GWAs. One source of gene variance of particular interest was single-nucleotide polymorphisms (SNP*), entailing an inherited mutation in one nucleotide. At first GWAs targeted hundreds of thousands, and subsequently millions, of gene locations to see if they could find SNPs that correlated with particular mental illnesses.

An alternative target for the fishing trip was copy number variants (CNV*). A CNV is where there has been duplication, insertion, or deletion of stretches of DNA base pairs. These CNVs are mostly not inherited, developing independently of the genes that were passed on from parents. In fact, all of us have CNVs spread around our DNA, up to and including the absence of whole genes, usually without any discernible consequence.

CNVs could not be a major way of identifying genetic inheritance of mental illness, but they might be locations of genetic material differing between the ill and the well.

As techniques became more sophisticated and cheaper, and researchers increasingly pooled their results, larger and larger samples became available, especially in the last five years. In due course, numbers of both SNPs and CNVs were found to be associated with many mental illnesses (Plomin & Simpson, 2013). But individually, the variants explained only minuscule amounts of heritability. When their effects were added all together they continued to explain very little. This cannot be stressed enough: added together, the polygenic findings of GWAs studying SNPs and CNVs continue to be able to explain no more than 1–5 per cent of differences in psychological traits, despite the major investment in large samples (Plomin & Simpson, 2013; Wray et al., 2014).

Psychiatrists were excited to find that most SNPs and CNVs that were associated with schizophrenia were also associated with bipolar disorder. Some of those clusters of both SNPs and CNVs have further been found to overlap in people with autism, and attention deficit hyperactivity disorder (ADHD). Interestingly, GWAs have not had success in finding genes for unipolar depression, despite using very large samples (Major Depressive Disorder Working Group of the Psychiatric GWAs Consortium, 2013). Leaving aside the crucial fact that these clusters provide tiny heritability estimates for any of these mental illnesses, even if the clusters were proven to be more than merely 'noise' from a large fishing trip, it has been pointed out that they seem to undermine the notion of discrete, biologically based illnesses that underpins the Diagnostic and Statistical Manual of mental illnesses.

If all people with numerous major mental illnesses share the same genetic variants, where does that leave the idea of discrete diagnoses of biologically based particular 'illnesses'?

In fact, recent formulations by leading psychiatric scientists suggest that there are no genes that are unique to people with mental illnesses.

For example, Kenneth Kendler, perhaps the most highly regarded such psychiatrist, states that:

> The efforts to ground a categorical model of schizophrenia in Mendelian genetics have failed. The genetic risk for schizophrenia is widely distributed in human populations so that we all carry some degree of risk. (Kendler, 2014)

If that is true, it is difficult to see in what sense particular genes are the cause of schizophrenia in one person but not in another.

The scientists continue to argue that they need ever-larger samples in order to identify what they assume to be hundreds or thousands of tiny differences in nucleotide sequences that will eventually make up the missing heritability. Because whole-genome sequencing will become feasible and affordable for each individual before long, it should be possible to establish definitively what combinations of sequences are associated with which traits, and what contribution they make to them, if any. The scientists believe that when cheap enough technology is available to scan all of the three billion nucleotide base pairs in large samples of people, the genetic truth will out. They now tend to believe that, rather than there being clusters of genetic profiles for specific traits, the profiles will be for a variety of interrelated psychologies a proneness to a variety of mental illnesses overlapping with a variety of mental capacities and personality traits. In this Brave New World, the geneticists continue to dream of the day when all newborns are routinely given a genome-wide scan in order to help advise parents on which kind of environment to provide, physically and emotionally (Plomin & Simpson, 2013, p. 1274).

So far, the HGP has proved the extreme improbability of such a scenario, because it has been wholly incapable of demonstrating a significant relationship (explaining beyond 1–5 per cent of the variance) between any patterns of specific DNA variants and any particular psychological traits in the parts of the genome that would be at all likely to prove this, or any other. They have already searched in most of the places that significant effects would be expected to be found (the 2 per cent of the genome that codes for the proteins that cause amino acid metabolisation). They are now beginning to kick the possibility of finding significant genes into the distant future, at best (Maughan & Sonuga-Barke, 2014), or clutch at straws.

The only way in which scientists have managed to extract significant heritability estimates from the data has been to give up altogether on the idea that any particular genes are linked to any particular outcomes. Genome Wide Complex Trait Analysis (GCTA) was developed when it became increasingly clear that significant effects were not going to emerge from the conventional model, where specific gene variants should have direct effects. GCTA looks for the average impact of genes in a group of people on a trait, without identifying any specific DNA variants that explain it. Using elaborate mathematical formulae, it compares how different the variants are in one sample overall, with the overall pattern in another. By this means, it has been possible to extract significant heritability estimates for mental illnesses (and other traits, like personality, political beliefs, and economic behaviour), although these are rarely more than half those found in twin studies (Plomin & Simpson, 2013). These findings often remain to be replicated – repeated in studies using the same method – and have already drawn a blank in a large and telling study of psychopathology in children (Trzaskowski, Dale, & Plomin, 2013). There are also suspicions that the results will not stand up when they are done on different populations.

Because the GCTA method does not demonstrate that specific genetic variants reliably cause differences it is of no practical use and it is not a test of the main HGP hypothesis. That its heritabilities are half or less of those of twin studies is suspicious, although attempts have been made to explain this (Plomin & Simpson, 2013). It is interesting that GCTAs are rarely used in the introductory or discussion sections of scientific papers to support the contention that genes are a significant cause of mental illness. Perhaps this is because the scientific community knows that GCTA studies will prove to be a red herring.

A final area which some geneticists hold out hope for is the 'dark matter' that makes up 98 per cent of the genome (Johnson et al., 2005). Only 2 per cent of DNA is in a gene's 'coding region', the portions of gene that code for proteins. Until the HGP, it was believed that the 'junk DNA' of dark matter played no role in affecting what we are like. Since then, studies in mice and other mammals have suggested that the dark matter may affect the transcription* of DNA into RNA (Pennisi, 2012). In doing so, they could have an effect on how DNA is expressed, including, in theory, vulnerability to mental illness. To date, there is no solid evidence that this is so, it is primarily a hypothesis.

It may be seen from this brief review that the HGP findings might lead a truly independent scientist to incline towards acceptance of the null hypothesis: that genetic variations play little or no part in explaining individual differences in human psychology. If the whole-genome sequencing studies continue to find only 1–5 per cent, it is hard to see where the scientists will be able to turn in order to avoid that conclusion. However, there are two areas that some scientists still hold out hope for.

Remaining areas of research that some believe could identity missing heritability: gene-environment interactions

Although GWAs have been the main method for finding missing heritability, there have also been attempts to look for gene-environment interactions where candidate genes have been identified. These are specific genes, or parts thereof, associated with particular traits, in which the genetic variant is supposed to create a vulnerability whose fulfilment depends on environmental factors.

The most promising of these seemed to demonstrate that certain variants of the 5-HTT gene created vulnerability to depression when combined with childhood maltreatment (Caspi et al., 2003). People with a functional polymorphism in the promoter region of the serotonin transporter gene (5-HTT) possess one or two short alleles* associated with lower transcriptional efficiency of the promoter than those with one or two long alleles. The study found that those with one or two copies of the short version who were maltreated as children, or who had suffered stressful life events, were more likely to be depressed. The relationship between the possession of the short alleles and depression was linear: having one short allele increased the risk, having two increased it even more, having one long allele reduced it, having two did so even more. Most startlingly of all, people with two long alleles who were severely maltreated were at no greater risk of depression than those with two long alleles who were not maltreated: two long alleles meant degree of maltreatment made no difference to risk of depression, for depression to occur you needed to possess one or two short alleles. One short allele combined with severe maltreatment increased the risk by half, and two short alleles doubled it.

These dramatic findings inspired a flurry of further studies, some of them epidemiological.

At the simplest level, it might be assumed from the theory that groups of depressed people would be more likely to have more of the (depression-conferring) short alleles than the non-depressed. This was quickly shown not to be so in large samples (Lasky-Su, 2005; Mendlewicz et al., 2004). An international study compared presence of the short alleles in nations with high and low prevalence of depression, finding that, if anything, there was more likelihood of short alleles in the relatively non-depressed nations (Chiao & Blizinsky, 2010). Interestingly, while the short allele did not predict depression, degrees of individualism or collectivism of the society did.

However, it can be objected that such epidemiological studies do not directly address the gene-environment interaction that was proposed by Caspi and colleagues (2003). This was examined in a review of the 14 best studies to date. It found that the short allele combined with stress did not increase risk for depression (Risch et al., 2009). An attempt was made to re-evaluate the evidence for several gene-environment interactions, not just the 5-HTT serotonin transporter (Belsky et al., 2009). It maintained that genetic variants should be understood as making people both more likely to be upset by adversity and to benefit from supportive experience. This made better sense of the existing evidence, it was argued. However, in 2011, a study was published reviewing the 103 gene-environment studies published between 2000 and 2009 (Duncan & Keller, 2011). This found that only 27 per cent of attempts to replicate initial findings proved positive. Several analyses of the gene-environment interaction since then have led many to doubt their validity (Manuck & McCafferty, 2014; Munafo et al., 2014), although debate still continues (Rutter, 2014).

Overall, the case for gene-environment interactions is weak in the light of so many studies that do not replicate original findings. What is more, for all kinds of illness, physical as well as mental, when candidate genes are tested in GWAs, they mostly do not emerge as significant (Siontis, Patsopoulos, & Ioannidis, 2010). This study reviewed them in 100 GWA studies and came up with very little.

A final area that has attracted a great deal of interest is that of epigenetics. This is the theory that environmental experiences cause the release of chemicals that either activate or suppress certain genes. There is some evidence that this pattern of chemicals can be passed down the germline to the next generation, although most of the evidence for this is in experiments performed on non-human mammals (Roth, 2014).

It should be stressed that epigenetics cannot solve the missing heritability problem. It is essentially a mechanism by which the environment causes outcomes through activation or suppression of genes. For example, there is considerable evidence for hypermethylation of key genes in adults who were abused as children and have developed psychiatric conditions (Roth, 2014, p.1281). Methyl is a chemical group that can inactivate genes.

Contrary to some of the claims made for epigenetics, it is not evidence for the argument that psychiatric outcomes are caused by both genes and environment, the 'bit of both' theory. In the epigenetic studies, it is primarily the presence of childhood maltreatment or adult stress that is the causal factor, not variations in genes. As such, it is an account of how mal-treatment or stress can affect outcomes, a mechanism no different in kind from the considerable evidence that these adversities can cause changes in key neurotransmitters or hormones. For example, cortisol regulation is strongly affected by adversities, resulting in psychiatric problems (e.g., reviewed by Hunter, Minnis, & Wilson, 2011).

Taken overall, gene-environment theories are highly unlikely to solve the missing heritability problem. No candidate genes have been unequiv-ocally shown to interact with childhood maltreatment or stress to be a major cause of mental illness. Epigenetics is not a theory that could explain missing heritability.

A reinterpretation of the results of twin studies in the event of acceptance of the null hypothesis of the HGP: twin studies' 'heritability' is shared environment (THISE)

Molecular geneticists continue to believe that the HGP may discover significant effects of genetic variation on mental illness through whole-genome sequencing studies. Within a very few years we shall find out if they are right. Given the findings of GWAs so far, there is good reason to doubt that they will be.

Let us suppose that no further significance is revealed and the null hypothesis of the HGP is accepted. In that eventuality, how would we interpret the findings of high heritabilities in twin studies?

Numerous studies of twins have concluded that half or more of impor-tant traits, like intelligence, major depression, schizophrenia, and bipolar disorder, are heritable (James, 2005; Plomin, 1990). Lower heritabilities are found for minor depression, anxiety disorders, and personality traits, in the range of 10–30 per cent (James, 2005; Plomin, 1990). These twin studies are the primary scientific foundation for the belief that genes are a major cause of individual differences. The positing of a missing heritabil-ity is based on them (Plomin & Davis, 2009).

If the HGP null hypothesis were to be accepted, then it would be necessary to re-evaluate the findings of twin studies. All scientists accept that direct evidence from measurement of the genome is much more reliable than the indirect evidence of twin studies. Writing in 2009, Robert Plomin stated that 'The future of genetics belongs to molecular genetics...' (Plomin & Davis, 2009). If the HGP null hypothesis were accepted, it would have to be further accepted that the heritabilities of twin studies are suspect at best, or more likely, simply incorrect. For example, the much-publicised results of Thomas Bouchard's study of twins reared apart would begin to look highly suspect (Bouchard et al., 1990). Indeed, grave doubts have been cast on the reliability of Bouchard's methods and of his findings (see James, 2005, Appendix 1). He and his colleagues would have to permit independent scrutiny of their data, something Bouchard has refused (Wright, 1997), an unfortunate refusal in the light of the history of deception in this area of research (Macintosh, 1995).

That twin studies turn out to be incorrect in their assessment of heritability would come as no surprise to long-standing critics of the method (James, 2005; Joseph, 2004, 2006). They maintain that flaws in the method exaggerate the role of genes, or that it is simply impossible to estimate heritability using this method. What is more, closer inspection of the twin method offers an intriguing alternative view of what their results demonstrate, one other than heritability.

The twin study method compares the degree of concordance (similarity) for a trait between samples of identical twins and same-sexed, non-identical twins. Whereas identical twins have identical genomes, non-identical twins have only half their segregating genes in common. If the identical twins are more concordant than the non-identical twins, it could be that this difference is caused by the differing degrees of genetic concordance. However, this requires an assumption, known as the equal environments assumption (EEA): that identical and non-identical twins are as likely to be treated similarly by parents, carers, and other significant people in their environment. If the identical twins are treated more similarly, then greater similarities in traits could be caused by that environmental influence, rather than genes. Breaching of the EEA would make it impossible to disentangle shared environmental effects and those of genes.

As Joseph (2013) has fully documented, from the 1960s onwards most scientists accepted that the EEA was, indeed, false: identical twins are treated more similarly than non-identical twins. This is unsurprising, given that they look the same, are often dressed similarly, have the same haircut, and so on. However, twin researchers maintained that this breach of the EEA did not disqualify the method, for two reasons (discussed by Joseph, 2004, 2006, 2013).

First, they maintained that genetic similarities in the psychology of identical twin psychology cause parents and others to respond to them more similarly; it is not just a matter of their physical similarity causing the more similar treatment. For example, children born with a sunny or grouchy disposition might cause positive or negative responses to them. It is held that their, allegedly genetical caused, more similar psychology causes them to choose more similar environments, which in turn creates greater concordance. Children both born with high or low aptitude to sport, for example, would consequently be more or less likely to be engaged with sporting environments, with all the feedbacks that would entail.

Second, it was maintained that, although the identical twins do have more similar treatment, that treatment is not necessarily more similar for environmental factors relevant to outcomes of particular traits being studied. For example, persons diagnosed with schizophrenia are three times more likely to have suffered childhood maltreatment (Varese et al., 2012) but that does not mean identical twins are necessarily equally likely to be subjected to it, so genes could still be the primary cause of that illness.

Joseph (2013) provides compelling evidence and arguments for rejecting these propositions.

A particularly telling study suggested that when identical twins are concordant for psychotic experience, they are also significantly more likely to have suffered childhood adversity (Alemany et al., 2013). If twins were discordant, the one who had not suffered adversity was significantly less likely to have psychotic symptoms. The study was able to show that adversity was directly causing psychotic symptoms, independent of genes. There are other studies with related findings. For example, Ball and colleagues (2008) found that being bullied before the age of five correlated at r = 0.77 in identical twin boys but only at 0.41 in fraternal twin boys; there were similar findings for girls.

This is by no means the whole of the evidence relating to this issue, and there are studies that support defenders of the EEA, beyond the scope of this paper. But if the EEA is false as an assumption and if the ancillary arguments to protect it are also false, it suggests that a great deal of what has previously been ascribed to the role of genes is in fact due to shared environment.

The causes of variance in outcome in twin studies are partitioned into three factors (Plomin, 1990): shared environment, the role of shared experiences in the environment; non-shared environment, the role of experiences that are different between the pair; and heritability, the role of genes. Using this partitioning of variance, twin studies find very little role for shared factors, much higher estimates of the effect of non-shared ones (Plomin & Daniels, 1987).

However, this method for apportioning variance requires the EEA to be valid, or for its protective arguments to be so. If they are false, it is very possible that a great deal of what has up until now been assumed to be caused by genes, currently partitioned as heritability, is in fact caused by shared environment. That leads to a fascinating alternative interpretation of twin study findings: where high 'heritabilities' have been found in twin studies, rather than the role of genes, they are actually demonstrating that there is greater similarity of treatment for that trait. Equally, where 'heritability' is low, it suggests a large non-shared environment contribution. I characterise this re-analysis as THISE (twin studies' 'heritability' is shared environment).

Given a null hypothesis for the HGP, a THISE analysis can make the assumption that much of what was previously regarded as heritability in twin studies is shared environment. While it is impossible to use twin studies to identify the small role genes may play, given that the HGP does find 1–5 per cent heritability, it is reasonable to assume that the great majority of supposed heritability is shared environment.

If we take schizophrenia, heritabilities of at least 50 per cent are frequently found in twin studies. In the THISE interpretation, this would be taken to show that the adverse childhood environmental factors that cause 'heritability' are more likely to be shared than for less 'heritable' traits, like minor depression. For example, maltreatment is three times more common in schizophrenics compared with controls (Varese et al., 2012). Of the various kinds of maltreatment, emotional abuse was shown to be the largest cause in Varese and colleagues (2012) review. THISE analysis would suggest that where there are twins and where there is emotional abuse in the family, it is more likely to be shared than other kinds of maltreatment, like emotional neglect, for which the review found less of an effect. That would be in accord with a finding by Bornovalvova and colleagues (2013) that emotional abuse was more shared by identical (any gender, r = 0.53) than fraternal twins (r = 0.36).

Where there is relatively low twin study 'heritability' for a trait, a THISE analysis suggests low concordance in environmental influence – a large non-shared environmental contribution. The case of the causes of attachment is particularly interesting in the light of THISE because there is substantial evidence that attachment patterns have little or no heritability during childhood, if one interprets twin studies as measuring genetic factors (see Introduction in Fearon et al., 2014). But rather than heritability, THISE re-analysis of those findings would indicate that parents do not treat children similarly in regard to the environmental factor known to affect attachment pattern, namely, availability (divided into responsiveness and accessibility) (Bowlby, 1978). In other words, what twin studies may prove about childhood attachment patterns is that they are very largely the product of non-shared environmental availability.

A recent report of a twin study suggested relatively high heritability for attachment patterns in adolescence, around the 40 per cent mark (Fearon et al., 2014). THISE reanalysis of these findings would suggest that environmental factors affecting attachment in adolescence are more shared by siblings, compared with in childhood. Fearon and colleagues (2014) present their findings as proof of heritability, yet they make no acknowledgement anywhere in their paper of the tiny heritability findings of the HGP. With an HGP null hypothesis accepted, a THISE analysis seems much more probable – the study by Fearon and colleagues (2014) has raised the possibility (subject to replication) that shared environment becomes a more significant cause of attachment patterns in adolescence compared with childhood. An interesting, more general implication of a THISE analysis is that shared environment plays a greater role in causing major mental illness than minor mental illness, which would seem to be more caused by non-shared environment: twin studies find much higher heritability for major, rather than minor, mental illness. It could be that the adversities that cause major mental illness are more likely to be shared than those that cause minor mental illness.

Conclusion

What evidence will molecular geneticists accept as a basis for accepting the null hypothesis of the HGP? It seems probable that even if whole-genome sequencing studies produce similar findings to those of existing GWAs, and studies of SNPs and CNVs, there will be continued attempts to find genetic alternatives.

In the newspaper article in which Robert Plomin acknowledged that 'I've been looking for these genes for 15 years and I don't have any', Peter Wilby, his interviewer, ended with a further question. Wilby wrote that, in answer to the question 'What if the genes he's looking for are never found?' Plomin replied 'I will still believe that heritability is true' (Wilby, 2014).

This response by Plomin may be an indication of how hard it will be to persuade behavioural geneticists (who conduct twin studies) or molecular geneticists to accept the null hypothesis of the HGP. Robert Plomin is rightly regarded as a man of integrity and as a major scientist in this field. Yet he states that he will continue to believe that 'heritability is true' even if no genetic material can be found to explain significant amounts of variance. It would be interesting to know what Plomin would regard as evidence that, on the balance of probabilities, the null hypothesis of the HGP should be accepted.

For while it is impossible to prove a negative, balances of probability can be used to evaluate the likelihood of a null hypothesis. If the whole-genome studies of sequencing in large samples are unable to find greater significance than existing GWAs and other methods, that will surely be the point at which the null hypothesis must be seriously considered, if not provisionally accepted.

In the meantime, papers reporting studies of twins continue to ignore the HGP null evidence when introducing their studies, or in discussing them. Equally, reports of HGP findings continue to flatly state at their outset that the traits under investigation 'are' highly heritable, citing twin studies. Neither of these practices should continue.

Equally, students at all stages of education continue to be taught that traits are highly heritable, with little or no reference to either the flaws of twin studies or to the null findings of the HGP. At the very least, it is time for teachers in secondary and higher education, and in clinical trainings, to begin teaching that there are strong reasons to doubt that traits are highly heritable.

If the whole-genome sequencing studies are as null as previous HGP investigations, it will be time for the next generation of students to be taught that the HGP is probably proving that genes play very little role in causing differences in traits. In this eventuality, students should also be taught that the findings of twin studies can no longer be regarded as safe and that a parsimonious Occam's Razor would lead us to a THISE interpretation.

More generally, there are momentous implications for parents, society, and psychotherapists if the null hypothesis of the HGP is accepted. Not the least of these is that no psychopathologies should be treated as immutable genetic destinies. For those of us engaged in the task of using an attachment informed relational therapy to help people troubled by past maltreatment, it is a highly optimistic spur to promote ever more emotional health. And also a spur for us as psychotherapists knowing the possibilities for therapeutic change.

Brief glossary of basic molecular genetic terms

Allele: an alternative form that a gene may have from other versions of it that may be associated with a particular behavioural or other phenotypic outcome.

Base pair: the double helix of DNA is like a staircase each of whose steps is a base pair made up of various bonded chemicals.

Copy number variants (CNV): a CNV is where there has been duplication, insertion, or deletion of stretches of DNA base pairs. These CNVs are mostly not inherited, developing Independently of the genes that were passed on from parents. In fact, all of us have CNVs spread around our DNA, up to and including the absence of whole genes, usually without any discernible consequence. CNVs could not be a major way of identifying genetic inheritance of mental illness, but they might be locations of genetic material differing between the ill and the well.

Deoxyribonucleic acid (DNA): the double-stranded molecule that contains information.

Gene: a sequence of DNA that codes for particular outcomes.

Single-nucleotide polymorphism (SNP): a polymorphism has more than one allele. An SNP has a mutation in a single nucleotide in a base pair.

Transcription: occurs in the cell nucleus when DNA becomes synthesised into the RNA that instructs specific bodily change.

References

Alemany, S., Goldberg, X., van Winkel, R., Gastó, C., Peralta, V., & Fañanás, L. (2013). Childhood adversity and psychosis: examining whether the association is due to genetic confounding using a monozygotic twin differences approach. *European Psychiatry*, 28: 207–12.

Ball, H. A., Arseneault, L., Taylor, A., Maughan, B., Caspi, A., & Moffitt, T. E. (2008). Genetic and environmental influences on victims, bullies and bully-victims in childhood. *Journal of Child Psychology and Psychiatry*, 49(1): 104–12.

BBC *Today* programme (2014). 22 July, 2014.

Belsky J., Jonassaint, C., Pluess, M., Stanton, M., Brummett, B., & Williams, R. (2009). Vulnerability genes or plasticity genes? *Molecular Psychiatry*, 14: 746–54.

Bornovalova, M., Brooke, A., Huibregtse, M., Hicks, B. M., Keyes, M., McGue, M., & Iacono, W. (2013). Tests of a direct effect of childhood abuse on adult borderline personality disorder traits: a longitudinal discordant twin design. *Journal of Abnormal Psychology*, 122(1): 180–94.

Bouchard, T. J., Lykken, D. T., McGue, M., Segal, N. L., & Tellegen, A. (1990). Sources of human psychological differences: the Minnesota study of twins reared apart. *Science*, 250: 223–28.

Bowlby, J. (1978). *Attachment: Attachment and Loss, Volume One.* London: Penguin.

Caspi, A., Sugden, K., Moffitt, T. E., Taylor, A., Craig, I. W., Harrington, H., McClay, J., Mill, J., Martin, J., Braithwaite, A., &

Poulton, R. (2003). Influence of life stress on depression: moderation by a polymorphism in the 5-HTT gene. *Science*, 301: 386–89.

Chiao, J., & Blizinsky, K. D. (2010). Culture-gene coevolution of individualism–collectivism and the serotonin transporter gene. *Proceedings of the Royal Society B*, 277: 529–37.

Deary, I. J., Johnson, W., & Houlihan, I. M. (2009). Genetic foundations of human intelligence. *Human Genetics*, 126: 215–32.

Duncan, L. E., & Keller, M. C. (2011). A critical review of the first 10 years of candidate gene-by-environment interaction research in psychiatry. *American Journal of Psychiatry*, 168: 1041–49.

Fearon, P., Shueh-Goetz, Y., Viding, E., Fonagy, P., & Plomin, R. (2014). Genetic and environmental influences on adolescent attachment. *Journal of Child Psychology and Psychiatry*, 55: 1033–41.

Harter, N., Butcher, L. M., Meaburn, E., Sham, P., Craig, I. W., & Plomin, R. (2005). A behavioral genomic analysis of DNA markers associated with general cognitive ability in 7-year-olds. *Journal of Child Psychology and Psychiatry*, 46: 1087–1107.

Hunter, A. L., Minnis, H., & Wilson, P. (2011). Altered stress responses in children exposed to early adversity: a systematic review of salivary cortisol studies. *Stress*, 14: 614–26.

James, O. W. (2005). *They F*** You Up*. London: Vermilion.

Johnson, J. M., Edwards, S., Shoemaker, D., & Schadt, E. E. (2005). Dark matter in the genome: evidence of widespread transcription detected by microarray tiling experiments. *Trends in Genetics*, 21: 93–102.

Joseph, J. (2004). *The Gene Illusion: Genetic Research in Psychiatry and Psychology Under the Microscope*. Ross-on-Wye: PCCS Books.

Joseph, J. (2006). *The Missing Gene: Psychiatry, Heredity and the Fruitless Search for Genes.* New York: Algora.

Joseph, J. (2013). The use of the classical twin method in the social and behavioral sciences: the fallacy continues. *Journal of Mind and Behavior*, 34: 1–40.

Kendler, K. (2001). Twin studies of psychiatric illnesses: an update. *Archives of General Psychiatry*, 58: 1005–14.

Kendler, K. (2014). A joint history of the nature of genetic variation and the nature of schizophrenia. Molecular Psychiatry Available at: www. nature.com/mp/journal/vaop/ncurrent/abs/mp201494a.html (accessed 20 August, 2014).

Lasky-Su, J. A. (2005). Meta-analysis of the association between two polymorphisms in the serotonin transporter gene and affective disorders. *American Journal of Medical Genetics*, 133b: 110–15.

Macintosh, N. J. (1995). *Cyril Burt: Fraud or Framed?* Oxford: Oxford University Press.

Major Depressive Disorder Working Group of the Psychiatric GWAs Consortium, Ripke, S., Wray, N. S., Lewis, C. M., Hamilton, S. P., Weissman, M.M., & Sullivan, P. F. (2013). A mega-analysis of genome-wide association studies for major depressive disorder. *Molecular Psychiatry*, 18: 497–511.

Manuck, S. B., & McCafferty, J. M. (2014). Gene-environment interaction. *Annual Review of Psychology*, 65: 41–70.

Maughan, B., & Sonuga-Barke, E. J. S. (2014). Editorial: Translational genetics of child psychopathology: a distant dream. *Journal of Child Psychology and Psychiatry*, 55(10): 1065–67.

Mendlewicz, J., Massat, I., Souery, D., Del-Favero, J., Oruc, L., Nöthen, M. M., Blackwood, D., Muir, W., Battersby, S., Lerer,

B., Segman, R. H., Kaneva, R., Serretti, A., Lilli, R., Lorenzi, C., Jakovljevic, M., Ivezic, S., Rietschel, M., Milanova, V., & Van Broeckhoven, C. (2004). Serotonin transporter 5-HTTTPLR polymorphism and affective disorders: no evidence of association in a large European multicenter study. *European Journal of Human Genetics*, 12: 377–82.

Munafo, M. R., Zammit, S., & Flint, J. (2014). Practitioner review: A critical perspective on gene-environment interaction models – what impact should they have on clinical perceptions and practice? *Journal of Child Psychology and Psychiatry*, 55(10): 1092–1101.

Pennisi, E. (2012). ENCODE project writes eulogy for junk DNA. *Science*, 337: 1159–61.

Plomin, R. (1990). *Nature and Nurture – An Introduction to Behavioural Genetics*. Pacific Grove, CA: Brooks/Cole.

Plomin, R., & Crabbe, J. (2000). DNA. *Psychological Bulletin*, 126: 806–28.

Plomin, R., & Daniels D. (1987). Why are children from the same family so different from each other? *Behaviour and Brain Science*, 10: 1–16.

Plomin, R., & Davis, O. S. P. (2009). The future of genetics in psychology and psychiatry: microarrays, genome-wide association and non-coding RNA. *Journal of Child Psychology and Psychiatry*, 50: 63–71.

Plomin, R., Owen, M. J., & Mcguffin, P. (1994). The genetic basis of complex human behaviors. *Science*, 264: 1733–39.

Plomin, R., & Simpson, M. A. (2013). The future of genomics for developmentalists. *Development and Psychopathology*, 25: 1263–78.

Risch, N., Herrell, R., Lehner, T., Liang, K. Y., Eaves, L., Hoh, J., Griem, A., Kovacs, M., Ott, J., & Merikangas, K. R. (2009). Interaction between the serotonin transporter gene (5-HTTLPR), stressful life events and risk of depression: a meta-analysis. *Journal of the American Medical Association*, 301: 2462–71.

Roth, T. L. (2014). Epigenetic mechanisms in the development of behavior: advances, challenges and future promises of a new field. *Child Development*, 25: 1279–92.

Rutter, M. (2014). Commentary: GxE in child psychiatry and psychology: a broadening of the scope of enquiry as prompted by Munafo et al. (2014). *Journal of Child Psychology and Psychiatry*, 55(10): 1102–04.

Schizophrenia Working Group of the Psychiatric Genomics Consortium (2014). Biological insights from the 108 schizophrenia-associated genetic loci. *Nature*, 511: 421–27.

Siontis, K. C., Patsopoulos, N. A., & Ioannidis, J. P. (2010). Replication of past candidate loci for common diseases and phenotypes in 100 genome-wide association studies. *European Journal of Human Genetics*, 18: 832–37.

Sonuga-Barke, E. J. S. (2010). Editorial: "It's the environment, stupid!" On epigenetics, programming and plasticity in child mental health. *Journal of Child Psychology and Psychiatry*, 51: 113–15.

Trzaskowski, M., Dale, P. S., & Plomin, R. (2013). No genetic influence for childhood behavior problems from DNA analysis. *Journal of the American Academy of Child and Adolescent Psychiatry*, 52: 1048–56.

Varese, F., Smeets, F., Drukker, M., Lieverse, R., Lataster, T., Viechtbauer, W., Read, J., van Os J., & Bentall, R. P. (2012). Childhood adversities increase the risk of psychosis: a meta-analysis of patient-control, prospective and cross-sectional cohort studies. *Schizophrenia Bulletin*, 36: 661–71.

Wilby, P. (2014). Psychologist on a mission to give every child a learning chip. *The Guardian* newspaper, 18 February, 2014, London:

Guardian newspaper, www.the guardian.com/cducation/2014/feb/18/ psychologist-robert-plomin-says-genes-crucial-education (accessed 6 September, 2014).

Wray, N. R., Lee, S. H., Melita, D., Vinkhuyzen, A. A., Dudbridge, F., & Middeldorp, C. M. (2014). Research review: polygenic methods and their application to psychiatric traits. *Journal of Child Psychology and Psychiatry*, 55(10): 1068–87.

Wright, L. (1997). *Twins, Genes, Environment and the Mystery of Identity*. London: Weidenfeld & Nicholson.

Appendix 2

Twin Studies: A Discredited Method

Twin and adoption studies are the foundations upon which the behavioural genetic edifice is built. Given the null findings of the Human Genome Project, the contention that genes are a significant cause of individual differences in human psychology relies wholly on their findings.

The twin study method compares the degree of concordance (similarity) for a trait between samples of identical twins and same-sexed, non-identical twins. Whereas identical twins have identical genomes, non-identical twins have only half their segregating genes in common. If the identical twins are more concordant than the non-identical twins, it could be that this difference is caused by the differing degrees of genetic concordance.

Such studies have a chequered past. The controversy surrounding the deceptions played by the psychologist Cyril Burt (who was proven to have invented results when doing twin studies) was unfortunate and serious doubts still remain about the validity of the methods employed by the influential schizophrenia researcher, Franz Kallman (Marshall, 1984). But actual fraud is not the main objection to such studies. It is the numerous problems that have been raised by highly respected scientists in this field concerning the validity of the scientific methods and assumptions made in such studies.

Behavioural geneticists tend either to ignore or to make the most fleeting of reference to the problems that this body of literature raises (e.g., see Plomin, 1997, a key textbook that hardly refers to them). As Jay Joseph has chronicled in great detail (Joseph, 2015), if they were more commonly considered, the over-confident assertions about the findings of behavioural genetics would be modified and greater caution emphasized regarding the overall validity and generalizability of both twin and adoption studies.

Problem 1: The assumption of equivalent environments (Baumrind, 1993; Joseph, 1998, 2015)

This is the single most significant issue. In estimating heritabilities from comparisons between samples of identical and fraternal twins, behavioural geneticists make a critical assumption: that the environments of the two kinds of twins do not differ systematically and therefore, that any differences found between the two groups are not due to environmental differences such as the kind of parenting, reactions from peers or schoolteachers and so on, but are solely due to the differences in zygosity.

There is, however, substantial and incontrovertible evidence to suggest that this assumption is false and that identical and fraternal twins are not as likely to be treated in the same way (Joseph, 2015). Indeed, it is now widely accepted that the equivalent environments assumption has been proven to be false: identical twins do have more similar environments. A simple example of this is appearance. A large body of research demonstrates that reactions to individuals are substantially influenced by physical attractiveness. Attractive people are more likely to be judged pleasant and be successful than unattractive ones (Etcoff, 1999). Since identical twins look exactly the same, their attractiveness will affect responses to them in the same way, whereas fraternal twins – who do not look identical – will receive different reactions. It follows that, in the light of the HGP findings, the higher concordances in psychology between identical compared with fraternal twins is very likely to reflect the impact of similarity of appearance on the way they are treated and not genetically inherited differences in psychology.

That the assumption of equivalent environments may be invalid makes estimates of heritability unreliable. Whilst it does not invalidate twin studies altogether – the findings of the HGP do that – it creates an unknown degree of effect on the concordance rates which lie at the heart of the twin method.

Problem 2: The low estimates of Shared Environment from twin and adoption studies (Stoolmiller, 1900; Joseph, 2015)

Behavioural geneticists subdivide the effects of environment into shared and non-shared effects. Shared effects are those which are experienced by all offspring, whereas non-shared ones are those which are unique to the individual. Hence, if a parent is depressed and expresses this behaviour equally to all offspring it is a shared effect, whereas if the depression is especially directed towards one offspring and not the others, it is a non-shared effect

It is frequently contended by behavioural geneticists that, overall, twin studies demonstrate that shared environments have minimal effects. This is more debatable than is often claimed on two grounds.

Firstly, there are many soundly conducted twin studies which do not confirm this claim, finding significant shared effects.

Secondly, there are numerous studies of the impact of families and socio-economic status on development and psychopathology that find shared effects.

Now that we know the results of the Human Genome Project, I have proposed an alternative interpretation of the results of twin studies (James, 2014).

The causes of variance in outcome in twin studies are partitioned into three factors (Plomin, 1990): Shared Environment, the role of shared experiences in the environment; Non-shared Environment, the role of experiences which are different between the pair; and Heritability, the role of genes. Using this partitioning of variance, twin studies find very little role for shared factors, much higher estimates of the effect of non-shared ones (Plomin et al., 1987).

However, this method for apportioning variance requires the EEA to be valid, or for its protective arguments to be so. If they are false, it is very possible that a great deal of what has up until now been assumed to be caused by genes, currently partitioned as heritability, is in fact caused by Shared Environment. That leads to a fascinating alternative interpretation of twin study findings: where high 'heritabilities' have been found in twin studies, rather than the role of genes, they are actually demonstrating that there is greater similarity of treatment for that trait. Equally, where 'heritability' is low, it suggests a large Non-shared Environment contribution. I characterise this reanalysis as THISE (Twin studies' 'Heritability' Is Shared Environment).

Given a null hypothesis for the HGP, a THISE analysis can make the assumption that much or all of what was previously regarded as genetic in twin studies is Shared Environment. Whilst it is impossible to use twin studies to identify the small role genes may play, given that the HGP does find 1–5 per cent heritability, it is reasonable to assume that the great majority of supposed heritability is shared environment.

Problem 3: The generalisability of findings from studies using twin samples (Schacter, 1982; Hay & O'Brien, 1987)

A fundamental query about studies based on comparisons of samples of identical and non-identical (fraternal) twins is whether the unique experience of being twins and their unusual genetic origins make them a population upon which generalisation to other populations can legitimately be based.

The evidence is equivocal. For example, studies of twins have suggested that their parents are forced to devote less time to each individual, that their language may be delayed and that there is a process of 'de-identification' in which parents make abnormal (compared with parents of singletons) attempts to create difference out of twin offspring. These, and other similar findings call into doubt the generalisability of estimates of heritability based on twin samples to singletons, who make up the vast majority of all humans.

Problem 4: Mathematical assumptions made in analysing twin data (Wahlstein, 1990, 1994)

Behavioural genetic analyses of twin data make assumptions in calculating the partitioning of heritability between shared and non-shared environmental effects and between additive and non-additive effects. These assumptions create an insensitivity to interactive effects between heredity and environment.

Problem 5: The impact of prenatal factors on identical twins (Devlin, 1997)

In reanalysing 212 twin studies, Devlin demonstrated that maternal womb effects may account for substantial amounts of the concordance between twins, concordances that are currently assumed to be due to genetics.

Problem 6: The lack of measures of the environment in behavioural genetic studies (Baumrind, 1993)

Nearly all twin and adoption studies either make no attempt at all to measure the possible impact of environmental factors or use measures that environmentalists find inappropriate or inadequate. It is widely believed that if the environment were to be properly measured in twin studies, its effect would be shown to be much greater than geneticists currently claim, creating a contradiction between the results from comparing concordance rates in samples with differing zygosities and environmental measures.

Problem 7: Cautions in the interpretation of adoption studies (Stoolmiller, 1999)

When twins are placed for adoption a considerable effort is often made to find families that are of similar socio-economic status and race as the biological family of origin, known as 'selective placement'. Both class and race of family have well-established, consistent effects on what children are like. Since adoption studies test the similarity of biological parents with their adopted offspring, some of the similarities found between them could be caused by selective placement.

A further worry about adoption studies is the crudity, from an environmental standpoint, of the comparisons made. It is assumed by geneticists that all similarities between biological parent and adoptees are caused by genes whereas differences between them are environmental. It is further assumed that similarities between adoptee and non-biological parents are environmental. But none of these assumptions can be safely made for a great many traits. For example, some children react against what their non-biological parents are like – an environmental effect that would not be treated as such by geneticists.

A final and fundamental problem is that geneticists make no allowance for the well-established fact that being adopted has a profound effect on psychology in its own right. Children who are taken into care have different outcomes from adoptees and adoptees are more at risk of a host of problems than children raised by biological parents.

References

Baumrind, D., 1993, 'The average expectable environment is not enough: a response to Scarr', *Child Development*, 64, 1299–1317.

Devlin, B. et al., 1997, 'The heritability of IQ', *Nature*, 388, 468–71.

Etcoff, N., 1999, *The Survival of the Prettiest*, London: Little Brown.

Hay, D.A. and O'Brien, P.J., 1987, 'Early influences on the school social adjustment of twins', *Acta Genetica Medica Gemellol*, 36, 239–48.

James, O.W., 2014, 'Not in Your Genes — Time to Accept the Null Hypothesis of the Human Genome Project?', *Attachment: New Directions in Psychotherapy and Relational Psychoanalysis*, 8, 281–96.

Joseph, J., 1998, 'The equal environments assumption of the classical twin method: a critical analysis', *Journal of Mind and Behaviour*, 19, 325–58.

Joseph, J., 2015, *The Trouble With Twins*, London: Routledge

Marshall, J.R., 1984, 'The genetics of schizophrenia revisited', *Bulletin of the British Psychological Society*, 37, 177–81.

Plomin, R., 1990, *Nature and Nurture – An Introduction to Behavioural Genetics*, Pacific Grove: Brooks/Cole.

Plomin, R. et al., 1987, 'Why are children from the same family so different from each other?', *Behaviour and Brain Science*, 10, 1–16.

Plomin, R. et al., 1997, *Behavioural Genetics*, San Francisco: Freeman.

Schacter, F.F. et al., 1982, 'Sibling de-identification and split-parent identification: a family tetrad', in Lamb, M.E. et al., *Sibling Relationships: Their nature and significance across the lifecycle*, NJ: LEA.

Stoolmiller, M., 1999, 'Implications of the restricted range of family environments of heritability and non-shared environment in behaviour-genetic adoption studies', *Psychological Bulletin*, 125, 392–409.

Wahlstein, D., 1990, 'Insensitivity of variance to heredity-environment interaction', *Behaviour and Brain Sciences*, 13, 109–61.

Wahlstein, D., 1994, 'The intelligence of heritability', *Canadian Psychology*, 37, 244–58.

Appendix 3

The Fatal Flaws of the Minnesota Twins Reared Apart Study

Starting in 1979, Professor Thomas Bouchard and colleagues used the media to invite twins from across America who were separated in childhood to come forward for testing. On being accepted for the study, the twins underwent 50 hours of assessment answering over 15,000 questions at Bouchard's unit in the University of Minneapolis, Minnesota. For a full critique of the scientific problems with the study, I strongly recommend Jay Joseph's scholarly book *The Trouble With Twins* (2015).

The Minnesota study has hugely influenced popular conceptions of the impact of genes upon behaviour through newspaper articles, books and television documentaries. In most cases, these report seemingly astonishing similarities between twins who have never met each other. For example, the journalist Lawrence Wright (Wright, 1997, p. 45) reports of two of Bouchard's twins who were separated at birth that they liked their coffee black and cold, had fallen down the stairs aged 15 and had weak ankles as a result, at 16 had met the man they were to marry at a local dance, laughed more than anyone else they knew, and so on. Even Bouchard admits that such similarities are purely coincidental, but that has not stopped them from being endlessly purveyed to the media by Bouchard and his colleagues as spooky evidence of genetics.

A fundamental concern is that Professor Bouchard refuses to allow his data to be examined by independent assessors. He told Lawrence Wright (Wright, 1997, p. 60) that he is not willing to release or allow for inspection the raw data on which his scientific papers are based, though he has allowed access to selected colleagues whom he considers supportive. Given the history of fraudulent findings in this field of research, it is a particularly unfortunate refusal and some scientists reject any of his findings as valid until such an assessment is permitted. Suspicions about Bouchard's genuine open-mindedness are compounded by the fact that in order to carry it out he has received grants to the value of $1.3 million from the Pioneer Fund of New York, which has its roots in the eugenics movement and which backs projects that advocate racial segregation (Wright, 1997, p. 50).

The published results contain several worrying and puzzling omissions in the data, and serious absences of basic, vital information in the scientific reports from Bouchard's group. Ideally, for such a study, the twins would be separated at birth and given for adoption to parents who differ greatly in the ways they rear their children. Yet average ages at which the twins were separated are not provided. The amount of time that they have been in contact and the form that this has taken are not reported in any detail. In many cases, the twins seem to have had extensive telephone contact before they visited Bouchard in Minnesota, which could have led them to convince themselves of their similarity. The only information provided is that the twins spent an average of over two years either together or in contact prior to being studied, with a large range in the amounts that conceals a great variation. One pair of these supposedly reared-apart twins had known each other for 23 years (Joseph, 2015, p. 106).

The key shortcomings of the study were summarised by Joseph (2015) as follows:

> 〉 Many twin pairs experienced late separation, and many pairs were reared together in the same home for several years. This is

extremely important: it is not at all the study that most of the public imagine, in which the twins were separated at birth. It is not a real test of the role of nature and nurture.

⟩ Most twin pairs grew up in similar socioeconomic and cultural environments. This means it is impossible to disentangle the impact of nurture and nature.

⟩ Similarities between the twins were inflated by non-genetic cohort effects, based on common age, common sex, and other factors. Again, that makes it hard to disentangle nature from nurture.

⟩ Twins share a common pre-natal (intrauterine) environment, and the pre-natal environment of identical twins is more similar than that of non-identical twins' pre-natal environment. Some of the greater similarities of the identical twins could be due to this rather than their identical genes.

⟩ In studies based on volunteer twins, a bias was introduced because pairs had to have known of each other's existence to be able to participate in the study. This was a major weakness in the design of the study. It means it is highly probably that those volunteering to join it were biased towards wanting to find similarities with their twin siblings.

⟩ The particular sample of identical twins were biased in favor of more similar pairs, meaning that they are not representative of identical twins in general.

⟩ The similar physical appearance and level of attractiveness of identical twins will elicit more similar nurture from parents and from peers. This is completely discounted as a factor by researchers, yet it has been proven many times over to have a large effect.

⟩ Twins sometimes had financial and other types of incentives to exaggerate or lie about their degree of separation and behavioural similarity, and their accounts are not always reliable. Some of the twins made money from having their lives turned into feature films, others were paid by television companies to appear on talks shows and in documentaries to talk about their 'amazing' similarity. There have been countless newspaper interviews with the twins, who were made available for this by the researchers. Some of the twins have admitted they deliberately lied about their similarity. For example, one pair known as 'the giggle twins' admitted that they both told the researchers that they longed to be opera singers, when this was not true (Joseph, 2015, p. 119).

〉 There were several questionable or false assumptions underlying the statistical procedures used in the studies.

〉 Before the researchers began their work, they are on record as having been strongly biased towards making genetic interpretations of the data. This meant that evidence proving the role of the environment was ignored or suppressed.

〉 There were problems with the IQ and personality tests used.

〉 In cases where evaluations and testing were performed by the same person, there was a potential for experimenter bias in favor of twin similarity. In short, the experimenters may have cheated by encouraging the twins to exaggerate similarity and underplay difference.

Another issue is the parameters that Bouchard has studied. He has focused on ones most likely to provide support for genetic theories, according to studies of twins reared together, like IQ, but there is very little about the huge swathes of psychology which appears to have little or no heritability, if studies of twins reared together are to believed, like choice of mate, violence or attachment patterns. Mysteriously, no attempt was made to assess the twins' mental health.

Bouchard rejects calls for detailed case histories on the grounds that it would be a breach of confidentiality. Yet there is a long tradition of publication of full reports without any such problem being raised (Farber, 1981) and doubtless he could easily obtain permissions if he felt this were necessary.

The truth about this study is that it is extremely suspect. The findings of the Human Genome Project are proving the findings to be false and the manner in which this falsehood was achieved needs to be exposed by full disclosure of the data.

References

Farber, S.L., 1981, *Identical Twins Reared Apart*, New York: Basic Books.

Joseph, J., 2015, *The Trouble With Twins*, London: Routledge.

Wright, L., 1997, *Twins*, London: Weidenfeld and Nicholson.

Appendix 4

The Perils of Geneticism: The Advantages of Believing in a Flexible Psychology

Beware of 'the little devil' attribution to your offspring

Assuming that your child's attributes are unchangeable, genetically determined destiny tends to be accompanied by the feeling that you have little control in the relationship. Mothers who attribute a lot of power to their children are at greater risk of maltreating them.

Two studies (Bugenthal, 1989, 2004) show that parents with low perception of control of their babies are more likely to attribute blame for negative interactions or behaviour to the child. This leads to greater harshness and more likelihood of physical abuse, as well as correlating with higher rates of depression in such mothers. Rather than seeing themselves as having greater power than their under-ones, such parents saw themselves as victims of the child, at its mercy. They believed they could do little to prevent negative outcomes, whereas the baby could do so. If the baby was independently measured as being born with a relatively difficult temperament (e.g. fussy, irritable), abuse was more likely from parents with low perceived control (Bugenthal, 2004). However, the studies were able to demonstrate that the way the parent perceived the baby was not to do with what the baby was actually like: extent of perceived control was measured before the birth and did not change according to independently measured temperament after the birth. Indeed, there is good evidence that how mothers perceive their babies is strongly linked to their own early childhood experiences (Grusec et al., 1995).

A further literature, discussed below, indicates that perceiving children as wilful and intentionally bad, the 'oh they can be little devils' way of thinking, is associated with abusive parenting and adverse outcomes. Such thinking tends to presume genetic causality for the badness. Conversely, there is also evidence (Himmelstein et al., 1991) that parents are more likely to attribute positive attributes, like doing well on tests, to their nurture rather than nature.

One study (Guzell et al., 2004) showed that parents who have low perceived control also tend towards 'categorical' thinking about their child's psychology, labelling them as having traits that are unchangeable, possibly because they believe they are caused by genetics. In a sample of 66 parents with one-year-olds, the mothers with low perceived control were more likely to be directive if they perceived their child to be difficult. They were more prone to urge, remind, restrain, question and correct their child during a play situation, reflecting adult-centred rather than child-centred ways of relating. Such directive mothers were also less sensitive to their children's needs.

Another study (Chavira et al., 2000) illustrated this. It examined 149 mentally retarded children from the ages of 3 to 19 and showed that most of their mothers did not view problematic behaviour by their children as the child's fault. However, the more that parents did do so, attributing wilfulness to them, the greater the likelihood of the mother reporting anger and frustration, and responding with aggressive or harsh reactions.

Another study (Kiang et al., 2004) shows how maternal assumptions feed into a lack of empathy with toddlers and subsequent lack of curiosity in the toddler. It investigated maternal preconceptions of mothering before birth and about a child's temperament at six months, and then measured her sensitivity to the child at 12–15 months and the inquisitiveness of the child at 21–24 months in a sample of 175 mother–child dyads. Mothers with prenatal negative preconceptions (measured as low perceived control, unrealistic expectations about being a mother, expected empathy level with child and expected use of physical punishment) were more likely to report a difficult temperament in their six-month-old. Such mothers were less sensitive to their toddlers at 12–15 months and had less inquisitive children at 21–24 months. Conversely, mothers who were sensitive at 12–15 months had more inquisitive children at the later age.

A final study (Maniadaki et al., 2005) of 634 parents showed that attributing deliberate wilfulness to behaviour increased harsh, abusive parenting. The parents were given a hypothetical story to read about a child who displayed many of the symptoms of Attention Deficit and Hyperactivity Disorder (ADHD). Half were given a version of the story in which the child was a boy, half given one with a girl. The ones with a boy were much more likely to label the problem ADHD but most importantly, having done so, they were more likely to assume the boy's difficult behaviour was expressing his intentions, was wilful. If so, these parents advocated harsh responses: attributing wilfulness increased the likelihood of authoritarian parenting.

This body of evidence provides strong grounds for parents to avoid assuming their child has a genetically caused trait that cannot be changed. Further, it suggests it is best not to assume that your baby or toddler is deliberately, wilfully and/or intentionally seeking to behave badly (based on this unchangeable trait) because you are more likely to react angrily and with frustration if you think they are trying to wind you up, and you are at greater risk of responding with harsh, aggressive and even abusive parenting behaviour. As countless studies have proven (James, 2002), it is that kind of parenting (and not genes) that causes children to become aggressive, hostile, violent and to have attention deficits.

Encouraging your child to see themselves as malleable – not fixed by their genes – can improve their abilities

Believe it or not, a crucial determinant of how your child performs at school is whether they themselves think their intelligence is fixed or changeable. Indeed, it has now been shown that just four lessons devoted to cultivating a malleable, 'I am what I choose' mindset (not to be confused with that overrated 'science', positive psychology), significantly improves performance.

A 1990 study (Henderson et al., 1990) showed that first-year secondary pupils who took a malleable view of their abilities got significantly higher grades than ones who believed they were fixed. This was true after allowing for the predictive power of prior academic performance.

Tipped off by this finding, two studies of teens and undergraduates put it into practice (Good et al., 2003). They taught samples to think of themselves as being malleable rather than fixed. Compared with groups given no such tuition, the malleable got significantly better grades as a result of the tuition, regardless of their prior SAT scores.

What was needed was more detail of how this works: are kids who see themselves as changeable made optimistic by this belief or are they already cleverer tryers? And would it work with all kinds of children, even that notorious thicko at the back of your class? Cue two studies putting theoretical flesh on the bones (Blackwell et al., 2007).

The first looked at 373 children aged 13, following them over a two-year period. To measure the malleability/fixity of their beliefs, they were asked how much they agreed or disagreed with statements like 'You have a certain amount of intelligence, and you really can't do much to change it' or 'You can always greatly change how intelligent you are'. Then they were tested as to motivations: attitude to learning (e.g., 'I do school work best when it makes me think hard'), confidence that effort brings results ('If you're not good at a subject, working hard won't make you good at it'), and when faced with failure, tendencies towards helpless or positive reactions.

Sure enough, during the two years of study, children who subscribed to malleable beliefs steadily improved in their maths performance. The malleable were more successful than the fixed because they liked being made to think, redoubled efforts if not succeeding and did not feel helpless. But which came first, the try-hard motive or the malleable belief?

This time, 91 13-year-olds, mostly from low income homes and doing badly at maths, were followed over a year. Half of them were given four lessons in malleability, the others were taught about other matters during those hours.

As before, the intervention group became more likely to subscribe to malleable beliefs as a result of the teaching and the average maths score of that group rose, whereas the control group continued to do badly. The greatest improvement over the year was found in the children who had started with a fixed view of their abilities and been taught to think of it as malleable: fixity is bad for performance. But above all, the sequence was clear: change the belief, you change the motivation, and that improves the grades.

The implications seem considerable: set aside four lessons for teaching the malleability of talents! But more than this, it is important that both you and the parents of your pupils also develop a malleable view.

Studies of teachers with fixed views show that they are more likely to let their expectations for pupils' performance bias how they treat them (Lee, 1996). Regarding parents, one study showed clearly that mothers need to avoid fixed ideas (Pomerantz et al., 2006). If they had a negative view of the child's capacities, a year later such offspring were the most likely to have done badly. True, offspring of fixed parents with high expectations did well, but if the child faltered, there could be big trouble.

The danger of perceiving mental illness in yourself or your children as being caused by genes

Whether it's you, your child or a professional, if genes are believed to be the cause of a mental illness there are worse outcomes in a number of respects: parents with this belief react less helpfully if their child is diagnosed with schizophrenia; patients who believe it's genetic do worse, and professionals subscribing to that ideology are also less effective.

A key factor identified in parents of schizophrenics is whether they relate to their child with what is known as high 'expressed emotion' (EE – controlling, angry, condemnatory reactions). Parents who do so are more likely to explain their child's problem as being an illness (Read et al., 2013, p. 263) – encouraged by the medical profession, they absorb the story that schizophrenia should be seen as a purely mechanical defect, one no different in kind from a broken arm. Labelling the problem as an illness increases the likelihood of having a biogenetic view of causation. Held by parents, the biogenetic view is associated with much more negative attitudes and behaviour. The patient behaves less well and the parent develops a lower opinion of their behaviour, becoming increasingly pessimistic about recovery (Read et al., 2013, p. 138–9).

Professional staff with a biogenetic view are more likely to interpret the patient as disturbed and to involve the patient less in the planning of treatment. By contrast, if staff or patients have a psychosocial view of causality, both are more likely to make a greater effort to achieve a recovery. The less the patient believes they can change, the greater their risk of alcoholism and depression, and the more passive they become about their management, leaving it to the experts.

Thankfully, the majority of populations in most developed nations tend to assume that extreme mental illness, like schizophrenia, is caused by such entities as 'trauma' or 'childhood abuse' (Read et al., 2006). However, the efforts of the drug companies and their pharmacists, the psychiatric establishment, are constantly seeking to persuade the public of a genetic model. It should never be underestimated how much the drug companies drive matters in this field. A worrying example is that studies of the efficacy of psychotropic drugs show that the proportion of them sponsored by drug companies rose from 25 per cent in 1992 to 57 per cent in 2002 (Kelly et al., 2006). This is worrying because there is good reason to suspect bias: 78 per cent of studies sponsored by drug companies report positive outcomes compared with only 48 per cent doing so where there is no such sponsorship.

People living in traditional societies in the developing world are both much less likely to develop schizophrenia and if they do so, are much more likely to recover. Part of the reason for this may be that much fewer families react to a child having that illness with what is known as high EE. Only 8 per cent do so, compared with 54 per cent in families of developed nations (Read et al., 2013, p. 255).

Another interesting fact is that people living in East Asian nations are much less likely than those in the developed Western ones to attribute personality and emotional dispositions to fixed, non-malleable traits. In Eastern Asia, they are more likely to explain what someone is like by reference to their social context, including their family background. It is also true that the amount of mental illness in East Asian countries is much lower than in Western ones. There are many reasons for this (as discussed in Chapter 3, James, 2007 and Chapter 1, James, 2008; see also Chiao et al., 2009). But it is possible that lesser adherence to biogeneticism is one of the reasons.

References

Blackwell, L.S. et al., 2007, 'Implicit theories of intelligence predict intelligence', *Child Development*, 78, 246–63.

Bugenthal, D.B. et al., 1989, 'Perceived control over caregiving outcomes: implications for child abuse', *Developmental Psychology*, 25, 532–9.

Bugenthal, D.B. et al., 2004, 'Predicting infant maltreatment in low-income families', *Developmental Psychology*, 40, 234–43.

Chavira, V. et al., 2000, 'Latina mothers' attributions, emotions and reactions to the problem behaviours of their children with developmental disabilities', *Child Development*, 41, 245–52.

Chiao, J.Y. et al., 2009, 'Culture-gene coevolution of individualism-collectivism and the serotonin transporter gene', *Proceedings of the Royal Society B*, February 22, 2010 277: 529–537.

Good, C. et al., 2003, 'Improving adolescents' standardized test performance: An intervention to reduce the effects of stereotype threat', *Journal of Applied Developmental Psychology*, 24, 645–62.

Grusec, J.E. et al., 1995, 'Features and sources of parents' attributions about themselves and their children', in Eisenberg, N., *Social Development* (Review of Personality and Social Psychology, 15, 49–73), Thousand Oaks, CA: Sage.

Guzell, J.R. et al., 2004, 'Parental perceived control over caregiving and its relationship to parent-infant interaction', *Child Development*, 75, 134–46.

Henderson, V.L. et al., 1990, in Feldman, S. et al., *At The Threshold: The Developing Adolescent*, MA: Harvard University Press.

Himmelstein, S. et al., 1991, 'An attributional analysis of maternal beliefs about the importance of child-rearing practices', *Child Development*, 62, 301–10.

Kelly, R.E. et al., 2006, 'Relationship between drug company funding and outcomes of clinical psychiatric research', *Psychological Medicine*, 36, 1647–56.

Kiang, L. et al., 2004, 'Maternal preconceptions about parenting predict child temperament, maternal sensitivity and children's empathy', *Developmental Psychology*, 40, 1081–92.

Lee, K., 1996, 'A Study of Teacher Responses Based on Their Conceptions of Intelligence', *Journal of Classroom Interactions*, 31, 1–12.

Mandiaki, K. et al., 2005, 'Parents' causal attributions about attention deficit/hyperactivity disorder: the effect of child and parent sex', *Child: Care Health and Development*, 31, 331–40.

Pomerantz, E. M. et al., 2006, 'The effects of mothers' perceptions of children's competence: The moderating role of mothers' theories of competence', *Developmental Psychology*, 42, 950–61.

Read, J. et al., 2006, 'Prejudice and schizophrenia: a review of the 'mental illness is an illness like any other' approach', *Acta Psychiatrica Scandinavica*, 113, 1–16.

Read, J. et al., 2013, *Models of Madness*, London: Routledge.

Endnotes

Introduction

1   genetic variants can only explain a tiny amount (1–5 per cent) of our individuality . . . See pp 208–9 of Joseph, 2015 for references to recent admissions of this fact for cognitive ability, personality, behaviour, and psychiatric disorders.

2   The scientists have invented something called 'The Missing Heritability' . . . Manolio et al., 2009.

3   there had been 115 studies . . . Collins et al., 2013.

4   the believers in genes are beginning to admit defeat . . . e.g. Sonuga-Barke, 2014; Munafo et al., 2014.

5   a single study of identical twins that were reared apart . . . Segal, 1999.

6   chemicals that switched certain genes on or off . . . for a readable account of epigenetics, see Carey, 2011.

7   it is a fact that some children are born with autism . . . Johnson et al., 2015.

8   there is some evidence that it may be so, in some cases . . . . e.g. Hadjikhani, 2010.

9   29 per cent of mental illness, worldwide, is attributable to it . . . Kessler et al., 2010.

10   the single best study found that 90 per cent . . . p 189, Sroufe et al., 2005.

11   there is strong evidence that children who suffer no maltreatment very rarely develop mental illness . . . e.g. Sroufe et al., 2005.

12 The presence of early love and responsiveness creates emotional health…Belsky et al., 2005; Lieberman et al., 2005; David et al., 2009; Hofferth et al., 2012.

13 just by believing its abilities are not fixed…see Appendix 4.

14 Fully 40 per cent of the websites on the Internet…Read et al., 2013.

Chapter 1: The Real Reasons Children are Like Their Parents

1 Human beings have the longest period of dependence…Bjorklund, 2007.

2 One of the most famous individual instances was Patti Hearst… Hearst, 1989.

3 to feel torn between doing so and meeting their own needs…Trivers, 1974.

4 At times, for most mothers…'Mother and Baby Sleep Survey', 2002.

5 no wonder so many become depressed and furiously angry…Fair-brother, 2008.

6 Indeed, is it any wonder that about two babies a week…Wolfe et al., 2014.

7 and ingratiate themselves, otherwise they can die…Trivers, 1974.

8 Parents implicitly and explicitly coach their children in the 'right' ways…Grusec, 1992; Simpkins et al., 2015.

9 children carefully study how parents behave and scrupulously copy it from a young age…Bandura, 1976; Simpkins et al., 2015.

10 identification is the child experiencing some aspect of the parent as being them…Ryan et al., 1989.

11 identification occurs out of love or out of fear…Ryan, R et al., 2000, 'Self-determination theory and the facilitation of intrinsic motivation, social development and well-being', *American Psychologist*, 55, 68–78.

12 an exceptionally successful doctor and dentist…see http://www.ncbi.nlm.nih.gov/pmc/articles/PMC2311865/?page=1 accessed 20 May, 2015.

13 it sets in motion a desperate and compulsive tendency to repeat the past...Levy, 2000.

14 The content of the depressive ideas may be identical....Hadwin et al., 2005; Murray et al., 2008.

15 In studies, such emotional abuse is emerging as the single most destructive maltreatment...Lanius et al., 2010; Varese et al., 2012.

16 But it is particularly damaging when done repeatedly and extremely by parents...Goldstein, 1985.

17 We use each other as dustbins for unwanted emotions in this way on a daily basis...Laing et al., 1964; Greatrex, 2002; Seligman, 2006; Fontes, 2015.

18 It becomes an intimate terrorism... Johnson, 2008, Fontes, 2015.

19 These patterns on the part of the parent usually result from having been subjected to them by their own parents...Quinton et al., 1984; Dowdney et al., 1985; Huesmann et al., 1984; Caspi et al., 1988; Chen et al., 2001; Thornberry et al., 2003; Capaldi et al., 2003; Conger et al., 2003; Smith, 2004; Neppi et al., 2009.

20 a high proportion of abusers of both kinds were themselves abused in that way... Quinton et al., 1984; Dowdney et al., 1985; Huesmann et al., 1984; Caspi et al., 1988; Chen et al., 2001; Thornberry et al., 2003; Capaldi et al., 2003; Conger. et al., 2003; Smith, 2004; Sroufe et al., 2005; Neppi et al., 2009; Read et al., 2013a.

21 The Traumagenic Model...Read et al., 2014.

22 The latest evidence proves that there is no simple mapping from one kind of maltreatment to one kind of mental illness...van Nirop, 2015.

23 It now seems clear that many of the hallucinations of psychosis are simply versions of memories...Bentall et al., 2012; Geekie, 2013.

24 All those positives shine through in later life, every bit as much as the consequences of maltreatment and other negatives...Chen et al., 2001; Thornberry et al., 2003; Sroufe et al., 2005; Belsky et al., 2005; Lieberman et al., 2005; David et al., 2009; Hofferth et al., 2012.

25 Nearly a quarter of Britons are suffering from a mental illness, mostly anxiety or depression, at any one time...ONS (Office of National Statistics), 2007.

26 In just 6 to 16 sessions, CBT claims to be able to convert you from depressed or anxious, to 'recovered'...Layard et al., 2014.

27 it has led to 'recovery' in around 40 per cent of people who complete the treatment...Layard et al., 2014.

28 In their book *Thrive*...Layard et al., 2014.

29 the extensive evidence...Westen et al., 2001; Westen et al., 2004; Westen et al., 2005; Durham et al., 2008; Shedler, 2010.

30 Proper therapy – such as psychodnamic therapy - can treat the causes...Leichsenring et al., 2008; Shedler, 2009.

31 Major reviews of the evidence...Leichsenring et al., 2008; Shedler, 2009.

32 Studies prove this...Shedler, 2009.

Chapter 2: Why Was Peaches Geldof So Like Her Mother?

1 this psychosomatic reaction...Kim et al., 2008.

2 Such prolonged separations from their main carer...Bowlby, 1975.

3 There is strong evidence...Read et al., 2013a.

4 While in the case of addiction...Kelly et al., 2009.

5 only insight into the true childhood causes can bring about profound change...Moos et al., 2006.

6 Like so many survivors...for an explanation of why trauma remains hidden, see Corstens et al., 2013; for explanation of how the mind organises trauma through buried selves, see p. 96, Corstens et al., 2012; for fuller scientific explanation of the meaning of symptoms of trauma, particularly auditory hallucination, see Longden et al., 2012.

7 very common in the childhoods of people with personality disorder...Bradley et al., 2005, Lahti, 2009; Velikonja et al., 2015.

8   emotional abuse is the strongest predictor of severe mental illness...Varese et al., 2012.

9   For example, one in three exceptional achievers...Eisenstadt, 1989.

10   Like so many personality disordered and well-known people...Young et al., 2006.

11   It is common for the emotionally abused...Widom et al., 2006.

12   Repeated overdoses are not attempts to die but they indicate a wilful lack of concern about living...Bohnert et al., 2012.

13   A study of the whole Swedish population...Wilcox et al., 2010.

14   We know this from suicidal clusters identified in groups of doctors, police and farmers...Coleman, 1987.

15   a student suicide increases the risk of further ones...Poijula et al., 2001.

16   When celebrities or characters in television fictions...Sudak et al., 2005.

17   Fans of the same gender and age...Phillips, 1974; Hittner, 2005.

18   Studies show that if the mother...Geulayov et al., 2012.

19   Even more specifically, the daughter of a suicidal mother...Table 2, Garssen et al., 2011.

20   On top of all this, women who have been sexually abused...Springs et al., 1992.

21   There is also evidence that sexual abuse...Hadland et al., 2012.

22   The fact of her equation with her mother...the AGA magazine article was reproduced in *The Sunday Times*, 13 April 2014, http://www.thesundaytimes.co.uk/sto/newsreview/article1399071.ece accessed 2 July, 2015.

23   In later life, FIfi was to report suffering from depression...*The Independent* newspaper, 31 August, 2014, http://www.independent.co.uk/news/people/news/fifi-trixibelle-geldof-i-have-suffered-from-clinical-depression-since-the-age-of-11-9702133.html accessed 2 July, 2015.

24 There is good evidence that premature death . . . Felitti et al.; Dube et al., 2001.

25 One study examined a sample of 1,210 . . . Bellis et al., 2012.

26 Having four or more ACE makes you seven times more liable to abuse alcohol . . . Anda et al., 2006.

27 which, in turn, have been proven to be more common among both fame-seekers and the famous . . . for fame-seekers, see Green et al., 2014; for the famous see Young et al., 2006.

28 If you had such a childhood . . . Hesse, 2008.

29 However good their early years . . . Geulayov et al., 2012.

30 Prior maltreatment and adversity . . . Melhem et al., 2008.

31 But most of us sometimes use 'drugs of solace' . . . Cameron et al., 1985.

32 R. D. Laing wrote that . . . Laing, 1971.

Chapter 3: Not In Your Genes

1 He stated that . . . p. 1, *The Observer* newspaper, London, 11 February, 2001.

2 it was established to everyone's satisfaction that no one gene existed . . . Plomin et al., 2003.

3 In 2010, some of the leading molecular geneticists . . . Haworth et al., 2010.

4 Twin studies had produced heritability estimates of 50 per cent or more for some traits . . . for intelligence see Deary et al., 2009; for schizophrenia and depression see Kendler, 2001.

5 the scientists dubbed the yawning gulf . . . Manolio et al., 2009.

6 a 2010 editorial in a key scientific journal . . . Sonuga-Barke, 2010.

7 For example, a 2014 study . . . Schizophrenia Working Group of the Psychiatric Genomics Consortium, 2014.

8 In the case of severe depression . . . Major Depressive Disorder Working Group of the Psychiatric GWAs Consortium, 2013.

9 I could quote several hundred scientific papers…See pp 208–9 of Joseph, 2015 for references to recent admissions of this fact for cognitive ability, personality and behaviour, and psychiatric disorders.

10 Professor Robert Plomin, told *The Guardian* newspaper…Wilby, P, 'Psychologist on a mission to give every child a learning chip', *The Guardian* newspaper, 18 February, 2014, London: *Guardian* newspaper, www.theguardian.com/education/2014/feb/18/psychologist-robert-plomin-says-genes-crucial-education accessed 15 May, 2015.

11 It was heralded on the BBC Radio 4 *Today* programme…*BBC Today* programme, 22 July, 2014.

12 I appeared on a BBC Radio 4 *Today* programme……*BBC Today* programme, 30 September, 2010.

13 only 1–3% of ADHD is explained by genetic variants…Nigg, 2012.

14 the BBC Radio 4 *Feedback* programme…BBC *Feedback*, 17 March, 2013.

15 some scientists are now trying to reclassify the junk ones as being important after all…Pennisi, 2012.

16 schizophrenia is at least partly caused by childhood maltreatment…Varese et al., 2012.

17 more likely to have both been maltreated in ways that cause schizophrenia, such as sexual or emotional abuse…Table 4, Fosse et al., 2015.

18 the abused one is much more likely to develop problems in adulthood…Kendler et al., 2000.

19 the twin where parental engagement is lowest…Ruttle et al., 2014.

20 But respected journals are finally now beginning to admit, e.g., Sonuga-Barke, 2014; Munafo et al., 2014.

21 certain key parts of his brain are underdeveloped and that this is unchangeable…van Rooij et al., 2015.

22 people who have suffered childhood maltreatment are three times more likely to smoke than ones who suffered none…Felitti et al., 2007.

Chapter 4: Maltreatment and Love (Why Siblings Are So Different, Pt 1)

1   good early care has as benign consequences as unresponsive care is damaging...Chen et al., 2001; Thornberry et al., 2003; Sroufe et al., 2005; Belsky et al., 2005; Lieberman et al., 2005; David et al., 2009; Hofferth et al., 2012.

2   they get a significantly different deal from each parent...McGuire, 2003.

3   but they do not do so nearly as much as we often imagine...this statement and the succeeding assertions about sibling difference in this paragraph are supported by: Plomin et al., 2011a; Plomin et al., 2011b.

4   In all families, to some degree, there are similarities in the treatment provided...Rose et al., 1990; Burt, 2009; Simpkins et al., 2015.

5   it's no puzzle that the children tend to be similar in their views...Jennings et al., 2009.

6   You do not have to posit genes as the reason...Conley et al., 2008.

7   The Traumagenic Model of mental illness...Read et al., 2014.

8   When such vulnerable people lose their job...Varese et al., 2011; Bentall et al., 2012; Longden et al., 2012.

9   All of us sometimes get a bit paranoid...Bentall et al., 1991.

10   The hormone cortisol plays a key role in priming us to overreact...Tarullo et al., 2006; Anderson et al., 2008.

11   with those tendencies usually having their roots in childhood maltreatment...Van Der Kolk, 2014.

12   A large body of evidence now proves that your baseline cortisol level is set by early childhood care...Hunter et al., 2011; Van Der Kolk, 2014.

13   at least half of the symptoms of the other disorder in common...Rommelse et al., 2011; Johnson et al., 2015b.

14   Scientific papers discussing them almost invariably begin...e.g. Nikolas et al., 2015.

15 This is despite the fact that the much more reliable evidence . . . Nigg, 2012.

16 Mothers who are stressed or anxious in pregnancy . . . Van Den Bergh et al., 2004; Rice et al., 2008; Glover et al., 2011; Korhonen et al., 2012; O'Connor et al., 2014.

17 Perhaps most tellingly . . . Grizenko et al., 2012.

18 When pregnant mothers are anxious or depressed . . . Winser et al., 2015; see also Lahti et al., 2009.

19 For example, birth weight has a significant effect . . . Petterson et al., 2015.

20 It is possible that the large number of serotonin-raising antidepressants . . . Sarkar et al., 2008.

21 increased amounts of autism . . . de Theije et al., 2011.

22 There are 13 studies . . . Curran et al., 2015.

23 one study identified 34 people . . . Fein et al , 2013.

24 If introduced early on, the right kind of support for carers . . . Dawson, 2008.

25 Prematurity is a predictor of a host of problems in babies . . . Siagal et al., 2008.

26 a very preterm newborn is two and a half to four times more likely to develop ADHD . . . Aylward, 2005; Delobel-Ayoub et al., 2006; Reijneveld et al., 2006.

27 it is harder for mothers to tune into babies who are difficult . . . Aagaard et al., 2008.

28 Responsive sensitivity to the infant's signals . . . Lanius et al., 2010.

29 Unresponsive care in early infancy . . . Chapters 4 and 5, James, 2005; Sroufe et al., 2005; Lanius et al., 2010.

30 A review of the 23 best studies . . . Weich et al., 2009; see also McEwen, 2010; Font, SA et al., 2015.

31 Rene Spitz in the 1940s . . . Spitz, 1946.

32 39 documented cases of children . . . Zingg, 1940.

33   Since then, it has been proven definitively...pp 158-9, James, 2005; Esther et al., 2009; Rutter et al., 2010; Mccall et al., 2011.

34   For example, they are at much greater risk of ASD and ADHD...For autism, see Rutter et al., 1999; Levin et al., 2015; For ADHD see Zeanah et al., 2009.

35   more prone to 'indiscriminate friendliness'...Zeanah et al., 2015.

36   Psychopathy has its roots in maltreatment, not genes...Weiler et al., 1996; Gao et al., 2010.

37   40 per cent of the British prison population spent time in local authority care during their childhoods...Singleton et al., 1998.

38   80 per cent of the prison population have at least one mental illness...Singleton et al., 1998.

39   but they (and not genes) create the vulnerability...Bradley et al., 2005; Lahti et al., 2009; Velikonja et al., 2015.

40   sexual and physical abuse well proven to be predictors...Read et al., 2003; Read et al., 2005; Varese et al., 2012.

41   Interestingly, where one identical twin is sexually abused...Kendler et al., 2000.

42   There are huge variations in the amount between nations...Foster et al., 2003.

43   with America having over 50 times more impulsivity disorder... Table 26.1, Chapter 26, Kessler et al., 2008.

44   Whereas the individualistic American culture...Foster et al., 2003.

45   Reviews of the evidence show that, stressed by unresponsive care...Teicher et al., 2003; Karl et al., 2006; Anda et al., 2006; McEwen, 2010; Lim et al., 2014; Teicher et al., 2014.

46   At 15 months, if a child has had unresponsive earlier care...Dawson et al., 2001.

47   have key parts of their brains that have not grown properly...Chugani et al., 2001.

48 This means they do not make eye contact and other relational problems...Tottenham et al., 2011.

49 If the child is insecure at 18 months old...Moutsiana et al., 2014.

50 Likewise, insecurity at 18 months is proven to affect the size... Moutsiana et al., 2015.

51 Unresponsive care before aged two has been demonstrated to predict dissociation ...Ogawa et al., 1997.

52 and personality disorder...Quinton et al., 1988.

53 When mothers are asked if their child was wanted before the birth or shortly afterwards...Matejcek et al., 1978; Matejcek et al., 1980; Myrhrman et al., 1996; McNeil et al., 2009; Broussard et al., 2010.

54 For example, the speed with which a baby's cortisol levels settle down....Albers et al., 2007.

55 Cortisol levels of toddlers can be adversely affected by being left with strangers...Appendix 3, James, 2010.

56 In one study of 18 month olds...Ahnert et al., 2004.

57 This is one of ten studies...Nine studies are reviewed in Vermeer et al , 2006; the tenth study is Bernard et al., 2015.

58 having to care for numerous other small children...Appendix 3, James, 2010.

59 Children of disharmonious parents are more likely to display symptoms of what are known as 'externalising' problems...Amato, 2001.

60 How distressed the child is and precisely how that distress is expressed...Ruttle et al., 2014; Jaffee et al., 2015.

61 For example, a study of 1,100 mothers and babies...Hibel et al., 2010.

62 The earlier the maltreatment the more severe the damage...Lansford et al., 2002; fn p156 on p 335, James, 2005; English et al., 2005a; English et al., 2005b; Kaplow et al., 2005; Sternberg et al., 2006; Kaplow et al., 2007; Lansford et al., 2007; Kim et al., 2009; Alameda et al., 2015.

63 For instance, in a study of 800 children . . . Manly et al., 2001.

64 There is strong evidence that if parents train their children in specific skills . . . Moreno et al., 2015.

65 There are numerous studies of identical twins . . . Fosse et al., 2015; Joseph, 2015.

66 For example, ADHD is found in the twin . . . Ruttle et al., 2014.

67 Large samples of children who were institutionalised . . . pp 158–9, James, 2005; Esther et al., 2009; Rutter et al., 2010; Mccall et al., 2011; Zeanah et al., 2015.

68 Institutionalised children are five to six times more likely . . . Rutter et al., 2010; Levin et al., 2015.

69 It has been shown that lengthy institutionalisation . . . Tottenham et al., 2010.

70 and cortisol levels . . . Rutter et al., 2010; Mccall et al., 2011.

71 If a mother gets depressed . . . Campbell et al., 1995; Teti et al., 1995; NICHD, 1999; Goodman et al., 2011.

72 It can lead to atypical brain development . . . Lupien et al., 2011.

73 The younger a child is when the depression begins . . . pp 472–3, Goodman et al., 1999.

74 There are numerous studies showing that the more severe the maltreatment, the worse the subsequent outcome . . . Shevlin et al., 2007; Felitti et al., 2010; Varese et al., 2012; Read, 2013a.

75 In the case of sexual abuse . . . e.g. Clemmons et al., 2007.

76 The most common comment preceding a city centre violent crime . . . Poyner, 1980.

77 He joined the 80 per cent of prisoners who qualify for a diagnosis of at least one mental illness . . . Singleton et al., 1998.

78 Multiple combinations of maltreatment are more harmful . . . Dong et al., 2004; English et al., 2005 b; Clemmon et al., 2007; Finkelhor et al., 2007; Sullman et al., 2009; Kim et al., 2009.

79 A comprehensive study of adverse childhood events (ACE) . . . Felitti et al., 2010.

80 A person who has five or more ACEs ... Shevlin et al., 2007.

81 Dozens of studies have shown ... Dawson et al., 1999; Diego et al., 2010.

82 For example, adults who were traumatised as children have decreased activity ... Hopper et al., 2007; Lanius et al., 2007.

83 Multiple studies have identified reductions ... Teicher et al., 2002; Teicher et al., 2006; Teicher et al., 2010; Bremner et al., 2010; McCrory et al., 2010.

84 Stress chemicals can cause the loss of neurones ... De Bellis, 2001; De Bellis, 2010.

85 It is an incontestable fact that societies and cultures have huge effects on how mentally ill we are ... James, 2008.

86 there is twice as much in English-speaking nations (23 per cent) compared with mainland Western Europe (11.5 per cent) ... James, 2008.

87 There is much less depression in collectivist Asian countries ... Chiao. J.Y., 2009.

88 America has the highest rate of mental illness ... Kessler et al., 2008.

89 An American is over fifty times more likely to be impulsive and aggressive ... Table 26.1, Chapter 26, Kessler et al., 2008.

90 It is true that World Health Organization evidence shows ... Kessler et al., 2010.

91 The opening line of a definitive account of the history of childhood ... De Mause, L., 1974, *The History of Childhood*, London: Souvenir Press.

92 Compared with American mother–baby dyads ... James, 1979.

93 For example, in a definitive study of schizophrenia ... World Health Organization, 1979.

94 In such collectivist societies, your identity is conferred upon you by virtue of your gender ... Sahlins, 2003; Konner, 2005.

95 A study of the impact of maltreatment in Nigeria ... Oladeji et al., 2010.

96   There is six times less mental illness in Nigeria than in America...
Kessler et al., 2008.

97   For example, in one large American study...Afifi et al., 2009.

98   there are extended families which reduces the disruption to care of
the child...Konner, 2005.

99   Hence, her brother bore out the broad findings of the World Health
Organization...Kessler et al., 2010.

100 In our affluenza-stricken society...James, 2008.

101 In my book *How Not To F*** Them Up*...James, 2010.

102 taking each other's toys 8 times an hour at the age of 18 months...Hay
et al., 2000.

103 I developed Love Bombing...James, 2012.

Chapter 5: Your Role In The Family Drama
(Why Siblings Are So Different, Pt 2)

1   There is a finite amount of love, time and money for parents to devote
to children...Trivers, 1974; Daly, M et al., 1998, *The Truth About
Cinderella*, London: Weidenfeld & Nicolson.

2   In families, we are very much like actors in a play...Byng-Hall, J,
1985, Cornell, W.F., 1988.

3   As R.D. Laing put it ...p 78, Laing, R.D., 1971.

4   The firstborn has a radical effect, especially upon the mother...
James, 2010.

5   As the family grows, the amount of parental resources decrease...
Lawson et al., 2009.

6   Lastborn children get less attention...Lawson et al., 2009.

7   In their early years, triplets get less sensitive responses...Feldman, R
et al., 2004, 'Parent-infant synchrony and the social-emotional development of triplets', *Developmental Psychology*, 40, 1133–47.

8   resulting in lower scores on tests of mental development...
Feldman, R et al., 2005.

9   the remarkable fact is that most of each individual child's nur-
     ture...Plomin et al., 1987; Plomin et al., 2011.

10 All of these interact with each other, rarely is a single one criti-
     cal...Atzaba-Poria, N et al., 2008.

11 There have been over 2,000 studies...Beer, J.M. et al., 2000.

12 the studies show that firstborns...see Sulloway, F.J., 1996 for refer-
     ences on statements about birth order in the succeeding paragraphs,
     unless I mention a specific study. See also Sulloway, F.J., 'Birth order
     and sibling competition', Dunbar, R et al., *The Oxford Handbook of
     Evolutionary Psychology*, Oxford: OUP; Healey, M.D. et al., 2007.

13 They achieve more in their careers having done better at
     school...Hotz, 2013.

14 The firstborn in a four-children family is, on average, approximately
     ten percentage points...Hotz, 2013.

15 although they are liable to have been forced to submit to older sib
     lings...Healey et al., 2007.

16 One major reason firstborns are different...Lawson, D.R. et al., 2009.

17 Another reason firstborns differ is that parents are generally stricter
     with them...Hotz, V J , 2013.

18 For example, on average, parents in two-child families...Price, J,
     2008.

19 It is no wonder that firstborns have higher scores...Hotz, 2013; Bu, F,
     2014.

20 Above all, they have less unfulfilled aspirations for the later-
     borns...Bu, F. 2014.

21 This is well illustrated by the story of Sir Vince Cable...My source
     for this analysis of Cable is his autobiography: Cable, V, 2010.

22 Misleadingly entitled *Free Radical*, he repeatedly admits...By the
     time Cable was an activist in 1970s Glasgow he had concluded
     that being two-faced was a necessary evil. He made a name for him-
     self by starting a strong campaign against the then Mrs Thatcher's

plan to end the provision of free milk in schools (the 'Thatcher Milk Snatcher' saga). He is quite explicit about having made a fuss of this policy as a way of advancing his career, more than because it was something he felt passionately about: 'This campaign established me, improbably, as a champion of the Glasgow left-wing and I milked the popularity it gave me. I rather foolishly confided to one of my colleagues that I found it incongruous to be promoting socialism in the council chamber and free-market economics in the university lecture rooms on the same day. I was reminded, unsympathetically, of a quote from Jimmy Maxton, that 'if you can't ride two horses at once you shouldn't be in the bloody circus'. I tried to assimilate this advice' (my emphasis, p 119, Cable, 2010).

Subsequently, he explains in his book that he deliberately developed a strategy of posing as Left Wing (having first of all tried out posing as more Right Wing) after Tony Blair was elected. Realising that mortgages and credit cards had come to play an ever-increasing role in voters' lives, he began writing newspaper articles and talking to financial journalists about the risks of such high levels of household debt and drawing attention to the methods commonly employed by High Street banks to jack up their profits. He proudly reports his greatest triumph as being when *Observer* Money ran the headline 'a lone hero stands up to the big banks'. He was delighted to get similar coverage in the *Mail on Sunday*.

After the resignation of Menzies Campbell in October 2007, he was made acting leader of the Liberal Democrats. The Northern Rock fiasco had happened the previous month. He consulted with his closest advisers in search of a way of making maximum impact during what would only be a two-month window of opportunity before the new leader was appointed. Now came the momentous publicity stunt which was to change the course of his career. 'Another opportunity was presented by the growing crisis in the banking sector, centring on the Northern Rock bank...we advocated temporary public ownership as the best way of protecting the state's enormous stake in the bank and ensuring that any upside would accrue to the taxpayer, not to someone like Richard Branson' (p 292, Cable, 2010).

Emboldened by the reception his pronouncements had received, he decided to give it as much welly as possible, completely conscious that the electorate would be deceived into thinking that he was far more of a Lefty than has ever been the case. In subsequent commentaries he insisted that 'the taxpayer must receive any profits in return for the rescue; the shareholders could not expect to have their equity investment protected; and the managers should be sacked. In effect, the banks should be nationalized. Matthew Oakshott and I debated the pros and cons of embracing full nationalization and I was encouraged to use the 'N' word without embarrassment, which became a telling point in the national news coverage' (p 329, Cable, 2010).

Far from Cable being an authentic warrior against bankers and the carnage they brought, he simply happened upon the financial crisis as an opportunity to market himself and his party. 'The Lib Dems will rarely be accommodated (ie, be given extensive coverage in the media) as of right, and so have to have something especially memorable to say or to have carved out a reputation as being the effective opposition, as Charles Kennedy did during the Iraq War and I have been trying to do in relation to the financial crisis' (p 307, Cable, 2010).

23 From birth onwards, parents respond differently to boys and girls...Hoyenga, K.B. et al., 1993, Eagly, A.H. et al., 2004.

24 In doing so she was not unusual, the most mentally ill group...Sweeting, H et al., 2009. 'GHQ increases among Scottish 15 year olds.

25 Two thirds of children claim their parents...Dunn, J et al., 1990.

26 Beauty or handsomeness... Etcoff, N, 1999.

27 But more commonly, favouritism is triggered by the parents' history... Atzaba-Poria et al., 2008.

28 Lucian Freud, the celebrated painter... see Greig, G, 2015.

29 the childhood of Janet Street-Porter... Street-Porter, J, 2005.

30 For example, in one study the negativity of mothers towards their babies... Broussard et al., 2010.

31 which means they would be nearly twice as likely to be mentally ill... Bakermans-Kranenburg, M.J. et al., 2009.

32 A rather clever Czechoslovakian study... Matejcek et al., 1978; Matejcek et al., 1980.

33 In accord with this, subsequent large studies... Myrhrman et al., 1996; McNeil et al., 2009.

34 A study of five- and seven-year-old siblings.... Atzaba-Poria et al., 2008.

35 Many studies show that children of depressed mothers... e.g. Cole, PM et al., 1992; Zahn-Waxler, C et al., 1990.

Chapter 6: Why Traits Run In Families

1 During their training, doctors are inducted into the biogenetic explanation of mental illness and studies show that this leads to a remarkable ignorance of the extensive evidence of environmental causes... Read et al., 2013b.

2 In the case of schizophrenia, 45 times more studies... Read et al., 2008.

3 The public are systematically misled... Read et al., 2013.

4 A first-degree relative of someone who is depressed... Sullivan et al., 2000.

5 For anxiety, depending on the kind... Hetteman et al., 2001.

6 Intelligence broadly runs in families... Bjorklund et al., 2009; Brown et al., 2009.

7 personality traits less so... Plomin et al., 2011a.

8   Schizophrenia runs in families...Mortenson et al., 1999.

9   but so does one of its main causes, sexual abuse...Langstrom et al., 2015.

10 Having a schizophrenic mother...Mortenson et al., 1999.

11 interestingly, though, having a schizophrenic father...p 99, Gottesman, I.I., 1992.

12 A review of 59 studies...Read et al., 2008.

13 the brother of a man convicted of a sexual crime...Langstrom et al., 2015.

14 Reviews of the evidence show that all kinds are two to three times commoner in the childhoods of schizophrenics...Varese et al., 2012.

15 The face that the impact of maltreatment is dose-dependent...Kelleher et al., 2013.

16 People who have endured...Shevlin et al., 2008.

17 This rises to 193 times more...Shevlin et al., 2008.

18 severely abused children are 48 times...Janssen et al., 2004.

19 like bipolar disorder (extreme mood swings)...Etain et al., 2008; Daruy-Filho et al., 2011.

20 and personality disorder (febrile emotions, me-me-me narcissism)...Bradley et al., 2005; Lahti et al., 2009; Steel et al., 2009; Velikonja et al., 2015.

21 It is also much more common in the depressed and anxious...for a review of the evidence on depression, see Nanni et al., 2012; for anxiety see Kuo et al., 2011.

22 Despite huge publicity...In the UK, Robert Plomin declared that his study of 11,000 twins had proven that more than half of GCSE results are attributable to genes: http://www.theguardian.com/science/2013/dcc/11/genetics-variation-exam-results1 accessed 27 June, 2015.

23 Since we now know that there are no genes for ability ...A major review of the latest evidence on intelligence stated that 'very little progress has been made in finding the genes that contribute to

normal variation' (in intelligence), p 135, Nisbett et al., 2012; what genes have been found seem to be false positives: Chabris et al., 2012.

24 For over a century, eugenicists...Galton, 1904.

25 low income homes have less books...Hart et al., 2003.

26 when children from low income homes are given extra help to boost their skills, it works...p 138, Nisbett et al., 2012.

27 Little attention is paid to the evidence that when children are adopted young...van Ijzendoorn et al., 2005.

28 Indeed, one study showed that children of heroin-addicted mothers...Ornoy et al., 2001.

29 But almost none has been given to a much more convincing study...Plomin et al., 1998.

30 Some reviews of the evidence suggest that certain variants ...Belsky et al., 2009; Karg et al., 2011.

31 or increase benign outcomes if care is good...Van Ijzendoorn et al., 2015.

32 However, this has been contradicted by so many other reviews of the evidence...Munafo et al., 2009; Risch et al., 2009; Munafo et al., 2014.

33 The same is true of other 'candidate genes'...Vassos et al., 2014.

34 There have been numerous studies...Maxfield et al., 1996; Farrington, 2005; Granic et al., 2006; Garber et al., 2007; Maikovich et al., 2008; Sheehan et al., 2008.

35 Their repeated 'nattering'...Patterson, 1982.

36 which has been proven to directly cause aggressive misbehaviour in childhood and subsequently, violence in adulthood, regardless of genes...Maxfield et al., 1996; Jaffee, 2004; Kaplow et al., 2007.

37 The reason such parents are like this is...Quinton et al., 1984; Dowdney et al., 1985; Huesmann et al., 1984; Caspi et al., 1988; Chen et al., 2001; Thornberry et al., 2003; Capaldi et al., 2003; Conger et al., 2003; Smith, 2004; Neppi et al., 2009.

38 Her behaviour was a form of what is known as intimate terrorism...Johnson, 2008.

39 There are at least ten studies...Quinton et al., 1984; Dowdney et al.,
1985; Huesmann et al., 1984; Caspi et al., 1988; Chen et al., 2001;
Thornberry et al., 2003; Capaldi et al., 2003; Conger et al., 2003;
Smith, 2004; Neppi et al., 2009.

40 For example, one study showed...Conger et al., 2003.

41 Half a century after the holocaust horror, offspring of survivors and
their children were still being made insecure by their ancestor's
trauma...Sagi et al., 2002.

42 A high proportion of survivors suffer post traumatic stress disorder
(PTSD) and that inevitably affects parenting, with more emotional
abuse and neglect...Yehuda et al., 2001.

43 The same is true of combat veterans...Dekel et al., 2008; Pearrow,
2009.

44 Eighty per cent of children with parents like this have what is called
a 'disorganised' pattern of attachment, in which they have confusing ways of coping with relationships...Lyons-Ruth et al., 2008;
Hesse et al, 2003.

45 Disorganised attachment in childhood often results in an unresolved
adult pattern which, in turn, leads to 80 per cent of their offspring having disorganised attachment...Liotti, 2004.

46 For example, in general, the kind of early care a monkey receives...for
references to the studies referred to here, see Suomi, 2008.

47 a study of over 1,700 maltreated children...Jaffee et al., 2007.

48 The classic demonstration of the importance...Van den Boom,
1994.

49 Overall, children born with low birth weights...Saigal et al., 2008.

50 For every pound less that an identical twin has...Pettersson et al., 2015.

51 children whose mothers drank a lot of alcohol...Saigal et al.,
2008.

52   the evidence shows that there is a strong tendency for mothers to care for their infants in similar ways to how they were nurtured ... Belsky et al., 2005; Neppi et al., 2009.

53   For example, in one study of 180 mothers ... Sroufe et al., 2009.

54   Several studies have observed the care children received when small ... Chen et al., 2001; Thornberry et al., 2003; Belsky et al., 2005; Lieberman et al., 2005; Campbell et al., 2007; Kerr et al., 2009; Neppi et al., 2009; Hofferth et al., 2012; Madden et al., 2015.

55   A particularly telling study ... Belsky et al., 2005.

56   The evidence clearly shows ... Lieberman et al., 2005.

57   Evidence from samples of mothers ... Hunter et al., 1979; Crockenberg, 1987; Egeland et al., 1987; Caliso et al., 1992.

58   These factors – a supportive other adult, therapy or a loving partner ... Belsky et al., 1990.

59   Loving partners are particularly shown to help .... Cohn et al., 1992; Das Eiden et al., 1995.

60   In a book on the subject ... Waugh, 2005.

61   In a moving documentary ... (https://www.youtube.com/watch?v=iAITT_K1rpU).

62   Transactional Analysis, created by Eric Berne ... Berne, 2001.

63   The quintuplet of Melrose novels ... St Aubyn, 2012.

Chapter 7: The Real Causes of Ability

1   The fact that less than one quarter of British children ... Goodman et al., 2010.

2   IQ scores are a proxy for privilege, not for inborn mental ability ... see Chapter 2, Skenk, 2010.

3   positive relative to negative feedback from parents than a working-class child ... Hart et al., 2003.

4   The vastly better educational performance ... OECD, 2012.

5   only 6 per cent in Denmark, for instance ... James, 2008.

6   The proportion of children in low-income families...James, 1995.

7   Many decades ago, the American psychologist Lewis Terman...Feldman, 1984.

8   It takes 10,000 hours of practice...Ericsson, 1996; pp 202–4, Skenk, 2010.

9   All prodigies, without exception, seem to be the product of hours practised, not some inbuilt capacity...Ericsson et al., 2007.

10   known as Deliberate Practice...Andersson et al., 1993.

11   many hours of learning required to acquire The Knowledge of different streets...Maguire et al., 2006.

12   myelin in the neurones of violinists, increasing the speed of passage of nerve signals...Hill et al., 2009,

13   Teaching children or students or teachers or parents...Dweck, 2012.

14   Take Wolfgang Amadeus Mozart's assiduousness...Sadie, 2006.

15   the Polgar family...Forbes, 1992; Polgar et al., 2005.

16   Interviewed recently, all three girls...see the documentary, *My Brilliant Brain*, 2012, New York: National Geographic Channel, https://www.youtube.com/watch?v=2wzs33wvr9E, accessed 30 June, 2015.

17   The term Tiger Mothering...Chua, 2011.

18   one in three of exceptional achievers lost a parent before the age of 15...Eisenstadt et al., 1989.

19   The evidence that high achievers of all kinds are more likely to suffer mental illness is now considerable...Young et al., 2006; Jamison, 2011; Bellis et al., 2012; Part One, James, 2013.

20   Chief executives in America are four times...Babiak et al., 2010.

21   British ones are significantly more likely...Board et al., 2005.

22   In the performing arts...Ando et al., 2014.

23   We know that children's fantasy narratives...Murray et al., 2014.

24   The physically abused make up different stories...Waldinger et al., 2001.

25 there are now a host of studies...e.g. Sroufe et al., 2005; Ruttle et al., 2014; van Nirop et al., 2015.

26 For example, sexual abuse correlates with auditory hallucinations...Bentall et al., 2012.

27 THE RISE AND FALL OF TIGER WOODS...Among others, a key source for assertions about Tiger Woods in what follows is Helling, S, 2010.

28 can be viewed on YouTube today...see https://www.youtube.com/watch?v=_wHkA_983_s accessed 1 July, 2015.

29 aged five he appeared on the network ABC show *That's Incredible!*...see https://www.youtube.com/watch?v=kfTY5xUFaJs accessed 1 July, 2015.

30 it is well proven to be caused by helicopter parenting...Blatt, 1995; Kawamura et al., 2002; pp 67–9, James, 2005; Soenes et al., 2005; Soenens et al., 2006; Craddock et al., 2009.

31 eating disorders...Franco-Paredas et al., 2005.

32 anxiety and depression...Stoeber et al., 2007; Harris et al., 2007.

33 loneliness...Laurenti et al., 2008; Sherry et al., 2008.

34 compulsiveness...Rheaume et al., 2000.

35 feelings of being an imposter...Thompson et al., 2000; Ferrari et al., 2006.

36 suicidal tendencies...O'Connor, 2007.

37 cortisol dysregulation...Wirtz et al., 2007.

38 In one study, samples of British and Italian families were compared...Raudino et al., 2013.

39 adaptive and maladaptive perfectionism...Stoeber et al., 2006.

40 a phenomenon which has been specifically tested in athletes...Stoeber et al., 2007b.

41 what is known as The Marketing Character...pp 13–14, 65–7, James, 2007.

42 Studies of such characters...Saunders et al., 2000; Saunders, 2001.

43 portrayed America as a Marketing Society...Fromm, 1955.

44 Pathological mourning takes two forms ... Bowlby, 1998.

45 Like most Scandinavians, as the studies show ... Thomsen et al., 2006.

46 In fact, there is a large body of evidence that we are attracted ... p 103, James, 2005.

47 The first study proving this was done in Hawaii in 1980 ... Jedlicka, 1980.

48 Subsequent studies show we are more likely to pick partners with the hair and eye colour ... Little et al., 2003.

49 It applies to traits as obvious as what our opposite-sexed parent's face looked like and as obscure as whether they smoked ... Facial resemblance: Bereczkei et al., 2009; Smoking: Kiado, 2011.

50 A study of 49 women ... Wiszewska et al., 2007.

51 A particularly telling study ... Bereczkei et al., 2004.

52 Indeed, there is evidence that women ... Pollet et al., 2009.

53 In a famous study ... Clark et al., 1989.

54 There is good evidence that a high proportion ... Young et al., 2006.

55 Narcissists are more prone to promiscuity ... Jonason et al., 2010a.

56 the Dark Triad of narcissism, psychopathy and Machiavellianism ... Jonason et al., 2010b.

57 The Twelve Steps Programme helpfully promotes ... Kelly et al., 2009.

58 although there can be problems in sustaining this for some people ... Moos et al., 2006.

59 childhood maltreatment puts them more at risk ... Dube et al., 2003; Dube et al., 2006.

60 In fact, over one hundred experiments (mostly conducted in the last decade) ... Hagger et al., 2010.

61 in one of four seminal experiments ... Baumeister et al., 1998.

62 Since those studies ... Baumeister et al., 2007.

63 When people choose water instead of alcohol ... Muraven et al., 2006.

64   When people put a positive gloss…Fischer et al., 2007.

65   Indeed, the evidence shows that people with good self-control….
Tangney et al., 2004.

66   Some studies have found that people…Gailliot et al., 2007.

67   However, other studies have not found…Bleedie et al., 2012; Kurzban, 2010.

68   It was with this model that Ryan approached…Ryan et al., 2008.

69   The self-determination model…Moller et al., 2006.

70   In the first of three experiments…Muraven, M.J. et al., 2007.

71   Two further studies supported those conclusions…Muraven et al.,
2008a; Muraven, 2008b.

72   Premature Ego Development…James, 1960.

73   Trescothick's autobiography…Trescothick, 2009.

74   Jonny Wilkinson's story is equally disheartening…Wilkinson, 2011.

Conclusion: It's The Environment, Stupid!

1   We need an education system like that in Finland…Sahlberg, 2007.

2   The *Lancet* medical journal…Cross-Disorder Group of the Psychiatric Genomics Consortium, 2013.

3   a telling example was published…Trzaskowski et al., 2013.

References

Aagaard, R.N., et al., 2008, 'Mothers' experiences of having a preterm infant in the neonatal care unit: a meta-synthesis', *Journal of Pediatric Nursing*, 23, e26–e36.

Afifi, T.O., et al., 2009, 'The relationship between child abuse, parental divorce and lifetime mental disorders and suicidality in a nationally representative adult sample', *Child Abuse and Neglect*, 33, 139–47.

Ahnert, L., et al., 2004, 'Transition to child care: Association with infant-mother attachment, infant negative emotion and cortisol elevations', *Child Development*, 75, 639–50.

Alameda, L et al., 2015, 'Childhood sexual and physical abuse: age at exposure modulates impact on functional outcome in early psychosis patients', *Psychological Medicine*, 45, 2727–36.

Albers, E.M., et al., 2007, 'Maternal behavior predicts infant cortisol recovery from a mild everyday stressor', *Journal of Child Psychology and Psychiatry*, 49, 97–103.

Amato, P.R., 2001, 'Children of divorce in the 1990s: an update of the Amato and Keith (1991) meta-analysis', *Journal of Family Psychology*, 15, 355–70.

Anda, R.F., et al., 2006, 'The Enduring Effects of Abuse and Related Adverse Experiences in Childhood: A Convergence of Evidence from Neurobiology and Epidemiology', *European Archives of Psychiatry and Clinical Neuroscience*, 256, 174–86.

Anderson, S.L., et al., 2008, 'Stress, sensitive periods and maturational events in adolescent depression', *Trends in Neurosciences*, 31, 183–91.

Andersson, K.A., et al., 1993, 'The role of deliberate practice in the acquisition of expert performance', *Psychological Review*, 100, 363–406.

Ando, V., et al., 2014, 'Psychotic traits in comedians', *British Journal of Psychiatry*, 204, 341–5.

Atzaba-Poria, N et al., 2008, 'Corelates of parental differential treatment: parental and contextual factors during middle childhood', *Child Development*, 79, 217–32.

Aylward, G.P., 2005, 'Neurodevelopmental outcomes of infants born prematurely', *J Dev Behav Pediatr*, 26, 427–40.

Babiak, P., et al., 2010, 'Corporate psychopathy: taking the walk', *Behavioral Science and the Law*, 28, 1–20.

Bakermans-Kranenburg, M.J. et al., 2009, 'The first 10,000 adult attachment interviews: distribution of adult attachment representations in clinical and non-clinical groups', *Attachment and Human Development*, 11, 223–63.

Bandura, A., 1976, *Social Learning Theory*, Cambridge: Pearson.

Baumeister, R.F., et al., 1998, 'Ego Depletion: Is the Active Self a Limited Resource?', *Journal of Personality and Social Psychology*, 74, 5, 1252–65.

Baumeister, R.F., et al., 2007 'The Strength Model of Self-Control', *Current Directions in Psychological Science* 16: 351.

Beer, J.M. et al., 2000, 'The influence of rearing order on personality development within two adoption cohorts', *Journal of Personality*, 68, 769–819.

Bellis, M.A., et al., 2012, 'Dying to be famous: retrospective cohort study of rock and pop star mortality and its association with adverse childhood experiences', *BMJ Open*, 2012; 2:e002089. doi:10.1136/bmjopen-2012-002089.

References

Belsky, J., et al., 1990, 'Childrearing history, marital quality and maternal affect: Intergenerational transmission in a low-risk sample', *Development and Psychopathology*, 1, 291–304.

Belsky, J., et al., 2005, 'Intergenerational transmission of warm-sensitive-stimulating parenting: a prospective study of mothers and fathers of 3-year-olds', *Child Development*, 384–96.

Belsky J., et al., 2009, 'Vulnerability genes or plasticity genes?', *Molecular Psychiatry*, 14: 746–54.

Bentall, R.P., et al., 1991, 'Paranoia and social reasoning: an attribution theory analysis', *British Journal of Clinical Psychology*, 30, 13–23.

Bentall, R.P., ct al., 2012, 'Do specific early-life adversities lead to specific symptoms of psychosis? A study from the 2007 The Adult Psychiatric Morbidity Survey', *Schizophrenia Bulletin*, 38, 534–40.

Bereczkei, T., et al., 2004, 'Sexual imprinting in human mate choice', *Proceedings of the Royal Society B: Biological Sciences*, 271, 1129–34.

Bereczkei, T., et al., 2009, 'Facialmetric similarities mediate mate choice: sexual imprinting on opposite-scxed parents', *Proceedings of the Royal Society B: Biological Sciences*, 276, 91–8.

Bernard, K., et al., 2015, 'Examining change in cortisol patterns during the 10-week transition to a new child-care setting', *Child Development*, 86, 456–71.

Berne, F., 2001, *Transactional Analysis in Psychotherapy: the classic handbook to its principles*, London: Souvenir Press.

Bjorklund, D.F., 2007, *Why Youth Is Not Wasted on the Young: Immaturity in Human Development*, Oxford: Blackwell Publishing.

Bjorklund, A., et al., 2009, *IQ and family background: are associations strong or weak?*, Discussion Paper 4305, Bonn: IZA.

Blatt, S.J., 1995, 'The destructiveness of perfectionism', *American Psychologist*, 50, 1003–20.

Bleedie, C.J., et al., 2012, 'The role of glucose in self-control: Another look at the evidence and an alternative conceptualization', *Personality and Social Psychology Review*, 16, 143–53.

Board, B.J., et al., 2005, 'Disordered personalities at work', *Psychology, Crime and Law*, 11, 17–32.

Bohnert, A.S.B., et al., 2012, 'Unintentional overdose and suicide among substance abusers: a review of overlap and risk factors', *Drug and Alcohol Dependence*, 110, 183–92.

Bowlby, J., 1975, *Attachment and Loss: Separation—anxiety and anger*, London: Penguin.

Bowlby, J., 1998, *Loss (Attachment and Loss Volume 3)*, London: Pimlico.

Bradley, R., et al., 2005, 'The psychodynamics of borderline personality disorder: a view of developmental psychopathology', *Development and Psychopathology*, 17, 927–57.

Broussard, E.R., et al., 2010, 'Maternal perception of newborns predicts attachment organization in middle adulthood', *Attachment & Human Development*, 12, 159–72.

Brown, S., et al., 2009, *Following in your parents' footsteps? Empirical analysis of matched parent-offspring test scores*, Discussion Paper 3986, Bonn: IZA.

Bu, F, 2014, 'Sibling configurations, educational aspiration and attainment', *Institute for Social and Economic Research*, 2014–11.

Burt, A.S., 2009, 'Rethinking environmental contributions to child and adolescent psychopathology: A meta-analysis of shared environmental influences', *Psychological Bulletin*, 135, 608–37.

Byng-Hall, J, 1985, 'The family script: a useful bridge between theory and practice', *Journal of Family Therapy*, 7, 301–5.

Cable, V, 2010, *Free Radical*, London: Atlantic Books.

Caliso, J., et al., 1992, 'Childhood history of abuse and child abuse screening', *Child Abuse and Neglect*, 16, 647–59.

Cameron, D., et al., 1985, 'An epidemiological and sociological analysis of the use of alcohol, tobacco and other drugs of solace', *Journal of Public Health*, 7, 18–29.

Campbell, J., et al., 2007, 'Intergenerational continuities and discontinuities in parenting styles', *Australian Journal of Psychology*, 59, 140–50.

Campbell, S.B., et al., 1995, 'Depression in first-time mothers: mother-infant interaction and depression chronicity', *Developmental Psychology*, 21, 349–57.

Capaldi, D., et al., 2003, 'Continuity of parenting practices across generations in an at-risk sample: A prospective comparison of direct and mediated associations', *Journal of Abnormal Child Psychology*, 31, 127–42.

Carey, N., 2011, *The Epigenetics Revolution*, London: Icon Books.

Caspi, A., et al., 1988, 'Emergent family patterns: The intergenerational construction of problem behavior and relationships' in R. Hinde., et al. (Eds.), *Relationships within families* (pp. 218–40), Oxford: Oxford University Press.

Chabris, G.F., et al., 2012, 'Most reported genetic associations with general intelligence are probably false positives', *Psychological Science*, 23, 1314–23.

Chen, Z., et al., 2001, 'The intergenerational transmission of constructive parenting', *Journal of Marriage and the Family*, 63, 17–31.

Chiao. J.Y., 2009, 'Culture-gene coevolution of individualism-collectivism and the serotonin transporter gene', *Proceedings of the Royal Society B*, doi:10.1098/rspb.2009.1650.

Chua, A., 2011, *Battle Hymn of the Tiger Mother*, London: Bloomsbury.

Chugani, H.T., et al., 2001, 'Local brain functional activity following early deprivation: a study of postinstitutionalized Romanian orphans', *NeuroImage*, 14, 1290–1301.

Clark, R.D., et al., 1989, 'Gender differences in receptivity to sexual offers', *Journal of Psychology and Human Sexuality*, 2, 39–55.

Clemmons, J.C., et al., 2007, 'Unique and combined contributions of multiple child abuse types and abuse severity to adult trauma symptomatology', *Child Maltreatment*, 12, 172–81.

Cohn, D., et al., 1992, 'Mothers' and fathers' working models of childhood attachment relationships, parenting styles and child behavior', *Development and Psychopathology*, 4, 417–31.

Cole, P.M. et al., 1992, 'Emotion displays in two-year-olds during mishaps', *Child Development*, 63, 314–24.

Coleman, L., 1987, *Suicide Clusters*, London: Faber.

Collins, A.L., et al., 2013, 'Genome-wide association studies in psychiatry: what have we learned?', *British Journal of Psychiatry*, 202, 1–4.

Conger, R., et al., 2003, 'Angry and aggressive behaviour across three generations: A prospective, longitudinal study of parents and children', *Journal of Abnormal Child Psychology*, 31, 143–60.

Conley, D., et al., 2008, 'All in the family: family composition, resources and sibling similarity in socioeconomic status', *Research in Social Stratification and Mobility*, 26, 297–306.

Cornell, W.F., 1988, 'Life Script Theory: a critical review from a developmental perspective', *Transactional Analysis Journal*, 18, 270–82.

Corstens, D., et al., 2012, 'Talking with voices: exploring what is expressed by the voices people hear', *Psychosis*, 4, 95–104.

Corstens, D., et al., 2013, 'The origins of voices: links between life history and voice hearing in a survey of 100 cases', *Psychosis*, 5, 270–85.

Craddock, A.E., et al., 2009, 'Family of origin characteristics as predictors of perfectionism', *Australian Journal of Psychology*, 61, 136–44.

Crockenberg, S., 1987, 'Predictors and correlates of anger toward and punitive control of toddlers by adolescent mothers', *Child Development*, 58, 964–75.

Cross-Disorder Group of the Psychiatric Genomics Consortium, 2013, 'Identification of risk loci with shared effects on five major psychiatric disorders: a genome-wide analysis', *The Lancet*, 28 February, 2013, http://dx.doi.org/10.1016/S0140-6736(12)62129-1.

Curran, E.A., et al., 2015, 'Birth by caesarean section and development of autism spectrum disorder and attention deficit/hyperactivity disorder: a systematic review and meta-analysis', *Journal of Child Psychology and Psychiatry*, 56, 500–8.

Daruy-Filho, L., et al., 2011, 'Childhood maltreatment and clinical outcomes of bipolar disorder', *Acta Psychiatrica Scandinavica*, 124, 427–34.

Das Eiden, R., et al., 1995, 'Maternal working models of attachment, marital adjustment and the parent-child relationship', *Child Development*, 66, 1504–18.

David, C., et al., 2009, 'A prospective three generational study of fathers' constructive parenting', *Developmental Psychology*, 45, 1257–75.

Dawson, G., et al., 1999, 'Infants of depressed mothers exhibit atypical frontal electrical brain activity during interactions with mothers and with a familiar non-depressed adult', *Child Development*, 70, 1058–66.

Dawson, G., et al., 2001, 'Autonomic and brain electrical activity in securely-and insecurely-attached infants of depressed mothers', *Infant Behavior and Development*, 24, 135–49.

Dawson, G., 2008, 'Early behavioral intervention, brain plasticity and the prevention of autism spectrum disorder', *Development and Psychopathology*, 20, 775–803.

Deary, I.J., et al., 2009, 'Genetic foundations of human intelligence', *Human Genet*, 126, 215–32.

De Bellis, M.D., 2001, 'Developmental traumatology', *Development and Psychopathology*, 13, 537–61.

De Bellis, M.D., 2010, 'The neurobiology of child neglect', in Lanius, R.A., et al., *The Impact of Early Life Trauma on Health and Disease*, Cambridge: CUP.

De Mause, L., 1974, *The History of Childhood*, London: Souvenir Press.

de Theije. C.G., et al., 2011, 'Pathways underlying the gut-to-brain connection in autism spectrum disorders as future targets for disease management', *European Journal of Pharmacology*, 668 (Suppl. 1), S570–80.

Dekel, R., et al., 2008, 'Is there intergenerational transmission of trauma? The case of combat veterans' children', *American Journal of Orthopsychiatry*, 78, 281–9.

Delobel-Ayoub, M., et al., 2006, 'Behavioral outcome at 3 years of age in very preterm infants: the EPIPAGE study', *Pediatrics*, 117, 1996–2005.

Diego, M.A., et al., 2010, 'EEG in 1-week, 1-month and 3-month old infants of depressed and non-depressed mothers', *Biological Psychiatry*, 83, 7–14.

Dong, M., et al., 2004, 'The interrelatedness of multiple forms of childhood abuse, neglect and household dysfunction', *Child Abuse and Neglect*, 28, 771–8.

Dowdney, L., et al., 1985, 'The nature and qualities of parenting provided by women raised in institutions', *Journal of Child Psychology and Psychiatry*, 26, 599–625.

Dube, S.R., et al., 2001, 'Childhood abuse, household dysfunction, and the risk of attempted suicide throughout the life span: Findings from the Adverse Childhood Experiences Study', *JAMA*, 286, 3089–96.

References

Dube, S.R., et al., 2003, 'Childhood abuse, neglect, and household dysfunction and the risk of illicit drug use: the adverse childhood experience study', *Pediatrics*, 111, 564–72.

Dube, S.R., et al., 2006, 'Adverse childhood experiences and the association with ever using alcohol and initiating alcohol use during adolescence', *Journal of Adolescent Health*, 38, 1–10.

DuMont, K.A., et al., 2007, 'Predictors of resilience in abused and neglected children grown-up: The role of individual and neighborhood characteristics', *Child Abuse and Neglect*, 31, 255–74.

Dunn, J et al., 1990, *Separate Lives: Why Siblings Are So Different*, New York: Basic Books.

Durham, R.C., et al., 2008, 'Long-term outcome of eight clinical trials of CBT for anxiety disorders: symptom profile of sustained recovery and treatment-resistant groups', *Journal of Affective Disorders*, 136, 875–81.

Dweck, C., 2012, *Mindset: How You Can Fulfil Your Potential*, London: Constable and Robinson.

Eagly, AH et al., 2004, *The Psychology of Gender* (2nd ed.). New York: Guilford Press.

Egeland, B., et al., 1987, 'Intergenerational continuity of abuse' in R. Colles., et al., *Child abuse and neglect: Biosocial dimensions* (pp. 255–76). New York: Aldine.

Eisenstadt, M., et al., 1989, *Parental Loss and Achievement*, Madison, Mass: IUP.

English, D.J., et al., 2005a, 'Defining maltreatment chronicity: Are there differences in child outcomes?' *Child Abuse and Neglect*, 29, 575–95.

English, D.J., et al., 2005b, 'Maltreatment's wake: the relationship of maltreatment dimensions to child outcomes', *Child Abuse and Neglect*, 29, 597–619.

Ericsson, K.A., 1996, *The Road To Excellence*, Abingdon, Oxon: Psychology Press.

Ericsson, K.A., et al., 2007, 'Giftedness and evidence for reproducibly superior performance: an account based on the expert performance framework', *High Ability Studies*, 18, 3–56.

Esther, J.M., et al., 2009, 'Impact of early childhood adversities on adult psychiatric disorders – a study of international adoptees', *Social Psychiatry and Psychiatric Epidemiology*, 44, 724–31.

Etain, E.B., et al., 2008, 'Beyond genetics: childhood affective trauma in bipolar disorder', *Bipolar Disorders*, 10, 867–76.

Etcoff, N, 1999, *The Survival of the Prettiest*, London: Little Brown.

Eyler, F.D., et al., 1999, 'Early development of infants exposed to drugs prenatally', *Clinics in Perinatology*, 26, 106–50; Saigal., et al., 2008.

Fairbrother, N., 2008, 'New mothers' thoughts of harm related to the newborn', *Arch Womens Ment Health*. 11, 221–29.

Farrington, D.P., 2005, 'Childhood origins of antisocial behaviour', *Clinical Psychology and Psychotherapy*, 12, 177–90.

Fein, D., et al., 2013, 'Optimal outcomes in individuals with a history of autism', *Journal of Child Psychology and Psychiatry*, 54, 195–205.

Feldman, D.H., 1984, 'A follow-up of subjects scoring above 180 IQ in Terman's genetic studies of genius', *Council for Exceptional Children*, 50, 518–23.

Feldman, R et al., 2005, 'Does a triplet birth pose a special risk for infant development? Assessing cognitive development in relation to intrauterine growth and mother-infant interaction across the first 2 years', *Pediatrics*, 115, 443–52.

Felitti, V.J., et al., 1998, 'Relationship of childhood abuse and house-hold dysfunction to many of the leading causes of death in adults',

References

American Journal of Preventive Medicine, 14, 245–58.

Felitti, V.J., et al., 2007, 'Adverse Childhood Experiences: lives gone up in smoke', *ACE Reporter*, 1, 5, 1–3.

Felitti, V.J., et al., 2010, 'The relationship of adverse childhood experiences to adult medical disease, psychiatric disorders and sexual behaviour: implications for healthcare', in Lanius, R.A., et al., *The Impact of Early Life Trauma on Health and Disease*, Cambridge: CUP.

Ferrari, J.R., et al., 2006, 'Impostor Fears: links with self-presentational concerns and self-handicapping behaviours', *Personality and Individual Differences*, 40, 341–52.

Finkelhor, D., et al., 2007, 'Poly-victimization: a neglected component of child victimization', *Child Abuse and Neglect*, 31, 7–26.

Fischer, P., et al., 2007, 'Ego Depletion and Positive Illusions: Does the Construction of Positivity Require Regulatory Resources?', *Pers Soc Psychol Bull*, 33: 1306–21.

Font, S.A., et al., 2015, 'Child maltreatment and children's development trajectories in early to middle childhood', *Child Development*, 86, 536–56.

Fontes, L.A., 2015, *Invisible Chains: Overcoming coercive control in your intimate relationships*, London. Guilford Press.

Forbes, C., 1992, *The Polgar Sisters: Training or genius?*, London: Batsford.

Fosse, R et al., 2015, 'Schizophrenia: A critical view on genetic effects', *Psychosis*, http://dx.doi.org/10.1080/17522439.2015.1081269

Foster, J.D., et al., 2003, 'Individual differences in narcissism: inflated self-views across the lifespan and around the world', *Journal of Research in Personality*, 37, 469–86.

Franco-Paredes, K., et al., 2005, 'Perfectionism and eating disorders: a review of the literature', *European Eating Disorders Review*, 13, 61–70.

Fromm, E., 1955, *The Sane Society*, 2nd ed, London: Routledge Classics.

Galton, F., 1904, 'Eugenics: its definition, scope and aims', *American Journal of Sociology*, 10, 1–25.

Gailliot, M.T., et al., 2007, 'Self-control relies on glucose as a limited energy source: Willpower is more than a metaphor', *Journal of Personality and Social Psychology*, 92, 325–36.

Gao, Y., et al., 2010, 'Early maternal and paternal bonding, childhood physical abuse, and adult psychopathic personality', *Psychological Medicine*, 1007–16.

Garber, J., et al., 2007, *The Development of Emotional Regulation and Dysregulation*, Cambridge: CUP.

Garssen, J., et al., 2011, 'Familial risk of early suicide: variations by and sex of children and parents', *Suicide and Life-Threatening Behavior*, 41, 585–93.

Geekie, J., 2013, 'Listening to the voices that we hear: clients' understanding of psychotic experiences', 178–90, in Read, J., *Models of Madness*, London: Routledge.

Geulayov, G., et al., 2012, 'The association of parental fatal and non-fatal suicidal behavior with offspring suicidal behavior and depression: a systematic review and meta-analysis', *Psychological Medicine*, 42, 1567–80.

Glover, V., et al., 2011, 'Prenatal stress and the programming of the HPA', *Psychophysiological Biomarkers of Health*, 35, 17–22.

Goldstein, M.J., 1985, 'Family factors that antedate the onset of schizophrenia and related disorders: the results of a fifteen-year prospective longitudinal study', *Acta Psychiatrica Scandinavia*, 319, 71, 7–18.

Goodman, A., et al., 2010, *Poorer Children's Educational Attainment: how important are attitudes and behaviour?*, York: Joseph Rowntree Trust.

References

Goodman, S.H., et al., 1999, 'Risk for psychopathology in the children of depressed mothers: a developmental model for understanding mechanisms of transmission', *Psychological Review*, 106, 458–90.

Goodman, S.H., et al., 2011, 'Maternal depression and child psychopathology: a meta-analytic review', *Clinical Child and Family Psychological Review*, 14, 1–27.

Gottesman, I.I., 1992, *Schizophrenia Genesis – the Origins of Madness*, New York: Freeman.

Granic, I., et al., 2006, 'Towards a comprehensive model of antisocial development: a dynamic systems approach', *Psychological Review*, 113, 101–31.

Greatrex, T.S., 2002, 'Projective identification: how does it work?', *Neuropsychoanalysis: an Interdisciplinary Journal for Psychoanalysis and the Neurosciences*, 4, 183–93.

Green, T., et al., 2014, 'Materialism and the tendency to worship celebrities', *North American Journal of Psychology*, 16, 33–42.

Greig, G, 2015, *Breakfast With Lucian*, London: Atlantic.

Grizenko, N., et al., 2012, 'Maternal stress during pregnancy, ADHD symptomatology in children and genotype: gene-environment interaction', *Journal of the Canadian Academy of Child and Adolescent Psychiatry*, 21, 9–15.

Grusec, J.E., 1992, 'Social learning theory and developmental psychology: The legacies of Robert Sears and Albert Bandura', *Developmental Psychology*, 776–86.

Hadjikhani, N., 2010, 'Serotonin, pregnancy and increased autism prevalence: is there a link?', *Medical Hypotheses*, 74, 880–83.

Hadland, S.E., et al., 2012, 'Childhood sexual abuse and risk for initiating injection drug use: a prospective cohort study', *Preventive Medicine*, 55, 500–4.

Hadwin, J.A., et al., 2005, 'The development of information processing biases in childhood anxiety: a review and exploration of its origins in parenting', *Clinical Psychology Review*, 26, 876–94.

Hagger, M.S., et al., 2010, 'Ego Depletion and the Strength Model of Self-Control: A Meta-Analysis', *Psychological Bulletin*, 136, 4, 495–525.

Hart, B., et al., 2003, 'The early catastrophe: the 30 million word gap by age 3', *American Educator*, 27, 4–9.

Harris, P.W., et al., 2007, 'The relationship between maladaptive perfectionism and depressive symptoms: the mediating role of rumination', *Personality and Individual Differences*, 44, 150–60.

Haworth, C.M.A., et al., 2010, 'Quantitative genetics in the era of molecular genetics: Learning abilities and disabilities as an example', *Journal of the American Academy of Child and Adolescent Psychiatry*, 49, 783–93.

Hay, D.F., et al., 2000, 'Toddlers' use of force against familiar peers: a precursor of serious aggression', *Child Development*, 71, 457–67.

Healey, M.D. et al., 2007, 'Birth order, conscientiousness and openness to experience tests of the family-niche model of personality using a within-family methodology', *Evolution and Human Behavior*, 28, 55–9.

Hearst, P., 1989, *The Patty Hearst Story*, London: Corgi Children's.

Heikkilä, K., et al., 2011, 'Breast feeding and child behaviour in the Millennium Cohort Study', *Archives of Diseases of Childhood*, 2011, doi:10.1136/adc.2010.201970.

Helling, S, 2010, *Tiger Woods: the real story*, Philadelphia: De Capo.

Hesse, E., et al., 2003, 'Unresolved states regarding loss or abuse can have "second-generation" effects: Disorganized, role-inversion and frightening ideation in the offspring of traumatized non-maltreating parents', in Siegel, D.J., et al., *Healing trauma: Attachment, mind, body and brain*, New York: Norton (pp. 57–106).

References

Hesse, E., 2008, 'The Adult Attachment Interview: protocol, method of analysis and empirical studies', in Cassidy, J., et al., *Handbook of Attachment (Second Edition)*, New York: Guilford.

Hetteman, J.M., et al., 2001, 'A review and meta-analysis of the genetic epidemiology of anxiety disorders', *American Journal Psychiatry*, 158, 10, 1568–78.

Hibel, L.C., et al., 2010, 'Maternal sensitivity buffers the adrenocortical implications of intimate partner violence exposure during early childhood', *Development and Psychopathology*, 23, 689–701.

Hill, N.M., et al., 2009, 'Brain changes in the development of expertise: Neuroanatomical and neurophysiological evidence about skill-based adaptations' in Ericsson, K.A., et al., *Cambridge Handbook of Expertise and Expert Performance*, Cambridge: CUP.

Hittner, J.B., 2005, 'How robust is the Werther effect? A re-examination of the suggestion-imitation model of suicide', *Mortality*, 10, 193–200.

Hofferth, S.L., et al., 2012, 'The transmission of parenting from fathers to sons', *Parenting: Science and Practice*, 12, 282–305.

Hopper, J.H., et al., 2007, 'Neural correlates of reexperiencing avoidance and dissociation in PTSD: symptom dimensions and emotion dysregulation in responses to script-driven trauma imagery', *Journal of Traumatic Stress*, 20, 713–25.

Hotz, V.J., 2013, *Strategic Parenting, Birth Order and School Performance*, Cambridge MA: NBER Working Paper Series no 19542.

Hoyenga, KB et al., 1993, *Gender-Related Differences: Origins and Outcomes*, London: Allyn.

Huesmann, L., et al., 1984, 'The stability of aggression over time and generations', *Developmental Psychology*, 20, 1120–34.

Hunter, R., et al., 1979, 'Breaking the cycle in abusive families', *American Journal of Psychiatry*, 136, 1320–2.

Hunter, A.L., et al., 2011, 'Altered stress responses in children exposed to early adversity: A systematic review of salivary cortisol studies', *Stress*, 14, 614–26.

Jaffee, S.R., 2004, 'Physical maltreatment victim to antisocial child: Evidence of an environmentally mediated process', *Journal of Abnormal Psychology*, 113, 44–55.

Jaffee, S.R., et al., 2007, 'Sensitive, stimulating caregiving predicts cognitive and behavioral resilience in neuro-developmentally at-risk infants', *Development and Psychopathology*, 19, 631–47.

Jaffee, S.R., et al., 2015, 'Interactive effects of early and recent exposure to stressful contexts on cortisol reactivity in middle childhood', *Journal of Child Psychology and Psychiatry*, 56, 138–46.

James, H.M., 1960, 'Premature ego development: some observations on disturbances during the first three months of life', *International Journal of Psychoanalysis*, 41, 288–92.

James, O.W., 1979, 'Anthropomorphization of infant behaviours in North West Ecuador', Thesis submitted for Masters Degree, Child Development Unit, Nottingham University.

James, O.W., 1995, *Juvenile Violence in a Winner-Loser Culture*, London: Free Association Books.

James, O.W., 2005, *They F*** You Up*, London: Bloomsbury.

James, O.W., 2008, *The Selfish Capitalist*, London: Vermilion.

James, O.W., 2010, *How Not To F*** Them Up*, London: Vermilion.

James, O.W., 2012, *Love Bombing: Reset your child's emotional thermostat*, London: Karnac Books.

James, O.W., 2013, *Office Politics: How to thrive in a world of lying, backstabbing and dirty tricks*, London: Vermilion.

References

Jamison, K.J., 2011, 'Great wits and madness: more nearly allied?', *British Journal of Psychiatry*, 199, 351–2.

Janssen, I., et al., 2004, 'Childhood abuse as a risk factor for psychotic experiences', *Acta Psychiatrica Scandinavica*, 109, 38–45.

Jedlicka, D., 1980, 'A test of the psychoanalytic theory of mate selection', *Journal of Social Psychology*, 112, 295–9.

Jennings, M.K., et al., 2009, 'Politics across generations: family transmission reexamined', *The Journal of Politics*, 71, 782–99.

Johnson, M.H., et al., 2015a, 'Infant development, autism and ADHD – early pathways to emerging disorders', *Journal of Child Psychology and Psychiatry*, 56, 228–47.

Johnson, M.H., et al., 2015b, 'Annual research review: Infant development, autism and ADHD – early pathways to emerging disorders', *Journal of Child Psychology and Psychiatry*, 56, 228–47.

Johnson, M.P., 2008, *A typology of domestic violence: Intimate terrorism, violent resistance, and situational couple violence*. Boston, MA: Northeastern University Press.

Jonason, P.K., et al., 2010a, 'The costs and benefits of the Dark Triad: implications for mate poaching and mate retention tactics', *Personality and Individual Differences*, 48, 373–8.

Jonason, P.K., et al., 2010b, 'The dirty dozen: a concise measure of the dark triad', *Psychological Assessment*, 22, 420–32.

Joseph, J., 2015, *The Trouble With Twins*, London: Routledge.

Kaplow, J.B., et al., 2005, 'Pathways to PTSD. Part II: Sexually abused children', *American Journal of Psychiatry*, 162, 1305–10.

Kaplow, J.B., et al., 2007, 'Age of onset of child maltreatment predicts long-term mental health outcomes', *Journal of Abnormal Psychology*, 116, 176–87.

Karg, K., et al., 2011, 'The serotonin transporter promoter variant (5-HTTLPR), stress and depression meta-analysis revisited: evidence of genetic moderation', *Archives of General Psychiatry*, 68, 444–54.

Karl, A., et al., 2006, 'A meta-analysis of structural brain abnormalities in PTSD', *Neuroscience and Biobehavioral Reviews*, 30, 1004–30.

Kawamura, J.Y., et al., 2002, 'The relationship of perceived parenting styles to perfectionism', *Personality and Individual Differences*, 32, 317–27.

Kelleher, I., et al., 2013, 'Childhood trauma and psychosis in a prospective cohort study: cause, effect and directionality', *American Journal of Psychiatry*, 170, 734–41.

Kelly, J.F., et al., 2009, 'How do people recover from alcohol dependence? A systematic review of the research on mechanisms of behavioral change in Alcoholics Anonymous', *Addiction Research and Theory*, 17, 236–59.

Kendler, K.S., et al., 2000, 'Childhood sexual abuse and adult psychiatric and substance abuse disorders in women: an epidemiological and cotwin control analysis', *Archives of General Psychiatry*, 57, 953–9.

Kerr, D.C.R., et al., 2009, 'A prospective three generational study of fathers' constructive parenting', *Developmental Psychology*, 45, 1257–75.

Kendler, K.S., 2001, 'Twin studies of psychiatric illnesses: An update', *Archives of General Psychiatry*, 58, 1005–14.

Kessler, R.C., et al., 2008, *The WHO World Mental Health Surveys: Global perspectives on the epidemiology of mental disorders*, Cambridge; New York: Cambridge University Press; Geneva: Published in collaboration with the World Health Organization.

References

Kessler, R., et al., 2010, 'Childhood adversities and adult psychopathology in the WHO World Mental Health Surveys', *British Journal of Psychiatry*, 197, 378–85.

Kiado, A., 2011, 'Parental influences on sexual preferences: the case of attraction to smoking', *Journal of Evolutionary Psychology*, 9, 21–41.

Kim, J., et al., 2009, 'Child maltreatment and trajectories of personality and behavioural functioning: implications for the development of personality disorder', *Development and Psychopathology*, 21, 889–912.

Kim, S.H., et al., 2008, 'The relationship between child and adolescent atopic dermatitis, attachment and the quality of parental life', *Korean Journal of Dermatology*, 46, 1457–62.

Konner, M., 2005, 'Hunter-gatherer infancy and childhood', in Hewlett, B.S., et al., *Hunter-Gatherer Childhoods*, Piscataway, NJ: Transaction Publishers.

Korhonen, M., et al., 2012, 'A longitudinal study of maternal prenatal, postnatal and concurrent depressive symptoms and adolescent well-being', *Journal of Affective Disorders*, 136, 680–92.

Kurzban, R., 2010, 'Does the brain consume additional glucose during self-control tasks?', *Evolutionary Psychology*, 8, 244–59.

Kuo, J.R., et al., 2011, 'Childhood trauma and current psychological functioning in adults with social anxiety disorder', *Journal of Anxiety Disorder*, 25, 467–73.

Lahti, J., et al., 2009, 'Early-life origins of schizotypal traits in adulthood', *British Journal of Psychiatry*, 195, 132–7.

Laing, R.D., et al., 1964, *Sanity, Madness and the Family*, London: Penguin.

Langstrom, N., et al., 2015, 'Sexual offending runs in families: A 37-year nationwide study', *International Journal of Epidemiology*, 44, 713–20.

Lanius, R.A., et al., 2007, 'Neural correlates of traumatic memories in posttraumatic stress disorder: a functional MRI investigation', *American Journal of Psychiatry*, 158, 1920–2.

Lanius, R.A., et al., 2010, *The Impact of Early Life Trauma on Health and Disease*, Cambridge: CUP.

Lansford, J.E., et al., 2002, 'A 12-year prospective study of the long-term effects of early child physical maltreatment on psychological, behavioral and academic problems in adolescence', *Archives of Pediatric Medicine*, 156, 824–30.

Lansford, J.E., et al., 2007, 'Early physical abuse and later violent delinquency: a prospective longitudinal study', *Child Maltreatment*, 12, 233–45.

Laurenti, H.J., et al., 2008, 'Social anxiety and socially prescribed perfectionism', *Personality and Individual Differences*, 45, 55–61.

Lawson, D.R. et al., 2009, 'Trade-offs in modern parenting: a longitudinal study of sibling competition for parental care', *Evolution and Human Behavior*, 30, 170–83.

Layard, R., et al., 2014, *Thrive – The Power of Evidence-Based Psychological Therapies*, London: Allen Lane.

Leichsenring, F., et al., 2008, 'Effectiveness of Long-term Psychodynamic Psychotherapy: A Meta-analysis', *JAMA*, 300, 1551–65.

Levin, A.R., et al., 2015, 'Social communication difficulties and autism in previously institutionalized children', *Journal of the American Academy of Child and Adolescent Psychiatry*, 54, 108–15.

Levy, M.S., 2000, 'A conceptualization of the repetition compulsion', *Psychiatry: Interpersonal and Biological Processes*, 63, 45–53.

Lieberman, A.F., et al., 2005, 'Angels in the nursery: the intergenerational transmission of benevolent parental influences', *Infant Mental Health Journal*, 26, 504–20.

References

Lim, L., et al., 2014, 'Grey matter abnormalities in childhood maltreatment: a vocel-wise meta-analysis', *American Journal of Psychiatry*, 171, 854–63.

Liotti, G., 2004, 'Trauma, dissociation and disorganized attachment; three strands of a single braid', *Psychotherapy: Theory, research, practice, training*, 41, 472–86.

Little, A.C., et al., 2003, 'Investigating an imprinting-like phenomenon in humans. Partners and opposite-sex parents have similar hair and eye colour', *Evolution and Human Behavior*, 24, 43–51.

Longden, E., et al., 2012, 'Dissociation, trauma and the role of lived experience: towards a new conceptualization of voice hearing', *Psychological Bulletin*, 138, 28–76.

Lupien, S.J., et al., 2011, 'Larger amygdala but no change in hippocampal volume in 10-year old children exposed to maternal depressive symptoms since birth', *Proc. of the National Academy of Sciences of the United States of America*, 108, 14324–9.

Lyons-Ruth, K., et al., 2008, 'Attachment disorganization: unresolved loss, relational violence and lapses in behaviour and attentional strategies', in Cassidy, J., et al., *Handbook of Attachment (Second Edition)*, New York: Guilford.

Madden, V., et al., 2015, 'Intergenerational transmission of parenting: findings from a UK longitudinal study', *The European Journal of Public Health*, ckv093.

Maguire, E.A., et al., 2006, 'London taxi drivers and bus drivers: a structural MRI and neuropsychological analysis', *Hippocampus*, 16, 1091–1101.

Maikovich, A.K., et al., 2008, 'Effects of family violence on psychopathology symptoms in children previously exposed to maltreatment', *Child Development*, 79, 1498–1512.

Major Depressive Disorder Working Group of the Psychiatric GWAs Consortium, 2013, 'A mega-analysis of genome-wide association studies for major depressive disorder', *Molecular Psychiatry*, 18, 497–511.

Manly, J.T., et al., 2001, 'Dimensions of child maltreatment and children's adjustment: contributions of developmental timing and subtype', *Development and Psychopathology*, 13, 759–82.

Manolio, T.A., et al., 2009. 'Finding the missing heritability of complex diseases', *Nature*, 461(7265): 747–53.

Markowitz, S.M., et al., 2011, 'Childhood sexual abuse and health risk behaviors in patients with HIV and a history of injection drug use', *AIDS Behavior*, 15, 1554–60.

Matejcek, Z., et al., 1978, 'Children from unwanted pregnancies', *Acta Psychiatrica Scandinavia*, 57, 67–90.

Matejcek, Z., et al., 1980, 'Follow-up study of children born from unwanted pregnancies', *International Journal of Behavioural Development*, 3, 243–51.

Maxfield, M.G., et al., 1996, 'The cycle of violence revisited 6 years later', *Archives of Pediatric Adolescent Medicine*, 150, 390–5.

Mccall, R.B., et al., 2011, *Children Without Permanent Parents: Research, Practice and Policy (Monographs of the Society for Research in Child Development)*, 301, 76, 4, Oxford: Wiley Blackwell.

McCrory, E., et al., 2010, 'Research review: the neurobiology and genetics of maltreatment and adversity', *Journal of Child Psychology and Psychiatry*, 51, 1079–95.

McEwen, B.C., 2010, 'Understanding the potency of stressful early life experiences on brain and body function', *Metabolism*; 57, S11–S15.

McGuire, S., 2003, 'Nonshared Environment Research', *Marriage & Family Review*, 33, 31–56.

McNeil, T.F., et al., 2009, 'Unwanted pregnancy as a risk factor for offspring schizophrenia-spectrum and affective disorders in adulthood: a prospective high-risk study', *Psychological Medicine*, 39, 957–65.

Melhem, N.M., et al., 2008, 'Antecedents and sequelae of sudden parental death in offspring and surviving caregivers', *Archives of pediatrics & adolescent medicine*, 162, 403–10.

Moller, A.C., et al., 2006, 'Choice and Ego-Depletion: The Moderating Role of Autonomy', *Personality and Social Psychology Bulletin*, 32, 8, 1024–36.

Moos, R.H., et al., 2006, 'Participation in treatment and Alcoholics Anonymous: a 16-year follow-up of initially untreated individuals', *Journal of Clinical Psychology*, 62, 735–50.

Moreno, S., et al., 2015, 'Short-term language and music training induces lasting functional brain changes in early childhood', *Child Development*, 86, 394–106.

Mortenson, P.B., et al., 1999, 'Effects of family history and place and season of birth on the risk of schizophrenia', *New England Journal of Medicine*, 340, 603–8

'Mother and Baby Sleep Survey', 2002, *Mother and Baby Magazine*, April.

Moutsiana, C., et al., 2014, 'Making an effort to feel positive: insecure attachment in infancy predicts the neural underpinnings of emotional regulation in adulthood', *Journal of Child Psychology and Psychiatry*, 55, 999–1008.

Moutsiana, C., et al., 2015, 'Insecure attachment during infancy predicts greater amygdala volumes in early adulthood', *Journal of Child Psychology and Psychiatry*, 56, 540–8.

Munafo, M.R., et al., 2009, '5-HTTLPR genotype and anxiety–related personality-related traits: a meta-analysis and new data', *American Journal of Medical Genetics: Part B Neuropsychiatric Genetics*, 150B, 271–81.

Munafo, M.R., et al., 2014, 'Research Review: polygenic methods and their application to psychiatric traits', *Journal of Child Psychology and Psychiatry*, 55, 1092–1101.

Munafo, M.R., et al., 2014, 'A critical perspective on gene-environment interaction models: what impact should they have on clinical perceptions and practice?', *Journal of Child Psychology and Psychiatry*, 55, 1092–1101.

Muraven, M., et al., 2006. 'The self-control costs of fighting the temptation to drink'. *Psychology of Addictive Behaviors*, 20, 154–60.

Muraven, M., et al., 2008a, 'Helpful self-control: Autonomy support, vitality and depletion', *Journal of Experimental Social Psychology*, 44, 573–85.

Muraven, M., 2008b, 'Autonomous self-control is less depleting', *Journal of Research in Personality*, 42. 763–70.

Muraven, M.J., et al., 2007, 'Lack of autonomy and self-control: Performance contingent rewards lead to greater depletion', *Motiv. Emot.*, 31, 311–22.

Murray, L., et al., 2008, 'The development of anxiety disorders in childhood: an integrative review', *Psychological Medicine*, 39, 1413–23.

Murray, L., et al., 2014, 'Socially anxious mothers' narratives to their children and their relation to child representations and adjustment', *Development and Psychopathology*, 26, 1531–46.

Myrhrman, A., et al., 1996, 'Unwantedness of a pregnancy and schizophrenia in the child', *British Journal of Psychiatry*, 169, 637–40.

Nanni, V., et al., 2012, 'Childhood maltreatment predicts unfavourable course of illness and treatment outcomes in depression: a metanalysis', *American Journal of Psychiatry*, 169, 141–51.

Neppi, T.K., et al., 2009, 'Intergenerational continuity in parenting behavior: mediating pathways and child effects', *Developmental Psychology*, 45, 1241–56.

NICHD, 1999, 'Chronicity of maternal depressive symptoms, maternal sensitivity and child functioning at 36 months', *Developmental Psychology*, 35, 1297–1310.

Nigg, J.T., 2012, Future directions in ADHD etiology research. *Journal of Clinical Child and Adolescent Psychology*, 41, 524–33.

Nikolas, M.A., et al., 2015, 'Parental involvement moderates etiological influences on Attention Deficit Hyperactivity Disorder behaviour in child twins', *Child Development*, 86, 224–40.

Nisbett, R.E., et al., 2012, 'Intelligence: new findings and theoretical developments', *American Psychologist*, 67, 130–59.

O'Connor, T.G., et al., 2014, 'Practitioner Review: maternal mood in pregnancy and child development', *Journal of Child Psychology and Psychiatry*, 55, 99–111.

O'Connor, R.C., 2007, 'The relations between perfectionism and suicidality: a systematic review', *Suicide and Life-Threatening Behavior*, 37, 698–714.

OECD, 2012, *PISA 2012 Results In Focus*, Geneva: OECD

Ogawa, J., et al., 1997, 'Development and the fragmented self: longitudinal study of dissociative symptomatology in a nonclinical sample', *Development and Psychopathology*, 9, 855–79.

Oladeji, B.D., et al., 2010, 'Family-related adverse childhood experiences as risk factors for psychiatric disorders in Nigeria, *British Journal of Psychiatry*, 196, 186–91.

Ornoy, A., et al., 2001, 'Developmental outcome of school-age outcome children born to mothers with heroin dependency: importance of environmental factors', *Developmental Medicine & Child Neurology*, 43, 668–75.

ONS (Office of National Statistics), 2007, *Adult Psychiatric Morbidity in England*, 2007, London: Office of National Statistics.

Patterson, G.R., 1982, *Coercive Family Processes*, Oregon: Castalia.

Patterson, G.R., 1990, *Antisocial Boys*, Oregon: Castalia.

Pearrow, M., 2009, 'The aftermath of combat-related PTSD: towards an understanding of transgenerational trauma', *Communication Disorders Quarterly*, 30, 77–82.

Pennisi, E., 2012, 'ENCODE project writes eulogy for junk DNA', *Science*, 337, 1159–61.

Peplau, L.A., 2003, 'Human Sexuality: how do men and women differ?', *Current Directions in Psychological Science*, 12, 37–40.

Petterson, E., et al., 2015, 'Birth weight as an independent predictor of ADHD symptoms: a within-pair analysis', *Journal of Child Psychology and Psychiatry*, 56, 453–9.

Phillips, D.P., 1974, 'The influence of suggestion on suicide: substantive and theoretical implications of the Werther effect', *American Sociological Review*, 39, 340–54.

Plomin, R., et al., 1998, 'Adoption results for self-reported personality: evidence for non-additive genetic effects?', *Journal of Personality and Social Psychology*, 75, 211–8.

Plomin, R., et al., 2003, 'Psychopathology in the postgenomic era', *Annual Review of Psychology*, 54, 205–28.

Plomin, R., et al., 2011a, Why are children from the same family so different from each other?', *International Journal of Epidemiology*, 40, 563–82.

Plomin, R., et al., 2011b, 'Commentary: Why are children from the same family so different from each other? Non-shared environment three decades later', *International Journal of Epidemiology*, 40, 583–92.

Poijula, S., et al., 2001, 'Adolescent suicide and suicide contagion in three secondary schools', *International Journal of Emergency Mental Health*, 3, 163–8.

References

Polgar, S., et al., 2005, *Breaking Through: How the Polgar sisters changed the game of chess*, London: Everyman Chess.

Pollet, T.V., et al., 2009, 'Partner wealth predicts self-reported orgasm frequency in a sample of Chinese women', *Evolution and Human Behavior*, 30, 146–51.

Polusny, M.A., et al., 1995, 'Long term correlates of child sexual abuse: Theory and review of the empirical literature', *Applied and Preventive Psychology: Current Scientific Perspectives*, 4, 143–66.

Poyner, B., 1980, *A Study of Street Crime*, London: Tavistock Institute (unpublished).

Price, J, 2008, 'Parent-Child Quality Time: Does Birth Order Matter?', *Journal of Human Resources*, 43, 240–265.

Quinton, D., et al., 1984, 'Parents with children in care: II. Intergenerational continuities', *Journal of Child Psychology and Psychiatry*, 25, 231–50.

Quinton, D., et al., 1988, *Parenting Breakdown*, Aldershot: Avebury.

Raudino, A., et al., 2013, 'Child anxiety and parenting in England and Italy: the moderating role of maternal warmth', *Journal of Child Psychology and Psychiatry*, 54, 1318–26.

Read, J., et al., 2003, 'Sexual and physical abuse during childhood and adulthood as predictors of hallucinations, delusions and thought disorder', *Psychology and Psychotherapy Theory, Research and Practice*, 76, 1–22.

Read, J., et al., 2005, 'Childhood trauma, psychosis and schizophrenia: a literature review with theoretical and clinical implications', *Acta Psychiatrica Scandinavica*, 112, 330–50.

Read, J., et al., 2008, 'Child maltreatment and psychosis: a return to a genuinely integrated bio-psycho-social model', *Clinical Schizophrenia and Related Psychoses*, October, 235–54.

Read, J., et al., 2013, *Models of Madness*, London: Routledge.

Read J., et al., 2013a, 'Psychosis and families: Intergenerational parenting problems', 276–91, in Read, J., *Models of Madness*, London: Routledge.

Read J., et al., 2013b, 'Prejudice, stigma and 'schizophrenia'', in Read, J., et al., *Models of Madness*, London: Routledge.

Read, J., et al., 2013c, 'A literature review and meta-analysis of drug company-funded mental health websites', *Acta Psychiatrica Scandinavica*, 128, 422–33.

Read, J., et al., 2014, 'The traumagenic neurodevelopmental model of psychosis revisited', *Neuropsychiatry*, 4, 65–79.

Reijneveld, S.A., et al., 2006, 'Behavioural and emotional problems in very preterm and very low birth weight infants at age 5 years', *Arch Dis Child Fetal Neonatal Ed*, 91, F423–8.

Rheaume, J., et al., 2000, 'The prediction of obsessive-compulsive tendencies: does perfectionism play a significant role?', *Personality and Individual Differences*, 28, 583–92.

Rice, F., et al., 2008, 'The impact of gestational stress and prenatal growth on emotional problems in offspring: a review', *Acta Psychiatrica Scandinavica*, 115, 171–83.

Risch, N., et al., 2009, 'Interaction between the serotonin transporter gene (5HTTLPR), stressful life events and risk of depression: a meta-analysis', *Journal of the American Medical Association*, 301, 2462–71.

Rommelse, N.N., et al., 2011, 'Shared heritability of attention-deficit hyperactivity disorder and autism spectrum disorder', *European Child and Adolescent Psychiatry*, 19, 281–95.

Rose, R.J., et al., 1990, 'Social contact and sibling similarity: facts, issues and red herrings', *Behaviour Genetics*, 20, 763–78.

Rutter, M., et al., 1999, 'Quasi-autistic patterns following severe early global privation', *Journal of Child Psychology and Psychiatry*, 40, 537–49.

References

Rutter, M., et al., 2010, *Deprivation-Specific Psychological Patterns: Effects of Institutional Deprivation: 300, 75-1 (Monographs of the Society for Research in Child Development)*, Oxford: Wiley Blackwell.

Ruttle, L., et al., 2014, 'Adolescent internalizing symptoms and negative life events: the sensitizing effect of earlier life stress and cortisol', *Development and Psychopathology*, 26, 1411–22.

Ryan, R.M., et al., 1989, 'Perceived locus of causality and internalization: examining reasons for acting in two domains', *Journal of Personality and Social Psychology*, 57, 749–61.

Ryan, R.M., et al., 2000, 'Self-determination theory and the facilitation of intrinsic motivation, social development and well-being', *American Psychologist*, 55, 68–78.

Ryan, R.M., et al., 2008, 'From Ego Depletion to Vitality: Theory and Findings Concerning the Facilitation of Energy Available to the Self', *Social and Personality Psychology Compass* 2/2, 702–17.

Sadie, S., 2006, *Mozart. The Early Years 1756–1781*, Oxford: OUP.

Sagi, A., et al., 2002, 'Disorganized reasoning in Holocaust survivors', *American Journal of Orthopsychiatry*, 72, 194–203.

Sahlberg, P., 2007, 'Education policies for raising student learning: the Finnish approach', *Journal of Education Policy*, 22, 147–71.

Sahlins, M., 2003, *Stone Age Economics*, London: Routledge.

Saigal, S., et al., 2008, 'An overview of mortality and sequelae of preterm birth from infancy to adulthood', *Lancet*, 371, 261–9.

Sarkar, P., et al., 2008, 'Maternal antenatal anxiety and amniotic fluid cortisol and testosterone: possible implications for foetal programming', *Journal of Neuroendocrinology*, 20, 489–96.

Saunders, S., et al., 2000, 'The construction and validation of a consumer orientated questionnaire (SCOI) designed to measure Fromm's (1955)

'Marketing Character' in Australia', *Social Behaviour and Personality*, 28, 219–40.

Saunders, S., 2001, 'Fromm's marketing character and Rokeach values', *Social Behaviour and Personality*, 19, 185–90.

Schizophrenia Working Group of the Psychiatric Genomics Consortium, 2014, 'Biological insights from the 108 schizophrenia-associated genetic loci', *Nature*, 511, 421–7.

Segal, N., 1999, *Entwined Lives: Twins and what they tell us about human behaviour*, New York: Dutton.

Seligman, S., 2006, 'Projective Identification and the Transgenerational Transmission of Trauma', in Wachs, C., et al., *Parent-Focused Child Therapy: Attachment, Identification, and Reflective Function*, NY: Aronson.

Shedler, J., 2010, 'The efficacy of psychodynamic psychotherapy', *American Psychologist*, 65, 98–109.

Sheehan, M.J., et al., 2008, 'Reciprocal influences between maternal discipline techniques and aggression in children and adolescents', *Aggressive Behavior*, 34, 245–55.

Sherry, S.B., et al., 2008, 'Social support as a mediator of the relationship between perfectionism and depression', *Personality and Individual Differences*, 45, 339–44.

Shevlin, M., et al., 2008, 'Cumulative trauma and psychosis: An analysis of the National Comorbidity Survey and the British Psychiatric Morbidity Survey', *Schizophrenia Bulletin*, 164, 166–9.

Simpkins, S.D., et al., 2015, 'The Role of Parents in Achievement-Related Motivation and Behavioral Choices', *Monographs of the Society for Research in Child Development*, 317, 80, 2, 1–169.

Singleton, N., et al., 1998, *Psychiatric Morbidity Among Prisoners in England and Wales*, Office of National Statistics.

References

Skenk, D., 2010, *The Genius In All Of Us*, London: Icon Books.

Smith, C., 2004, 'Continuities in antisocial behaviour and parenting across three generations', *Journal of Child Psychology and Psychiatry*, 45, 230–47.

Soenens, B., et al., 2005, 'The intergenerational transmission of perfectionism' parents' psychological control as an intervening variable', *Journal of Family Psychology*, 19, 358–66.

Soenens, B., et al., 2006, 'In search of the sources of psychologically controlling parenting: the role of parental separation anxiety and parental maladaptive perfectionism', *Journal of Research on Adolescence*, 16, 539–59.

Sonuga-Barke, S.J., 2014, 'Editorial: Translational genetics of child psychopathology: a distant dream?', *Journal of Child Psychology and Psychiatry*, 55, 1065–7.

Spitz, R., 1946, 'Hospitalism: a follow-up report', *Psychoanalytic Study of the Child*, 2, 113–17.

Springs, F.E., et al., 1992, 'Health risk behaviors and medical sequelae of child sexual abuse', *Mayo Clinic Proceedings*, 67, 527–32.

Sroufe, L.A., et al., 2005, *The Development of the Person: the Minnesota Study of Risk and adaptation from birth to adulthood*, New York: Guilford Press.

St Aubyn, E., 2012, *Edward St Aubyn Patrick Melrose Novels 5 Books Collection Pack*, London: Picador.

Steel, C., et al., 2009, 'Childhood abuse and schizotypal personality', *Social Psychiatry and Epidemiology*, 44, 917–23.

Sternberg, K.J., et al., 2006, 'Type of violence, age and gender differences in the effects of family violence on children's behavior problems: a mega-analysis', *Development Review*, 26, 89–112.

Stoeber, J., et al., 2006, 'Positive perfectionism: Conceptions, evidence, challenges', *Personality and Social Psychology Review*, 10, 219–319.

Stoeber, J., et al., 2007, 'Perfectionism in adolescent school students: Relations with motivation, achievement, and well-being', *Personality and Individual Differences*, 42, 1379–1389.

Stoeber, J., et al., 2007b, 'Perfectionism and competitive anxiety in athletes: differentiating striving for perfection and negative reactions to imperfection', *Personality and Individual Differences*, 42, 959–69.

Street-Porter, J, 2005, *Baggage: My Childhood*, London: Headline.

Sudak, H.S., et al., 2005, 'The media and suicide', *Academic Psychiatry*, 29, 495–9.

Sullivan, P.F., et al., 2000, 'Genetic epidemiology of Major Depression: review and meta-analysis', *American Journal of Psychiatry*, 157, 1552–62.

Sullman, S., et al., 2009, 'Cumulative effect of multiple trauma on symptoms of posttraumatic stress disorder, anxiety and depression in adolescents', *Comprehensive Psychiatry*, 50, 121–7.

Sulloway, F.J., 1996, *Born To Rebel*, London: Abacus.

Sulloway, F.J., 'Birth order and sibling competition', Dunbar, R et al., *The Oxford Handbook of Evolutionary Psychology*, Oxford: OUP.

Suomi, S.J., 2008, 'Attachment in Rhesus monkeys', in Cassidy., et al., *Handbook of Attachment* (second edition), New York: Guilford.

Sweeting, H et al., 2009, 'GHQ increases among Scottish 15 year olds 1987–2006', *Social Psychiatry and Psychiatric Epidemiology*, 44, 579–86.

Tangney, J.P., et al., 2004, 'High Self-Control Predicts Good Adjustment, Less Pathology, Better Grades, and Interpersonal Success', *Journal of Personality*, 72, 271–324.

Tarullo, A.R., et al., 2006, 'Child maltreatment and the developing HPA axis', *Hormones and Behavior*, 50, 632–9.

Teicher, M.H., et al., 2002, 'Scars that won't heal: the neurobiology of child abuse', *Scientific American*, March, 54–61.

Teicher, M.H., et al., 2003, 'The neurobiological consequences of early stress and childhood maltreatment', *Neuroscience and Biobehavioral Reviews*, 27, 33–44.

Teicher, M.H., et al., 2006, 'Sticks, stones and hurtful words: relative effects of various forms of childhood maltreatment', *American Journal of Psychiatry*, 163, 993–1000.

Teicher, M.H., et al., 2010, 'Neurobiology of childhood trauma and adversity', Chapter 11, in Lanius, R.A., et al., *The Impact of Early Life Trauma on Health and Disease*, Cambridge: CUP.

Teicher, M.H., et al., 2014, 'Childhood maltreatment: altered network centrality of cingulate, precuneus, temporal pole and insula', *Biological Psychiatry*, 76, 297–305.

Teti, D.M., et al., 1995, 'Maternal depression and the quality of early attachment: an examination of infants, preschoolers and their mothers', *Developmental Psychology*, 31, 364–76.

Thompson, T., et al., 2000, 'Impostor fears and perfectionistic concern over mistakes', *Personality and Individual Differences*, 29, 629–47.

Thomsen, L., et al., 2006, 'Interpersonal levelling, independence and self-enhancement: a comparison between Denmark and the US, and a relational practice framework for cultural psychology', *European Journal of Social Psychology*, 37, 445–69.

Thornberry, T., et al., 2003, 'Linked lives: The intergenerational transmission of antisocial behaviour', *Journal of Abnormal Child Psychology*, 31, 171–84.

Tottenham, N., et al., 2010, 'Prolonged institutional rearing is associated with atypically large amygdala volume and difficulties in emotional recognition', *Developmental Sciences*, 13, 46–61.

Tottenham, N., et al., 2011, 'Elevated amygdala response to faces following early deprivation', *Developmental Science*, 14, 190–204.

Trescothick, M., 2009, *Coming Back To Me – The Autobiography*, London: Harper Sphere.

Trivers, R., 1974, 'Parent-offspring conflict', *American Zoology*, 14, 249–64.

Trzaskowski, M., et al., 2013, 'No genetic influence for child behaviour problems from DNA analysis', *Journal of the American Academy of Child and Adolescent Psychiatry*, 52, 1048–56e.

Van Den Bergh, B.R.H., et al., 2004, 'High antenatal anxiety is related to ADHD symptoms, externalizing problems and anxiety in 8- and 9-year-olds', *Child Development*, 75, 1085–97.

Van den Boom, D., 1994, 'The influence of temperament and mothering on attachment and exploration: an experimental manipulation of sensitive responsiveness among lower-class mothers with irritable infants', *Child Development*, 65, 1457–77.

Van Der Kolk, B., 2014, *The Body Keeps The Score*, London: Allen Lane.

Van Ijzendoorn, M.H., et al., 2005, 'Adoption and cognitive development: A meta-analytic comparison of adopted and non-adopted children's IQ and school performance', *Psychological Bulletin*, 131, 301–16.

Van Ijzendoorn, M.H., et al., 2015, 'Genetic differential susceptibility on trial: meta-analytic support from randomized controlled experiments', *Development and Psychopathology*, 27, 151–62.

Van Nierop, M., et al., 2015, 'Childhood trauma is associated with a specific admixture of affective, anxiety and psychosis symptoms cutting across diagnostic boundaries', *Psychological Medicine*, 45, 1277–88.

van Rooij, S.J.H., et al., 2015, 'Smaller hippocampal volume as a vulnerability factor for the persistence of post-traumatic stress disorder', *Psychological Medicine*, 45, 2737–46.

References

Varese, F., et al., 2011, 'Dissociation mediates the relationship between childhood trauma and hallucination-proneness', *Psychological Medicine*, 42, 1025–36.

Varese, F., et al., 2012, 'Childhood adversities increase the risk of psychosis: a meta-analysis of patient-control, prospective- and cross-sectional cohort studies', *Schizophrenia Bulletin*, 38, 661–71.

Vassos, E., et al., 2014, 'Systematic meta-analyses and field synopsis of genetic association of violence and aggression', *Molecular Psychiatry*, 19, 471–7.

Vaughan, B.F., et al., 1999, 'Attachment and temperament', in Cassidy, J., et al., *Handbook of Attachment*, New York: Guilford.

Velikonja, T., et al., 2015, 'Childhoood trauma and schizotypy: a systematic literature review', *Psychological Medicine*, 45, 947–63.

Vermeer, H.J., et al., 2006, 'Children's elevated cortisol levels at daycare: a review and meta-analysis', *Early Childhood Research Quarterly*, 21, 390–41.

Waldinger, R.J., et al., 2001, 'Maltreatment and internal representations of relationships: core relationship themes in the narratives of abused and neglected preschoolers', *Social Development*,10, 41–58.

Waugh, A., 2005, *Fathers and Sons: the autobiography of a family*, London: Headline Books.

Weich, S., et al., 2009, 'Family relationships in childhood and common psychiatric disorders in later life: a systematic review of prospective studies', *British Journal of Psychiatry*, 194, 392–8.

Weiler, B.L., et al., 1996, 'Psychopathy and violent behavior in abused and neglected young adults', *Criminal Behaviour and Mental Health*, 6, 253–71.

Westen, D., et al., 2001, 'A multidimensional meta-analysis of treatments for depression, panic, and generalized anxiety disorder:

An empirical examination of the status of empirically supported therapies', *Journal of Consulting and Clinical Psychology*, 69, 875–99.

Westen, D., et al., 2004, 'The empirical status of empirically supported psychotherapies: assumptions, findings and reporting in controlled trials', *Psychological Bulletin*, 130, 632–63.

Westen, D., et al., 2005, 'Empirically supported complexity: rethinking evidence-based practice in psychotherapy', *Current Directions in Psychological Science*, 4, 266–71.

Widom, C.S., et al., 2006, 'Childhood victimization and illicit drug use in middle adulthood', *Psychology of Addictive Behaviors*, 20, 394–403.

Wilcox, H.C., et al., 2010, 'Psychiatric morbidity, violent crime and suicide among children and adolescents exposed to parental death', *Journal of the American Academy of Child and Adolescent Psychiatry*, 49, 514–23.

Wilkinson, J., 2011, *Jonny – My Autobiography*, London: Headline.

Winser, C., et al., 2015, 'Prospective associations between prenatal adversities and borderline personality disorder at 11–12 years', *Psychological Medicine*, 45, 1025–37.

Wirtz, P.H., et al., 2007, 'Perfectionism and the cortisol response to psychosocial stress in men', *Psychosomatic Medicine*, 69, 249–55.

Wiszewska, A., et al., 2007, 'Father-daughter relationship as a moderator of sexual imprinting: a facialmetric study', *Evolution and Human Behavior*, 28, 248–52.

Wolfe, I., et al., 2014, *Why children die: death in infants, children and young people in the UK*, London: Royal College of Paediatrics and Child Health and National Children's Bureau.

World Health Organization, 1979, *Schizophrenia: An International Follow-Up Study*, Chichester: Wiley.

References

Yehuda, R., et al., 2001, 'Childhood trauma and the risk for PTSD: relationship to intergenerational effect of trauma, parental PTSD and cortisol excretion', *Development and Psychopathology*, 3, 733–53.

Young, M.S., et al., 2006, 'Narcissism and celebrity', *Journal of Research in Personality*, 40, 463–71.

Zahn-Waxler, C et al., 1990, 'Patterns of guilt in children of depressed and well mothers', *Developmental Psychology*, 26, 51–59.

Zeanah, C.H., et al., 2009, 'Institutional rearing and psychiatric disorders in Romanian preschool children', *American Journal of Psychiatry*, 166, 777–85.

Zeanah, C.H., et al., 2015, 'Attachment disorders in early childhood – clinical presentations, correlates and treatment', *Journal of Child Psychology and Psychiatry*, 56, 207–22.

Zingg, R.M., 1940, 'Feral man and extreme cases of isolation', *American Journal of Psychology*, 53, 487–517.

Acknowledgements

Many thanks to my editor Samantha Jackson for her help in getting this book right. Her critiques enabled me to better understand how it might seem through the eyes of the reader. Thanks also to Susanna Abbott, Publishing Director of Vermilion, for her helpful and patient interventions in the final editorial stages.

Thanks also to my agents, Imogen Pelham, for her support and helpful suggestions in navigating our way to the best possible text, and as ever, to Gillon Aitken for his many kindnesses.

Particular thanks to Susannah Cox-Johnson for her careful reading of the text and steerage in the right direction.

I am grateful to Paul and Anita Bamborough for their largesse in providing me with accommodation to work in peace but most of all, for the debates we have had over the years about nature-nurture, helping me to see both sides of the argument. Thanks to Paul for permission to reproduce his witty version of 'This Be The Verse'.

I am very grateful to Guy Shepherd for his considerable help in clarifying the legalities of some of the text.

Thanks to the many individuals who have given me permission to tell their stories, anonymously. I hope they feel I have done them justice.

Thanks to the other members of the email thread in which I occasionally participate, who discuss the issue of geneticism, especially Jay Joseph, Jonathan Latham, John Read and Roar Fosse. Let us hope that the time is not too far away when the truth of the findings of the Human Genome Project will be public knowledge.

Thanks to Kate White, editor of ATTACHMENT: *New Directions in Psychotherapy and Relational Psychoanalysis*, for permission to reproduce my scientific paper, in Appendix 1.

Thanks to my daughter Olive and my son Louis for putting up with the inconvenience and hassle that my having to devote so much time to writing this book caused them, as well as the emotional absence and stroppiness that preoccupation with it sometimes occasioned. Likewise, thanks to my wife Clare for putting up with it and for never failing to challenge my assumptions. As always, her imagination and insights helped enormously, as well as her straight talking about bits of text that sent her to sleep.

Idbury, August, 2015

Index

ability, real causes of 10, 165–210
  ambitions for your children,
    having the right 204–6,
    208–10
  ego-depletion and 195, 196–9,
    206–8
  emotional health and pathology
    in exceptional achievers
    199–202
  genetics and 71, 165–6, 167,
    168, 170, 179, 181, 192–3,
    199, 202, 203
  hothousing of skills, healthy and
    unhealthy 167–74, 177–82
  intelligence and 143–4, 165–6
    see also intelligence
  loss of parent and 48, 177–3,
    186–7
  malleable view of ability,
    advantages of 8, 30, 71, 121,
    167–74, 260–2
  mental illness and high
    achievers 173–4, 195,
    199–204
  Tiger Woods, rise and fall of
    174–99
academic performance:
  birth order and 115, 118, 138
  institutionalised children
    and 92
  low-income families and 165–6
  malleable view of ability and 8,
    30, 71, 121, 260–2
  Oliver James and 19–21, 30,
    121, 161

  parents and 19–21, 30, 55,
    115, 118, 121–2, 138, 161,
    165–6, 260–2
  perfectionism and 121–2
  self-control and 194–5
achievers, exceptional see ability,
  real causes of
actors/comedians, mental illness
  and 173–4, 199
adoption studies 64, 91–2, 144, 190,
  218, 243, 244, 245–6, 247,
  248, 252
Adverse Childhood Experiences
  (ACEs) 54, 94–5
Allen, Woody 98, 157
ambitions:
  children as conduit for parents'
    unfulfilled 18–19, 21, 102,
    118, 120, 136, 138, 139–40,
    169, 201, 203, 208–9
  having the right ambitions
    for your children 204–6,
    208–10
America, mental illness and 87–8,
  94–5, 97–9, 100, 184
Amy (Oliver James client) 149–51,
  152, 162
Asian cultures, mental illness
  and 87–8, 97, 98, 100–1,
  122, 263
Attention Deficit Hyperactivity
  Disorder (ADHD) 66, 69,
  82–3, 84, 85, 86, 91, 108,
  144, 156, 199, 213, 215,
  222, 259

autism 5–6, 63, 82–3, 84–5, 86, 92,
    95, 108, 212–13, 215, 222
autistic spectrum disorder (ASD)
    82–3, 84–5, 86, 212–13

BBC 214–15, 219–20
Believe the Unbelievable 26–7, 46,
    32–5, 151
Berne, Eric 161
bipolar disorder 143, 173, 199, 218,
    222, 228
birth order 78, 112, 113–20, 128,
    132, 134, 138–9
Blair, Tony 117, 199
Bouchard, Thomas 67, 229, 251–5
Bowlby, John 85–6, 139, 232–3
brain:
    autism and 5–6
    changes in adulthood and
        elasticity of 8
    cortisol regulation and 81–4,
        88–90, 92, 96–7, 108,
        181, 228
    delusions/hallucinations
        and 28, 29
    differential maltreatment
        and 91–7
    early years effect upon baseline
        chemicals and patterns of
        brainwaves 72 hothousing
        of skills and 167–8
    Traumagenic Model of mental
        illness and 81–2, 85
Bremner, Rory 199
British Journal of Psychiatry 214
Burt, Cyril 243

Cable, Sir Vince 116–20
Caesarean births 85
Chua, Amy 171–2
Clark, Professor David 33, 34, 35
cognitive behavioural therapy
    (CBT) 33–5, 36, 55, 199,
    200, 207, 208, 213
Cohen, Tom 49, 51
collectivism 97, 98, 99–102, 226

Contented Dementia (James) 36–7
copy number variants (CNVs)
    221–2, 233, 235
cortisol regulation 81–4, 88–90, 92,
    96–7, 108, 181, 228

Daphne (Oliver James interviewee
    in Singapore) 100–2, 119
Dark Triad (narcissism, psychopathy,
    Machiavellianism) 192
Dawkins, Richard 7
Debney, Anita 42, 43, 44, 45, 47, 51
depression:
    ACEs and 95
    America and 97–8
    Asian cultures and 97
    brainwaves of infants and
        toddlers of depressed
        mothers 95
    CBT and 33–4, 35, 199–200, 213
    exceptional achievers and
        199–204
    familial traits and 142
    Geldof family and 53
    genetics and 63, 64, 71, 217,
        218, 222, 225–7, 228,
        232, 245
    Little Devil attribution
        and 71, 245
    Love Bombing and 107
    Marketing Character and 184
    perfectionism and 121–2
    performers and 173–4
    postnatal depression (PND)
        80, 81, 85, 92, 94, 118
DNA *see* genes

Ecuadorean jungle, child-care
    in 98–9
ego-depletion 195, 196–200, 206–8
epigenetics 6, 7, 67, 227–8
equal environments assumption
    (EEA) 229–32, 244–5
eugenicists 143, 252
experiential videos 28
externalising problems 89

Index

fame:
  Geldof family and 39–59
  mental illness and 173–4
  premature death and 54
  sexual attractiveness/
    promiscuity and 191–2,
    196–7, 198
  Tiger Woods and 179, 180,
    187–8, 191–2, 196–7, 198
Farrow, Mia 156
favouritism 78, 113, 123–30
Feedback, Radio 4 66, 215
Feilden, Tom 214–15
flexible psychology, advantages of
  believing in a 8, 70–2, 96,
  167, 168, 260–2
Fleximum, The (one half of
  mothers) 104–5
Ford, Gina 133–6
Freud, Clement 126, 127–8
Freud, Ernst 127
Freud, Lucian 126, 127–8, 130
Freud, Sigmund 11, 126, 193
Freud, Stephen 126, 127
Fromm, Erich 184
Fry, Stephen 173, 199

Galilei, Galileo 213–14
Geldof, Bob 9, 39, 41, 42, 43, 44,
  45, 48, 52, 53
Geldof, Fifi 42, 44, 53
Geldof, Peaches 11
  childhood 42–7
  death 39–40
  death of mother and 46
  takeaways from story of 53–9
  teenage years and adulthood
    47–9
  why was Peaches more like
    her mother than her sisters?
    51, 52–3
  why was Peaches' death so
    similar to Paula's? 49–52
  why was Peaches so like her
    mother? 39–59
Geldof, Pixie 42, 45, 48, 52, 53

Geldof, Tiger-Lily 39, 44
gender: role in family and 10, 78,
  112–13, 114, 120–3, 128,
  130, 132, 133, 138–9, 169,
  208–9
genes/geneticism:
  ability and *see* ability, real
    causes of
  assuming traits are not fixed by,
    positive effects of 8, 70–2,
    96, 167, 168, 260–2
  gene-environment interactions
    67, 225–8
  HGP and *see* Human Genome
    Project
  identify what you believe is
    genetic about yourself and
    think again 70–1
  income inequality and *see*
    income
  individual psychology, do not
    explain our 4–8, 62–5, 71,
    212–13
  intelligence and
    see intelligence
  limits of what is possible and
    72–3
  media reporting of discoveries
    in field of 62, 63, 65–6,
    143, 199, 200, 214–15,
    219–20
  mental illness and *see* mental
    illness
  'Missing Heritability' 4–5,
    63–70, 219, 223, 225–8
  perils of geneticism 257–60,
    262–3
  revising how we raise our
    children and 212–13
  twin studies and *see* twins
Genome Wide Association (GWA)
    studies 221, 222, 225, 227,
    228, 233, 234
Genome Wide Complex
    Trait Analysis (GCTA)
    224–5

George (Oliver James client) 90–1, 92, 95, 96–7, 101, 119
Guardian 48, 65, 70, 218

hallucinations 27, 28, 29, 55, 81, 95, 174
helicopter parenting 181
heroin 39, 40, 48, 49, 51, 52, 72, 144, 162
Hoffman Process 32, 58
Holocaust 152–3
hothousing of skills, healthy and unhealthy 121, 167–74, 177–82
How Not To F*** Them Up (James) 103
Hugger, The (about a quarter of mothers) 104
Human Genome Project (HGP) 1, 5, 83, 144, 146, 211, 214
  consensus view of findings of 62–5, 66
  gene-environment interactions and 225–8
  media reporting of 65–6, 215
  mental illness, findings of for 5, 220–5
  Missing Heritability/DNA Deficit and 4–5, 63–5, 225–8
  null hypothesis of, accepting 217–20, 233–5
  proves beyond little doubt that impact of genes on transmission of psychological characteristics is largely non-existent 5, 7, 9–10, 62– 5, 66, 83, 217–20, 233–5
  proving Dawkins emphatically wrong 7
  twin studies and 67, 68, 69, 77, 228–33, 235, 246
Hutchence, Michael 43, 44, 45, 50, 53

I'm Okay, You're Not mechanism 23–6, 29, 35–7, 56, 78, 133, 145, 151, 162
identification, child/parent 17–18, 21, 22, 29, 31, 50, 51–2, 57–9, 135–7, 145, 148, 168, 208, 247
Improving Access to Psychological Therapies (IAPT) 33
income, genetics and 77, 143–4, 165–6, 211, 261
individualism, me-me-me cultural 87–8, 97, 99, 100–1, 226
insight, importance of 53–9
institutionalised children 86–7, 88, 91–2, 139
intelligence:
  academic performance and *see* academic performance
  birth order and 115, 116, 129
  favouritism and 129, 133
  genetics and 62, 63, 64, 76, 77, 143–5, 146, 165–6, 214, 218, 228, 261
  institutionalised children and 92
  low-income families and 77, 143–4, 165–6, 261
  twin studies and 218, 228
  why traits run in families and 142, 143–5

James, Oliver:
  academic ability 18–22, 30, 121, 161
  acceptance of some personal traits 72–3
  childhood 3–4, 6–7, 16–22, 30, 40, 58, 121, 123
  father and 16–22, 30, 58, 121, 123, 161
  football dribbling skills, son's inheritance of 3–4, 6–7, 40

identification and 17–22, 58
modelling and 15–16, 58
mother and 7, 18, 19, 21, 22,
    73, 121, 127, 160–1
multiple sclerosis 4, 73
nicotine addiction 73
teaching and children of 15, 58
Japan 87, 98
Jeff and Carole (Love Bombing)
    109–10
Jill and George (Oliver James
    clients) 81, 95
junk DNA 66–7, 69, 225

Laing, R. D. 58, 111
Layard, Professor Richard 33, 34
Leach, Penny 137–3, 136
'The Little Devil' attribution 71,
    257–60
Love Bombing (James) 80, 95
Love Bombing (LB) 36, 80, 95,
    105–10, 151, 162

Machiavellianism 36, 192
Maines twins 61
maltreated children:
    dose dependent impact of
        maltreatment 143
    exceptional ability and
        see ability, real causes of
    mental illness linked to
        1, 7–8, 199
    similarities between children
        and parents and 22–32
    therapy and *see* therapy
    generational inheritance and
        136–7
    specific kinds of maltreatment
        relate to specific adult
        psychotic symptoms 174
maltreatment and love, sibling
    difference and 75–110
    broader context of childhood
        maltreatment/societal
        and cultural effects and
        97–102

cortisol regulation, impact of
    early care on 81–2, 88–90
differences between siblings
    76–8
different adults, how differential
    maltreatment makes us into
    91–7
differential maltreatment and
    love as causes of sibling
    difference 79–81
early years, crucial importance
    of 85–8
examples of differing love and
    maltreatment 75
love bombing and 105–10
prenatal experience, effect of
    83–5
real causes of mental illness
    81–3
stress chemicals caused by
    early maltreatment create
    a heightened sensitivity to
    threat 81–2
stress during pregnancy,
    avoiding 102–5
tune in to babies 105
Marketing Character/Marketing
    Society 184, 185, 187,
    188, 197
me-me-me narcissism/self-focus 47,
    84, 86, 97, 143
media:
    Geldof family and 40, 41, 42
    genetic inheritance reporting
        62, 63, 65–6, 143, 199, 200,
        214–15, 219–20, 251
    Tiger Woods and 178, 179,
        190, 191
meditation 32, 35, 182
Melrose novels (Edward St Aubyn)
    162–3
mental illness:
    childhood maltreatment as
        cause of 1, 7–10, 27–8,
        81–5, 174, 199
    early years and 85–90

mental illness: (*continued*)
fame and 173–4, 199
HGP studies of 5, 9–10, 214,
218, 220–5, 228
high achievers and 173–4,
199–204
nations/cultures and differences
between amounts of 97–102
perception of as fixed and
likelihood of continuation
or recurrence 71
prenatal experience and 73, 79,
83–5, 87, 102–5, 130, 131,
154, 156, 247, 259
real causes of 81–3
The Traumagenic Model of
27–8, 81–2, 88, 90
therapy and *see* therapy
UK amount and cost of 32–3
*see also under individual
type of mental illness*
Miranda and Tim (Love Bombing
case study) 107, 108
'Missing Heritability' 4–5, 63–5, 69,
219, 223, 225–8
modelling, children/parent 15–16,
17, 22, 29, 30, 31, 58, 136,
145, 148, 168, 188, 208
Mozart, Nanneri 169, 202
Mozart, Wolfgang Amadeus 169, 202

narcissism 36, 47, 54, 56, 87, 143,
173, 178, 180, 192, 198
Natalie (Oliver James client) 55–7
National Institute for Care
Excellence (NICE) 35
Nigeria, study of impact of child
maltreatment in 100–2
Nordegren, Elin 188–90, 198

Offspring Stockholm Syndrome
13–15, 23, 27, 29, 30, 31,
32, 45, 52, 59, 93, 94, 101,
118, 151, 160, 180
Organiser, The (about a quarter of
mothers) 103, 104

P-A-C (top tip for changing the
intergenerational record)
161–3
Pamela (Oliver James client) 123–6
paranoia 81, 174
parents:
ability and *see* ability, real
causes of
ambitions of 18–19, 21, 102,
118, 120, 136, 138, 139–40,
169, 201, 203, 204–9
disharmonious 84, 89–90, 96–7,
100, 119
how similar are you to your? 31–2
*I'm Okay, You're Not see I'm
Okay, You're Not*
identification, child/parent 17–
18, 21, 22, 29, 31, 50, 51–2,
57–9, 135–7, 145, 148, 168,
208, 247
maltreatment as a cause of
similarities between
children and 22–31
modelling, children/parent
15–16, 17, 22, 29, 30, 31,
58, 136, 145, 148, 168, 188,
208
*Offspring Stockholm Syndrome
and see Offspring Stockholm
Syndrome*
real reasons children are like
their 13–37
role in the family drama and
111–40
teaching, parental 15, 22, 29,
31, 58, 145, 168, 208
traits running in families and
141–63
perfectionism 108, 121, 122, 150,
168, 181–2, 201–3
personality disorder 47–8, 54, 84,
86, 87, 88, 143, 173
Plomin, Professor Robert 65, 70,
218, 220, 221, 222, 223,
224, 228, 229, 231, 233–4,
244

Polgar family 169–71, 172, 174, 179, 180, 181, 182, 202, 203
post traumatic stress disorder (PTSD) 27, 57, 125, 152–3
postnatal depression (PND) 80, 81, 85, 94, 118
pregnancy/prenatal experience 73, 79, 83–5, 87, 102–5, 130, 131, 154, 156, 247, 259
psychodnamic therapy 34, 35
psychopathy 36, 82, 87, 173, 192, 224, 235

Read, John 27
role in the family drama, sibling differences and 111–40
    birth order 113–20
    favouritism 123–30
    gender 120–3
    how did your birth order, gender and so on, affect the script of your role? 138–9
    positives of parents' unfulfilled ambitions 139–40
    stigmatization 130–7
    tease out your role in the family drama 137–8
Roth, Eli 48
Ryan, Richard 195, 196

Sam and Emma (Love Bombing case study) 108–9
schizophrenia 63, 64, 65, 68, 88, 99, 102, 131, 141–3, 173, 218, 219, 220, 222, 223, 228, 230, 232
self-restraint, good and bad 193–6
sexuality:
    ACEs and 95
    fame and 191–2, 196–7, 198
    instiutionalised children and 86–7
    Paula Yates/Peaches Geldof and 40–1, 47, 48, 49, 50
    secret 101, 102, 119

sexual abuse 23, 26, 27, 50, 55, 68–9, 72, 76–7, 87, 92, 94, 102, 124, 142–3, 162, 174
sexual attraction to opposite-sexed parent 189–90
    Tiger Woods and 174–5, 187–92, 193, 194, 196–7
Shedler, Jonathan 34
siblings, difference between 5, 23, 29, 53, 70, 75–141
    differential maltreatment and love as causes of sibling difference 75–110
    role in family and differences between 23, 111–40, 202
single-nucleotide polymorphism (SNP) 221, 222, 233
Spitz, Rene 86
stigmatisation 78, 113, 130–7, 138
Street-Porter, Janet 128–30
stress:
    cortisol regulation and 81–4, 88–90, 92, 96–7, 108, 181, 228
    pregnancy and 83–4, 102–5
    post traumatic stress disorder (PTSD) 27, 57, 125, 152–3
suicide 39, 44, 45, 49–50, 51, 54, 55, 56, 72, 95, 131, 160–1

teaching, parental 15, 22, 29, 31, 58, 145, 168, 208
temper tantrums 75, 81, 84, 90, 109–10, 116, 148, 149, 207
Terman, Lewis 166
Thatcher, Margaret 21, 94, 166
therapists 46, 54, 55, 57, 58, 77, 105, 135, 200–2, 212, 235
therapy 32–5, 46, 56, 57, 58, 72, 77, 92, 125, 141–2, 158, 201
    see also under individual type of therapy
This Be Yet Another Verse (Paul Bamborough (2014), pace Philip Larkin) v
Tiger Mothering 171–2, 174, 203

Today Programme, Radio 4 65, 66,
    214–15, 219–20
traits run in families, why 141–63
    embrace the angels in the
        nursery 160–1
    how traits run in families 145–52
    identify intergenerational patterns
        in your family 159–61
    intergenerational transmission
        of traits through parenting
        152–9
    P-A-C, a top tip for changing
        the intergenerational record
        161–3
transactional analysis 32, 161–2
transpersonal psychology 32
Traumagenic Model, The 27–8,
    81–2, 88, 90
Trescothick, Marcus 200–1,
    202, 203
twins:
    birth weight and 84, 156
    childhood maltreatment and
        differences in 68–9, 91
    childhood maltreatment and
        similarities in 68–9
    Colorado reared apart study
        144–5
    equal environments
        assumption (EEA) and
        229–32, 244–5
    generalisability of findings from
        studies using twin samples
        246–7
    HGP hypothesis and 64, 218–19,
        220, 221, 224, 228–33, 234,
        235
    impact of prenatal factors
        on 247
    Jim Twins 67
    lack of measures of
        environment in behavioural
        genetic studies 247–8
    low estimates of Shared
        Environment from twin and
        adoption studies 245–6
    mathematical assumptions
        made in analysing twin
        data 247
    Minnesota (Bouchard) reared
        apart study, 67–8, 144, 229,
        251–5
    Missing Heritability and 5,
        61–2, 64, 67–70, 83
    sexual abuse and 76–7, 87
    twin studies 'heritability'
        is shared environment
        (THISE) 228–33, 235
    twin studies: a discredited
        method 243–9

Van den Boom, Dymphna
    155, 156
Venter, Craig 62

Waugh, Alexander 160
Waugh, Evelyn 21, 160
Wilkinson, Jonny 200, 201–2, 203
Winnicott, Donald 86, 139
Woods, Earl 175–6, 177–8, 179–81,
    182–4, 186–8, 196, 198–9,
    202–3, 208
Woods, Kultida 176–7, 178, 181,
    182, 184, 196, 198, 202–3,
    208
Woods, Tiger 167, 174, 202–3
    brand 184–5
    childhood 174, 177–83, 191,
        192–3, 194
    Dark Triad traits and 192–3
    fame 179, 180, 187–8, 191–2,
        196–7, 198
    hothousing of 177–82
    Marketing Character 184, 185,
        187, 188, 197
    parents and *see* Woods, Earl
        and Woods, Kultida
    rise and fall of 174–99
    self-restraint 193–6
    sex life 174–5, 187–93, 196–7
World Health Organization 7, 97,
    98, 102

Yates, Paula:
  belief in inheritance of mental
    illness 9
  childhood of 9, 11, 46, 50
  death of 39–40, 44, 46, 49–52
  Hutchence and 43, 44, 45, 50, 53
  Peaches' childhood and 42–7

  similarity of death to Peaches'
    49–52
  similarities to Peaches Geldof
    39–42
  toxic identification with parents
    and 57–9